S0-AID-528

Entrepreneur MAGAZINE'S

FINANCING YOUR BUSINESS

made easy

Entrepreneur Press,
Ralph Alterowitz, and
Jon Zonderman

Ep Entrepreneur Press

Editorial Director: Jere Calmes
Cover Design: Beth Hansen-Winter
Editorial and Production Services: CWL Publishing Enterprises, Inc., Madison, Wisconsin, www.cwlpub.com

This publication is designed to provide accurate and authoritative information in regard to the subject matter covered. It is sold with the understanding that the publisher is not engaged in rendering legal, accounting, or other professional services. If legal advice or other expert assistance is required, the services of a competent professional person should be sought.

> —From a Declaration of Principles jointly adopted by a Committee of the American Bar Association and a Committee of Publishers and Associations

ISBN 1-59918-022-7

Library of Congress Cataloging-in-Publication Data
Alterowitz, Ralph.
  Financing your business made easy / by Entrepreneur Press, Ralph Alterowitz, and Jon Zonderman.
    p. cm.
  ISBN 1-59918-022-7 (alk. paper)
  1. New business enterprises—United States--Finance. I. Zonderman, Jon.
  II. Entrepreneur Press. III. Title.
  HG4027.6.A48 2006
  658.15'22--dc22

                                                        2006023690

11 10 09 08 07 06   10 9 8 7 6 5 4 3 2 1

Contents

Contents

Introduction

The Never-Ending Quest for Capital

MOST ENTREPRENEURS WHO START A BUSINESS THINK THE VEN-ture is going to make them rich. A few say they are primarily interested in seeing their ideas or visions become a reality, but they still want to build a lucrative, successful business.

This eternal optimism is spawned by America's unique blend of democracy and capitalism. America has the most robust and open flow of capital in the world, allowing almost anyone who would like to start a business to find the cash to do so.

But the reality of entrepreneurship, including the often difficult task of accessing capital, frequently undermines dreams. The hard truth is that half of all businesses created each year go out of business in the first four years. They succumb to competition, the lack of a viable market, an inability to take a technology past the prototype stage, or a lack of capital. Many close simply because the entrepreneur runs out of energy to maintain the business; after all, operating a small company is all-consuming, a 24/7 way of life.

Sometimes, if the company is good at what it does and gets lucky, it will be bought by a larger company that has the deep enough pockets to take the products or processes to the next level.

The majority of companies that make it past infancy into corporate adolescence do so without engaging in a public stock offering. Their stock remains closely held. Sometimes this is by design; other times it's because no investor is willing to help the entrepreneur realize the vision. Only a few entrepreneurs—perhaps one in 5,000 or 10,000—will ever get rich from the initial public offering of their company's stock. Most successful small business owners work hard, make a comfortable living, and enjoy the sense of freedom and accomplishment that comes from working for themselves.

What Is Capital?

Capital can be thought of either narrowly or broadly.

In the narrow definition, capital is money. Capital in the form of money is used to purchase the goods and services necessary to run a business.

In the broad definition, capital is money or the items money can buy. So if you need a physical plant in order to run your business and someone who owns space that you could use says, "I will provide you with one year's rent free in exchange for 5 percent of your company," you have just raised capital. If your sister-in-law, an attorney, says, "I will handle the work necessary to set up your company for free, and if your business takes off, you can start paying me for the legal work necessary for any small business," you have just raised capital. If you find a materials supplier who says, "For new businesses, I extend credit terms for 60 days rather than 30," you have just raised capital.

But regardless of how much non-cash capital you can raise, you will almost always have to raise capital in the form of money. This is done in any number of ways.

Where's the Money?

Every new company needs money to get started, whether it's $5,000 to launch a home-based crafts business, $500,000 to open a new restaurant, or $5 million to take a bit of technology developed at a university laboratory to the first stage of commercial development.

The business press likes to focus on the last of these three kinds of companies, because technology and innovation are sexy and innovation combined with the need for money attracts the most serious investors—professional venture capitalists—interested in nurturing such companies.

But again, the truth is far different from the dream. The vast majority of new business owners, like owners of small companies in general, will never meet a professional venture capitalist interested in their company. Most entrepreneurs have to look for less glamorous solutions for their capital needs. Owners of new, small, or growing companies who want to raise capital need to engage in a long process of understanding who they are, what their company is, what their capital needs are, and what the best solutions to these needs are.

This book is about venture funding in the real world, the world beyond the snazzy offices on Sand Hill Road, the world where mom and dad and the guy who sells supplies to you on credit are your venture capitalists, the world that most entrepreneurs really inhabit.

Finding the money to start a business is almost always more difficult than people think it will be.

First-time entrepreneurs looking to go into business may think of capital as "something the big guys do."

"I'm only starting a small business" sealing driveways, making home repairs, designing and making lamps, or whatever. "All I need is $5,000. How difficult can that be?" In truth, it can be as difficult as raising $5 million, depending on who you know, what your credit history is like, and any number of other factors.

Remember: if you can't draw on your own savings, there are only two ways to raise money for a business—borrow money or sell a portion of your business in exchange for the cash needed to run it and grow it.

If you sell a portion of your business to an investor, you have given the investor a share of the business and possibly a role in managing the business. The same can be true of a lender, who may also get a role in managing your business, depending on the size of the loan and if the lender feels that you need additional guidance in using the capital effectively.

There are a number of other ways to acquire capital to start a company or help your company grow, all of which we will discuss in this book. They include:

▶ Licensing your product to another company to sell it

▶ Borrowing on your credit cards or against the equity in your house or some other personal asset

▶ Borrowing from family or friends or letting them invest in your company

▶ Using the credit terms of your suppliers and the credit terms you offer your customer

Another way of looking at capital is that if you can keep your cash and use something else to trade for either a product or a service, that "something else" is capital. Bartering is the exchange of capital. Instead of using cash in the transaction, one party pays the other in the form of a product or a service. An attorney and a car dealer may trade legal services for a car lease. A home remodeling company and a wholesale food broker may trade the renovation of a bathroom for the food necessary for the remodeling business's annual company outing.

Small Business Capital Needs

According to federal government data, there are over 7 million small businesses (those with fewer than 500 employees) in the United States. Almost 80 percent of them have ten or fewer employees. Small businesses account for about 99 percent of all businesses in the United States, employ about 54 percent of workers, and generate about 52 percent of the country's gross domestic product (GDP). Most new jobs in the United States are created by businesses with under 500 employees.

These businesses and businesses that are being started have a never-ending need for capital. Because small business owners often live in the communities in which they operate their business and frequently have personal assets tied up in their businesses, financial institutions are willing to overlook other risk factors in lending to them and increasingly compete for their business. The economic output of small businesses also often stays within the communities in which they operate, so local and state governments are eager to help them start and survive through rough patches. And because many small businesses are family businesses, their pool of outside investors, if any, is usually small and supportive.

In short, small businesses, start-ups, and growing businesses are the economic engines that power local economies and keep the national economy running, even as large companies downsize or push more of their jobs offshore.

How This Book Is Organized

This book is structured to provide you with a wide spectrum of financing opportunities for a new or growing business. They are all, to one degree or another, sources of "venture" capital or "risk" capital in that they provide capital for risky, entrepreneurial ventures.

The book is divided into two sections: "Getting Started" and "Getting Bigger." Not every entrepreneur who gets started will want to, need to, or be able to get bigger, so we have teased apart those ways of raising capital that work best for each particular situation.

Contrary to much opinion, an entrepreneur getting started does not have fewer options for raising capital than does a business person seeking to grow his or her business to the next level. The difference between the two types of capital is that the new business owner often has to be more creative than the owner of a business seeking to take it to the next level. The business owner seeking to grow, however, often has more complex decisions to make, since growing more often means giving up a portion of the ownership than does starting out.

In each section, we divide the discussion into chapters indicating three levels of need—"Need Money", "Need More Money," and "Need a Lotta Money."

We have set the dollar amounts for these levels arbitrarily. The "Need Money" chapters focus on ways to raise under $100,000 of capital. The "Need More Money" chapters focus on techniques for raising between $100,000 and $1 million in capital. And the "Need a Lotta Money" chapters focus on raising over $1 million in capital.

At some point in your search for capital, you will be asked to invest the time, energy, and possibly money necessary to prepare a detailed business plan. While this book does not include a discussion of writing a business plan, there are dozens of books available on that subject.

We have also created a set of tools, forms, and exhibits that you can download from www.venturetechcorp.com to help you do some of the calculations for determining how much capital you need and what the best avenues for raising that capital are.

More Help

Are you interested in downloading the tools, forms, and reference materials found in this book so you can modify them for your personal use?

Visit **www.venturetechcorp.com.**

On this site you may also

▶ submit a question for an answer online

▶ view other people's questions and the answers provided

▶ view additional material of interest to entrepreneurs

▶ link to other sites for entrepreneurs

▶ provide your own "war stories" about raising capital

Copyright applies. Proper attribution is required for use of any materials downloaded.

Part One

Getting Started

ENTREPRENEURS HAVE IDEAS. THEY WANT TO MAKE THOSE IDEAS REAL. That means generating enough income to create a profitable business. Figuring out how to implement an idea means setting up the processes for realizing the business benefits of the idea. The prospective business owner must figure out how to create the following:

- ▶ **Infrastructure:** This is the staff and organizational dynamic necessary to carry out the business plan as well as all of the necessary activities to do the work and achieve the objectives. Infrastructure tasks run from the simple, such as doing the bookkeeping, to the complex, such as having an ordering process for supplies and raw materials and flowing them through the business processes.

- ▶ **Marketing and distribution:** As the famed business consultant Peter Drucker often pointed out, profits are generated outside the company walls. The business needs a marketing organization that provides the demand for the product or service by generating the interest that leads to orders. On the other end of the process, the business must have an effective and efficient distribution system that can get orders out the door and to the customers who have ordered them.

1

▶ **Use of funds:** An entrepreneur must be shrewd about the way he or she uses the company's financial resources, squeezing every penny until Lincoln cries out. Money is hard to obtain and there is a cost for every dollar of capital that is raised. The cost to the entrepreneur may be interest paid for borrowing money or the equity in the business sold for cash to operate. In every way, using someone else's money costs the entrepreneur some money.

Establishing these three core competencies—infrastructure, marketing, and proper use of funds—can improve an entrepreneur's probability of success. Although this book focuses on how to obtain money, entrepreneurs have to know how to use the capital they raise or they will have raised it for naught.

Chapter 1

Getting Started/Need Money, Part 1

E NTREPRENEURS WHO NEED LESS THAN $100,000 TO START A BUSINESS will typically be borrowing money rather than trying to recruit equity investors to purchase a piece of the company. And they will typically look for financing in three places, in the following order:

- ▶ Personal savings and assets
- ▶ Family and/or friends
- ▶ Third parties such as banks and finance companies

In this chapter we'll discuss the first two sources. The third we'll cover in Chapter 2.

Personal Savings: Invest in Yourself and in Your Business

The best piece of advice for any aspiring entrepreneur might be "Don't give up your day job."

At least until you have something tangible with which to approach those who might be interested in providing you with equity financing (buying stock

3

shares in your company), you should work on your idea or concept nights and weekends. Unless, of course, you have substantial personal savings.

Putting your own cash into your start-up or young business is the simplest way to go. You avoid using credit, keep your business affairs to yourself, and steer clear of any legal entanglements that come with either borrowing or selling an equity stake.

Show Yourself the Money

Many of us have personal savings we can access in places we might not think to look. Sometimes you have to borrow these savings, but you are in effect borrowing from yourself. In addition to your checking and savings accounts, the other places you can tap for cash include:

- ▶ Taxable investment accounts
- ▶ Tax-advantaged retirement accounts, such as 401(k) plans or IRAs
- ▶ Cash value in whole life insurance policies
- ▶ Lump-sum payout on leaving a job
- ▶ Trust fund
- ▶ Hard assets, such as art, antiques, or cars

Taxable Investment Accounts

Taxable investment accounts are those you hold with brokerage houses or mutual fund companies on which you must pay annual taxes for any capital gains and dividends.

Remember: if you liquidate such an account or cash out some of the investments, come April 15 of the next year you may have capital gain tax to pay on some of the proceeds. The best thing to do is to determine your capital gain liability when you cash out the funds and put that money aside to pay taxes (or leave enough in the account to remove next April 15).

Timing the removal of such funds is important. Since you owe no taxes on funds removed until April 15 of the year following the one in which you take the proceeds, the earlier in the calendar year you remove the funds, the longer you have before a tax payment is due.

If you tell your broker you are liquidating your account in order to start a business, he or she may suggest that you not do so and instead borrow against your assets by shifting your account to a "margin" account.

Don't do it.

While it may seem tempting, margin accounts are dangerous tools. They allow you to borrow 40 to 50 percent of the value of the assets in your account.

But if the value of the assets in your account falls (i.e., your stocks, bonds, or funds go down in price), your broker may be forced to sell some of those proceeds, then use them to pay off part of your loan in order to maintain the ratio of your account value to your loan. If the assets are sold for more than you bought them for, you will still have a capital gain tax to pay and you won't necessarily be able to time the disposal of assets and payment of taxes: the broker may have to sell out your position in December.

It's better to take the cash, put your tax liability into an account you won't be tempted to raid, and be done with it.

Tax-Advantaged Retirement Accounts

There are two options for removing funds from a tax-advantaged retirement fund.

First, you can liquidate assets the way you would from a taxable investment account. Second, you can borrow against the proceeds in some types of tax-advantaged funds. However, there are problems with both options.

Remember: these plans were set up to encourage saving for retirement. They allow you to earn interest and dividends and to obtain capital gains on investments that increase in value, without incurring any current tax liability. When you retire and begin taking distributions, they are taxed as ordinary income, at your effective tax rate. The theory is that most Americans spend their prime earning years in moderately high tax brackets but drop to lower brackets in their retirement years. They then pay taxes at the lower rates on the distributions they take from their tax-advantaged accounts.

So, if you take money out of a tax-advantaged retirement plan to capitalize your start-up or growing business, you will pay income taxes at your regular rate for the amount you withdraw. Therefore, timing is important. For instance, if you are starting a business in October and you need $50,000 for the first year of operations, you want to calculate your current year income tax liability (based on what you and your spouse have already earned) and determine your tax bracket. This helps you decide how much to withdraw this year and how much next year, when you will have earned income from a different job and may be in a lower bracket.

There's one more catch. There is a 10 percent penalty tax on all distributions from tax-advantaged retirement plans to individuals younger than 59 ½ or, if permanently disabled, 55. Again, when you determine how much

When buying equipment, tools, or other physical assets, stretch your money by buying from companies that are going out of business, secondhand stores, and distressed merchandise sales and auctions.

you need to take out of a tax-advantaged retirement plan to capitalize your business, you need to calculate your tax liability and take out enough to pay the liability or leave enough in the account to pay the taxes next April 15.

Many employer-sponsored 401(k) plans allow borrowing. You are limited to borrowing 50 percent of the amount in your plan account, to a maximum of $50,000. And you must repay the loan within five years.

Loans from a 401(k) have a low interest rate, but you are forgoing the tax-free growth on the money you borrow for the time you borrow it. If you have other borrowing options, pass on this one.

Also, you cannot borrow against 403(b) retirement annuities, IRAs, or Keogh or SEP plans if you are already self-employed.

Cash Value in Whole Life Insurance

Whole life, universal life, and variable-life insurance policies all have a cash value you can get by canceling the policy. Whole life policies also have provisions for borrowing.

Most entrepreneurs should not cancel any cash value life insurance; if anything, you should be increasing its death benefit when you strike out on your own.

If you are currently working and thinking about starting your own company, you may be able to take advantage of a company buyout program and walk away with a chunk of cash to fund your start-up.

Borrowing against the cash value in a policy is a viable option. Loans against cash value in life insurance come at a low interest rate (usually 4 to 6 percent). However, if you die while the loan is outstanding, its value will be deducted from the death benefit paid to your beneficiary or beneficiaries.

Here's a way to have your cake and eat it too. Use the built-up cash value to pay for the premium on the policy. This allows you to use for your business the cash you would have paid for the premium and maintain your life insurance at the same time.

Lump-Sum Payout from a Job

If you are currently working and thinking about starting your own company, you may be able to take advantage of a company buyout program and walk away with a chunk of cash to fund your start-up.

Many companies routinely offer buyout programs or are amenable to negotiating a separation package. These are usually aimed at middle-aged employees (45 to 60) as an early-retirement incentive program. Companies often offer from one to four weeks' pay for every year of service with the company, with a maximum of one or even two full years of pay. They will sometimes make these payments as a lump sum rather than weekly or biweekly.

Again, if you are able to maneuver into such a position, timing is critical. You want to accept a lump sum buyout as early in the calendar year as possible, to maximize the time you have to use the money until you have to pay taxes.

Trust Fund

We should all be so lucky!

Some people are beneficiaries of trust funds. Some of them receive funds when they reach a certain age. For others, the distribution of funds is at the trustees' discretion.

If you are the beneficiary of a trust fund with trustee discretion, make a pitch for your share just as you would to any other angel or venture capitalist. Trustees have a fiduciary responsibility to all the beneficiaries. By placing money in your business, they are reducing the trust's assets and therefore its growth potential. You may have to waive some or all of its possible future benefits if you receive a large amount of funding.

You may also see if the trust documents allow for an investment in a private venture and if the trust wishes to become an equity investor.

Hard Assets

Most people don't pawn the family jewelry to start a business, but it does happen. There are "high-end" pawnshops in some communities that lend sizable amounts of money to well-off people against quite substantial hard goods. That gold Rolex you got as a gift from your employer for the multimillion-dollar deal you made five years ago might have some real value after all.

Artwork, musical instruments, artistic rugs and carpets, and antique furniture all have a market and can sometimes be liquidated quickly to raise cash. Loans are usually given at a fraction of the price that would be paid in an outright sale.

Home Equity: Your Home Can Be Your Most Valuable Asset

Large companies that use the same kind of equipment as you need may have old equipment taking up space. They may be willing to sell it to you cheap or provide it as part of a strategic alliance.

For many Americans, their house is their largest and greatest asset. This is as true for entrepreneurs as for anyone else.

You may have enough equity in your house to get your business off the ground, especially if you have been living in it for a few years and are in an area where real estate prices have been booming rather than crawling upwards. Remember: equity is the difference between the market value of the house and the current balance of your loan.

If you bought a house seven years ago for $150,000 and took out a 30-year fixed-rate mortgage for 80 percent of the price ($120,000), you have paid down a few thousand dollars of the debt by now. Perhaps you owe $110,000.

At the same time, if your house has appreciated about 5 percent a year (compounded of course), today it is worth over $200,000—let's say $210,000. That means you have $100,000 of equity in it—$40,000 through your down payment and mortgage payments and $60,000 through appreciation.

There are two ways to get equity out of the house you own: to refinance with a new mortgage or to take out a home-equity loan or a home-equity line of credit against your available equity. There are a few variables to consider before deciding which route is better for you.

Among these are the interest rate of your current mortgage and the interest rates available now, how long you expect to live in your house, how much equity you would like to take out, and your ability to qualify for a new mortgage.

Refinancing

If interest rates are lower now than when you obtained your current mortgage, take a look at refinancing with a new mortgage first. In our example, you could borrow 80 percent of your $210,000 house value, or $168,000. After paying off your $110,000 mortgage, you would have $58,000 in cash.

Here's the rule of thumb for when to refinance: if today's interest rate is more than 1 percent lower than your current rate and you expect to live in your home at least another five to seven years, the lower interest payment (based on your current loan balance) will allow you to recoup your upfront fees for the refinancing. Use this as a first step to guiding your decision; if these conditions prevail, it's a point in favor of a new mortgage.

*W*ith many banks and finance companies looking for business in a slow economy, some may offer exceptionally good terms for a creditworthy borrower.

Given the fact that most home equity loans and lines of credit peg their interest rate to the prime rate banks charge their best corporate customers, mortgage interest rates are sometimes lower. If mortgage rates are lower than home equity rates, that's a point in their favor.

There is, of course, one big problem with applying for a new mortgage. If you didn't plan well and waited until you left your job and started your business to apply for the new mortgage, unless your spouse's income can swing the payments, the bank may not look favorably on you as a risk.

To counter this, you can apply for a mortgage for 70 percent of the house's value instead of the traditional 80 percent. This will allow you to get a "no-income verification" mortgage from many banks. The downside, of course, is that you've left equity in the house that you could have used for the business. (A 70 percent mortgage would mean you'd borrow only $147,000 and have only $37,000 after paying off your old loan.)

The lesson in this, of course, is that if you are thinking of refinancing your house in order to start a business, begin the process early while you can still show the bank a steady income stream.

The other downside of a new mortgage is the extra fees involved. Banks usually charge an application fee and a mortgage-origination fee called "points." A point is one percent of the amount of the loan. For instance, if you are taking out a $200,000 mortgage, with a charge of two points origination, the fee is $4,000. Some banks will allow you to add the points to the loan, but that raises the monthly cost and may reduce the amount of equity you can take out if you are borrowing the maximum for which your income will allow you to qualify.

Other fees include a new title search and title insurance (even though you own the house and demonstrated clear title the last time you borrowed) and the attorney's fees for closing on the loan. Points, fees, and other closing costs can run 5 to 6 percent of the loan value and reduce the cash available for your business by that much.

Tap the Equity

If you want to get at the equity without going through the hassle or expense of a new mortgage, banks and other financial institutions offer home equity loans written for a fixed term (usually 10 to 15 years) or home equity lines of credit.

Most home equity loans (either fixed term or line of credit) have minimal fees. They do not require a new title search or title insurance. They do not have origination points attached to them. The documentation is less complicated and the attorney's fees for closing on the loan are lower.

Whether you take a term loan or a line of credit, you should be able to take out the full difference between your current loan balance and 80 percent of your home's value (in this case $58,000). In either case, the bank or other institution would take a second mortgage on your home.

In the case of a term loan, the bank would write you a check for the same amount and you would begin making monthly payments on the note.

With an equity line of credit, you would get a checkbook on which you could write checks up to the amount of your credit line. You would receive monthly statements showing your balance available; your monthly payment would depend on how much of your credit line you have used. As long as you pay the monthly interest, you can pay all or part of the credit line as you are able.

Funding from Family or Friends

The second place to look for start-up funds after you have exhausted your own savings and assets is family or friends. There are three ways you can raise capital from these people. Each way has unique advantages, yet all the methods share the same potential disadvantages. The three ways are:

- ▶ Loan
- ▶ Gift
- ▶ Equity sale

One resource everyone has is an address book. Use yours.

In this chapter, we will only discuss loans and gifts, since these are the primary ways to raise less than $100,000. For entrepreneurs who need to raise between $100,000 and $1 million, family and friends often are the source of the first round of equity investments.

Loans

Nothing says you can't accept a loan from a family member or friend. In fact, family members probably loan as much money to their entrepreneur relatives as banks do.

A loan from a family member or friend has at least three advantages over a commercial loan.

First, the lender rarely asks for any collateral on the loan. It is purely a personal loan.

Second, the loan can be made quickly. You can have a discussion with your Uncle Mike one morning and deposit a check in your company's account that afternoon.

Third, many loans from family members or friends are written at a below-market interest rate. As long as the interest is equal to what the lender would receive on a comparable bank deposit, the difference between the loan rate and the market rate is a legitimate gift.

Gifts

Gift taxes, if any are due, are paid by the person making a gift. As of 2006, any individual is allowed to give a gift of up to $12,000 per year to any other individual without incurring a gift tax. That means that your parents, for instance, could give you a gift of $24,000 ($12,000 from each) to help jump-start your business. In fact, they could give you $24,000 on December 24 and another $24,000 two weeks later without incurring a gift tax. If they had the money, they could even give you gifts of $120,000 ($60,000 each), under a special provision of the federal tax code that allows five years' worth of gifts to be made in a single year, as long as no other gifts are given over the next five years.

Or, they could write you a loan for which your annual interest payment is under $24,000. Each year, after your company pays the interest on the loan, your parents could turn around and give you back the interest amount as a gift for that year. (You have to write the check for the interest and then they have to write you a new check for the gift, to make sure you have the proper paperwork for tax and accounting records.) If they wrote you a three-year loan with a 9 percent interest rate, they could loan you $100,000 and all the interest you paid annually could come back to you as a gift. (In order for them to return the interest to you as a gift, they need to set an interest rate that a bank would set for a comparable loan. Or, they could reduce the interest rate and consider the reduced rate as the gift, as discussed in the sidebar.)

The gift tax (a federal tax) is tightly intertwined with the federal estate tax. A person can choose to make gifts totaling the amount of the federal estate tax exemption while he or she is alive without incurring a gift tax. (However, in this case the estate tax exemption would have been waived.) Such gifts can be made over and above the annual $12,000 tax-free threshold.

That means that a person could give a total of $2 million in tax-free gifts in 2006, increasing to $3 million in tax-free gifts in 2009, as the federal estate tax exemption increases. Currently, the gift tax is slated to remain in some form even after the estate tax is repealed in 2010. With these tax law changes enacted in 2001, the timing of such large gifts must be well thought out. Careful planning among the giver, the recipient, and their respective tax advisors is important.

One way of presenting your business opportunity to friends and family is to give them an alternative—e.g., "Would you prefer to invest in my company or give me a loan?" This bounds the person's thinking so he or she is more likely to say yes to providing you with capital in some way.

A Gift of Reduced Interest

Family members and friends can combine a loan to an entrepreneur with a gift. They can do this by writing a loan at a reduced interest rate. The low interest rate is, in effect, a gift.

Banks earn income by taking deposits and paying interest on them, then loaning out the money at a higher rate of interest. The difference between the interest the bank pays on deposits and the interest it charges on loans is called the *spread*. As long as the person making the loan charges interest equal to the amount he or she would earn on a bank deposit of the same size and duration, the difference between that rate and the rate a bank would charge is a legitimate gift.

For example, your sister could lend you $100,000 for a period of three years. As long as she sets the interest rate equal to or above what her money would earn if placed in a three-year certificate of deposit (CD) (about 5 percent in 2006), the amount you save in not getting a $100,000 loan from a bank is a legitimate gift.

If you could get a bank to write you an unsecured loan for three years in 2006, the interest rate would probably be the prime rate plus 4 to 6 percent, or between 12 and 14 percent.

That's a difference between paying your sister $5,000 in interest and paying the bank between $12,000 and $14,000—at least $7,000 in savings. Even if your sister asked for a little above the bank CD rate to compensate for the risk, she still would charge you less than a bank would.

Chapter 2

Getting Started/Need Money, Part 2

AS MENTIONED AT THE START OF THE PRECEDING CHAPTER, ENTREPRE-neurs who need less than $100,000 to start a business will typically be borrowing money from three places:

- ▸ Personal savings and assets
- ▸ Family and/or friends
- ▸ Third parties such as banks and finance companies

We've discussed the first two. Now let's consider the third.

Banks and Finance Companies: Show the Lender Who You Are and What You're Made of

Getting a personal loan to start a business is very difficult. Here "personal" means a loan to your business (whether it's incorporated or not) based on an idea, concept, or business plan without any track record. In a way, every loan to a small business is a personal one, since you will be asked to personally sign a guarantee to repay the loan, even if the company is incorporated

13

and the loan is being guaranteed by the Small Business Administration (SBA) or another entity.

Despite the fact that banks are in the money-lending business, they are often leery about lending to unproven businesses. However, they are becoming less tightfisted. In fact, some banks have set up special small-business lending centers and trained bankers to lend to small businesses. They are also working more closely with the SBA and state and local economic development agencies to leverage their loans to start-up or growing small businesses in enterprise zones or other disadvantaged areas.

Banks can work with you to apply for an SBA guaranteed loan. (The SBA programs are discussed later in this chapter.) The SBA is constantly coming up with new ways to reduce the paperwork and hurdles for small businesses to acquire loans.

Microloans

Microloans are loans of up to $35,000 made by nonprofit community-based lenders to start-up, newly established, or growing small businesses. The funding comes directly from the SBA.

Each community-based lender establishes its own credit and collateral requirements. Personal guarantees are expected. The maximum term of a microloan is six years. Microloans are generally used for working capital, inventory, supplies, furniture, fixtures, machinery, and equipment.

In addition to funding, community-based intermediaries are required to provide business-based training and technical assistance to microloan recipients. They may require a prospective borrower to complete training and/or planning requirements before considering his or her application.

Hundreds of participating lenders in the Microloan Program will lend up to $35,000 to companies with little or no track record. (Appendix A is a complete list of participants in the Microloan Program as of June 2006.)

More than 30 percent of all loans to small and start-up businesses come not from banks but from commercial lenders such as Allied Capital or GE Credit. These companies are often willing to assume more risk than banks (and consequently they charge a higher interest rate) and may allow intangible factors like the personal integrity of the borrower to compensate when a business has little or no operating history.

A new form of lending is the Web-based "auction" model of small loans, created by companies such as *Prosper.com*. In this situation, a potential borrower enters a brief description of his or her reasons for borrowing and sub-

History of Microlending

When Muhammad Yunus lent a small sum of money to a struggling furniture maker, neither he nor possibly the world had a vision that he had initiated a major innovation in entrepreneurship.

In 1970, Yunus, a Bangladesh economics professor, thought there should be a better way to help struggling entrepreneurs who did not have access to capital. His initial small loans initiated the concept of microlending, which has since had a significant impact around the world, especially in major pockets of poverty. Besides the fact that his loans were very small, Yunas did not require collateral.

Yunus went on to found the Grameen Bank, which continues to make business loans to people who have no access to the financial system. Such micro-business owners are most likely to be denied any sort of a loan because of no credit or poor credit, often no collateral, and usually a need for less capital and therefore less interest than a lender would consider worth incurring the administrative and processing costs.

Since its start, Grameen Bank has distributed "more than $4 billion in small loans to millions" through a network of microfinance institutions. One measure that such loans are filling a need is the fact that the bank has grown to the point where it employs more than 11,000 people and has connections to entrepreneurs in more than 40,000 villages and towns throughout the less-developed world.

The "financing for the poor" Grameen style of entrepreneurial finance has been imitated by thousands and brought to the United States, where Accion International and others, such as the federal Small Business Administration (SBA), have implemented the concept.

The SBA's Microloan Program, described later in this chapter, was developed in 1992, about 20 years after microloans started in Third World countries. Until it became a permanent program in 1997, the SBA made more than 6,000 loans totaling more than $65 million. The loans range from $100 to a maximum of $25,000, with a maximum loan period of six years and an average repayment period of 37 months. The Microloan Program fills the gap for small business borrowers who need very small loans.

mits a credit history (just as with a bank or commercial lender) and the rate of interest he or she would like to pay on the loan. The Web site's mathematical algorithm then matches the borrower with individuals who have agreed to lend money at certain interest rates to borrowers who meet certain criteria. These loans are usually very small (under $10,000) and for short duration (less than two years) and not many lenders are yet willing to lend to start-up businesses.

From a Mircroloan to a Microbusiness

Garvyn Manganiello, a mother of two and pregnant again, wanted to begin a hot dog business. She thought it would be fun selling hot dogs on the beach of coastal New Hampshire while her older son played in the sand and water. Her first day of business in 1984 coincided with the Fourth of July parade in Bristol. Since then vice-president George H.W. Bush was the grand marshall, the crowd was huge. Garvyn sold 500 hot dogs and lots of soda.

Her pregnancy resulted in triplets, and soon she, her husband, and the five children moved to Canada when her husband was given a business assignment there. Wanting to do more than just talk about children with other mothers, she took a cooking class. At the first class, she learned how to make bread. She soon began baking more bread than the family could eat and gave the rest away.

Returning to New Hampshire a couple of years later, she decided to see if the local grocery store would sell her bread. Dave, the owner of the store, called her soon after she had dropped off the first loaves to say that her bread sold out and he needed more. With that kind of demand, she did not lack for anything to do. But her husband suggested that rather than bake bread to sell through another retailer, she should "do it for herself."

So she borrowed $2,000 and went searching for used equipment and for space in which to open her own bakery. Seventeen years later, her company, Basic Ingredients, still located in Bristol, carries an assortment of breads, pies, and other pastries, as well as soups and sandwiches. Sunday mornings the line stretches out the door. Garvyn now has a thriving summer-month micro-business, earning $50,000 each year, as she says, "one sticky bun at a time."

The Five C's of Credit

Lenders look at five major factors—often called the five C's of credit—when evaluating whether to loan you money:

- ▶ character
- ▶ capacity
- ▶ collateral
- ▶ capital
- ▶ contribution

Character

Character is considered a "soft" or subjective criterion. Lenders take into account who you are, whether you are a longtime resident or transient, and whether you are active in the community.

One element of character—your credit history—is objective. Credit history is a one-way street: good credit might get you a gold star, all things being equal; bad credit knocks you right out of the box.

Before you apply for a loan, be sure to obtain a copy of your credit history and do whatever you can to buff it up. Make sure it is correct (mistakes happen) and contact any individuals or companies that have entered negative information.

Banks will have some criteria that may seem unusual or even unfair. For example, one banker commented that any small business loan application that shows the applicant making child-support payments (court-mandated or not) automatically gets rejected.

Capacity (Cash Flow)

Capacity is a measure of your ability to repay a loan. If your business is a start-up, a lender will look at your business plan and projections for revenue and cash flow. If your business has a history, the lender will look at your previous two years' cash flow. It should be sufficient to meet the terms of the loan, pay all operating expenses, and provide a cushion for emergencies.

Projecting cash flow is tricky. Try to adhere to industry norms and provide sound reasoning if your projection departs from these norms.

Collateral

No lender writes loans based on collateral alone. But lack of collateral is a real problem. You will be asked to personally guarantee any loan you take for your business; by doing so you put your assets at risk. Even if the lender does not formally take a lien on your home (through an equity loan and second mortgage) to obtain repayment of the loan principal, the lender can go after your house if you pledge it as collateral on your loan.

The only way to protect assets from your personal guarantee is to put them in the name of a spouse or child. Assets held jointly can be taken by the creditor to pay a loan only if both parties have signed the loan documents; however, the creditor may be able to force the sale of jointly held assets to pay off the loan.

Capital

Lenders will scrutinize your net worth before making a loan. Your net worth is the amount by which your assets exceed your liabilities.

Contribution

Lenders want entrepreneurs to have a significant amount of equity in the business. When the entrepreneur has "skin in the game," it ensures that his or her interests are aligned with those of the lender. Lenders don't like to see people trying to start businesses using only other people's money.

The SBA uses a ratio of anywhere from 4 to 1 to 2 to 1. In order to guarantee a loan, it wants the business owner to have put in equity equal to 20 to 33 percent of the total loan amount. For instance, if you are seeking a $100,000 loan, the SBA wants you to have put between $20,000 and $33,000 in personal equity into the business, depending on which SBA program you are using.

Credit Cards: Careful Funds Management Keeps You from "Kiting"

Starting a business by using credit cards can be easy and enticing. But it can also be also extremely expensive and risky.

Credit cards are an easy, convenient way to buy the furniture and business equipment needed to start a business. For operating expenses, you can always get a cash advance.

If you think you can get a business up and running and earning income within a couple of months, "putting it on plastic" can save you the time and trouble that goes along with acquiring other kinds of financing. But with most cards charging 15 to 20 percent annual interest, unless your company is able to rack up sales quickly and get rid of the debt, credit card financing is not the way to go over the long haul.

That's not to say it hasn't been done. There are entrepreneurs who have put a quarter of a million dollars and more on credit cards to bootstrap a business.

But if you are going to use credit cards to that extent, you need a plan. The only way to beat the finance charges is to create a self-funding pyramid by acquiring new credit cards and using the account balance transfer provisions (usually offered at a discounted rate) to pay off the balances on the old cards in full, thereby avoiding interest charges.

The following seven steps outline a plan for a credit-card pyramid.

Set up a Spreadsheet

The first step to financing a business start-up with credit cards is to set up a spreadsheet and list every card you have (or acquire), the day of the month when the account closes, the grace period, the date when the discount rate on balance transfers ends, and your current balance on the card. This will be extremely important as you build your credit-card pyramid.

Acquire Two to Three New Cards Every Month

Never turn down an offer of a new credit card. If the application you receive has not been presorted with your name, use your middle initial on some and not on others. Many credit data bases will track the different names as two separate accounts, which can give you added leverage—higher maximum balances or more cards.

Using credit cards as well as checks enables you to track expenses.

Apply for every kind of card that offers credit: Visa, Mastercard, Discover, and American Express Blue, Optima, or AmEx Small Business Open.

Don't start using a new card as soon as you get it. Hold onto it for when other cards become old and stale.

Use Courtesy Checks

Courtesy checks can be used for things you can't do with a credit card, like paying employees or professional advisors and consultants. These checks that credit card issuers mail are very similar to cash advances. You usually pay an upfront fee to use them, pay a higher interest rate, and do not have a grace period.

Use Some Cards for Purchases, Others for Cash Advances

Remember: when you transfer a balance from one card to another, the interest starts ticking on the new account immediately. This is also true when you write a courtesy check, which is considered a cash advance.

You should therefore use some cards for purchases only and others for paying off the monthly balances on those cards by transferring the card balances. Use the cards with the lowest courtesy rates as the ones from which you will pay off other balances and write courtesy checks.

Many cards offer low-interest time-limited rates, often called "teasers," for a period of time after you acquire the card. Whenever possible, shift higher-interest balances to the cards with the teasers.

As long as you zero out the balance for the billing period shown on your card, there is no interest for any purchases made using the card after the account closed. But if you write a cash advance check or transfer a balance using that account, all of the purchases made with the card also incur interest charges.

Finally, use courtesy checks only on cards that do not impose a check fee, which is usually 3 percent of the face amount of the check. (This is equal to about two months of interest upfront of the amount you will be borrowing by using the check.)

Start Moving the Money Around

Now that you've set up your card accounts for purchases, as well as the accounts for courtesy checks to pay other expenses and the card-purchase account balances, you need to keep track of when the discounted rate ends on each of the accounts to which you are transferring balances or from which you are issuing courtesy checks.

When a discounted rate is about to expire, pay off the balance with one or more new cards that you have acquired and kept. Move the card with the expired discount rate into the group of cards you use for credit-card only purchases and keep it there until another low-rate transfer offer comes along.

Get Rid of High-Interest Stale Cards

Credit cards stop being useful after a time. Once you have many cards that you are using for only credit-card purchases, you can start culling out the ones that charge the highest interest rate or annual fee or that have not issued an offer for low-interest balance transfer checks in the previous six months.

Getting rid of credit cards frees up space on your credit report for you to acquire more cards.

Find Another Source of Funding

Unless you are a fan of Charles Ponzi (one of the greatest schemers and swindlers in American history) and three-card monte dealers, you will probably be able to stay sane and run a credit-card operation for only nine months or a year before it becomes enormously cumbersome.

If in that time your business isn't generating revenue to allow you to get bank or commercial financing or generating enough buzz that you become a candidate for angel or VC funding, you might want to close up and get a job.

Finally, during all this credit card wheeling and dealing, you should have been able to rack up some serious frequent flier miles. After you've recapitalized your business, treat yourself and your significant other to a vacation.

Most credit card companies will provide a quarterly management report that categorizes expenses by type and employee and provides a tax organization form.

Prompt payment will give you a good credit history that you can use in the future to support a loan application at a bank or finance company.

The Small Business Administration: Uncle Sam Targets Services for Small Businesses

The federal Small Business Administration (SBA) can be a key participant in your search for capital for a start-up or growing business through the following:

▶ Guarantees for loans made by banks and other lenders

▶ Equity investments made by small business investment companies or specialized small business investment companies

▶ Consulting and technical assistance provided by small business development centers

Most SBA-backed loans can be written for as much as $2 million. Many small businesspeople—especially those starting a business—find the SBA approval process complex. However, there are special SBA programs for those who need small loans or for those who are creating businesses in places where the government wishes to encourage new businesses.

When you go to a local lending institution, ask how frequently it works with the SBA. Even if you don't seek an SBA guarantee for a first loan, in the future you may wish to do so. The SBA is constantly tinkering with its programs to make them more efficient and effective at providing loan assistance to small businesses, so check the SBA Web site, *www.sba.gov,* frequently.

SBA Loan Programs

The SBA maintains two major loan programs, the Certified Development Company Loan Program, known as 504 loans, and the 7A loan-guarantee program, in addition to its new microlending program.

504 Loan Guarantees

The 504 Certified Development Company (CDC) program is designed to help small and growing businesses buy facilities and major equipment. The program provides funding for companies that will expand employment or meet one of a number of public policy objectives, including business district revitalization, job creation in rural areas, expansion of exports, or small business ownership by minorities, women, and military veterans.

Loans are written by the CDC for terms of 10 to 20 years at a fixed below-market rate. They are jointly underwritten by a CDC, a nonprofit corporation established to contribute to the economic development of its

The magic of SBA programs is that almost any type of business can apply.

21

region (which uses SBA funds), and a private-sector lender. There are approximately 270 CDCs in the United States, each of which covers a specific geographic region.

You can put together a 504 loan by working either with a CDC that in turn brings a bank into the project or with a bank that brings a CDC into the project. These loans are appropriate for projects with a total cost up to $2.5 to $3.0 million, but they can be written for as little as $50,000. Generally, the company acquiring the loan is obligated to either create or maintain one job for every $50,000 it borrows.

The typical project covered by a 504 loan is the purchase of a building or land for building, construction of a building, or the fitting of the building with machinery. The total package includes a loan of up to 50 percent of the project cost from a private-sector lender, covered by a senior lien, and a loan of up to 40 percent by the CDC, covered by a junior lien. The CDC loan is backed by a 100 percent SBA-guaranteed debenture.

The CDC's 40 percent can be up to $1 million for projects that create jobs and up to $1.3 million for projects that meet other public policy objectives. Technically, the bank's contribution can be unlimited.

Your contribution to the project is expected to be 10 percent of the cost. Project assets being financed are used as the collateral. You are also expected to personally guarantee the loan. You are eligible for a 504 loan if your company has a net worth of less than $7 million and did not have average net income of more than $2.5 million in each of the previous two years.

With three parties involved in making the loan and the myriad federal regulations, this transaction can be complex. Expect to pay a fee of 3 percent of the amount of the loan, which can be written in.

7A Loan Guarantees

Under the 7A loan-guarantee program, you apply for a loan through a bank or other lending institution. This program provides an SBA guarantee for a portion of the loan, helping the lender make a loan to a small business that otherwise would not be able to secure a loan on reasonable terms.

Over 800 lenders have been designated SBA Certified Lenders under the 704 program. These lenders have extensive experience with SBA-guaranteed loans and have agreed to take on many of the responsibilities for analyzing, structuring, servicing, and liquidating loans, responsibilities that normally fall to the SBA. This strong relationship allows the SBA to respond to loan applications approved by a certified lender within three days, as opposed to the weeks it takes with a uncertified lender. Certified Lenders account for about 10 percent of SBA guaranteed loans.

About 500 lenders have been designated SBA Preferred Lenders. They have full lending authority and the SBA responds to their approved loan applications in one day. Preferred Lenders account for an additional 30 percent of SBA guaranteed loans.

The SBA Web site has lists of Certified and Preferred Lenders in its "listings and directories" section, *www.sba.gov/library/listfoo.html*. It also has detailed explanations of the loan programs described briefly here.

For loans of under $150,000, the SBA will guarantee 85 percent. From $150,000 to $1 million, it will guarantee 75 percent. The maximum loan is $2 million, of which the SBA will guarantee $1.5 million.

Most types of businesses are eligible. Eligibility is determined by the size of the business, calculated either by the number of employees or net worth, depending on the industry.

Loan maturities of up to 25 years are available for purchasing real estate and capital equipment and up to seven years for working capital. The 7A program has some advantages over the 504 program for real estate purchases, including that the maturity is longer and there's no need to show public policy or job creation benefits.

Loans are also available for purchasing a business, buying a franchise, agricultural and fishing businesses, medical facilities, recreational facilities, and clubs. Loans cannot be used for speculative real estate, lending, or multilevel marketing (pyramid sales) companies.

Interest rates may be fixed or variable; the SBA sets maximum rates in relation to the prime rate that lenders can charge. Lenders are not allowed to charge many of the typical fees associated with borrowing, although there is a onetime guarantee fee.

Since 2003 the SBA has rolled a lot of pilot programs into the 7A program. As of the middle of 2006, the 7A program has six subsidiary programs:

You may apply for SBA programs while concurrently exploring other sources of capital.

- ▶ 7A CAPLine—Asset-Based Line of Credit
- ▶ 7A CAPLine—Contract Line of Credit
- ▶ 7A CAPLine—Seasonal Line of Credit
- ▶ 7A SBA Express
- ▶ 7A Community Express
- ▶ 7A Export Working Capital

7A CAPLine Programs

CAPLine is an umbrella program under which the SBA offers loan guarantees for five kinds of short-term working-capital needs. The guarantee is the same as on standard SBA-backed loans—85 percent on loans of under $150,000 and 75 percent on loans from $150,000 to $2 million for all of the lines. These are the three CAPLine programs:

▶ **Asset-based line.** A revolving line of credit (it can be reused as it is paid down, like a credit card) for cyclical growth, recurring needs, or short-term working capital, designed for businesses unable to meet credit standards associated with long-term lending. It is asset-based; repayment comes from converting short-term assets into cash, which is remitted to the lender to pay down the line. Asset-based lines of credit require continual servicing and monitoring and they may be subject to additional fees.

▶ **Contract line.** A revolving or nonrevolving line available to finance the material and direct labor costs of performing a particular assignable contract or contracts.

▶ **Seasonal line.** A revolving or nonrevolving line to advance funds against anticipated inventory or accounts receivable during peak season sales fluctuations.

CAPLines are available to businesses that meet type and size criteria for the 7A program.

CAPLines are available to businesses that meet type and size criteria for the 7A program. Maturity for a CAPLine asset-based loan can be up to five years. The contract fulfillment and seasonal loans have one-year maturities. The asset-based loan can be repaid with proceeds from sale of inventory, as in a factoring arrangement. (See Chapter 5 for a description of factoring.) Only one seasonal CAPLine loan can be in effect at any time.

The guarantee fee is the same as for any 7A loan. The SBA places no fee restrictions on lenders that write asset-based loans and imposes a 2 percent annual fee based on the outstanding balance on other CAPLine loans.

7A SBA Express

SBA Express loans are for less than $350,000 and are provided at rates consistent with 7A program guidelines. Borrowers must also meet SBA 7A size criteria for eligibility. Maturities of between five and ten years are standard for working capital loans, and loans up to 25 years for the purchase of real estate and/or equipment.

However, there are some differences between the SBA Express and other loans.

First, with the SBA Express the lender may use its own forms and processes. The lender may also take advantage of electronic loan processing.

Second, the SBA provides only a 50 percent guarantee of loans made under the SBA Express program.

Third, and most important, under the SBA Express, the SBA will provide a 50 percent guarantee for lender-approved unsecured credit lines of up to $25,000, and this loan can be revolving for up to seven years. This is the SBA's primary microlending program.

7A Community Express

Community Express provides loans of up to $250,000 for businesses located in designated areas in need of business improvement, such as urban or rural communities, or communities where household income is predominantly "moderate."

Community Express loans are made using the lender's own documents and procedures. The SBA guarantees decisions within 36 hours, and the guarantee is up to 85 percent for loans of under $150,000 and 75 percent for loans of $150,000 to $250,000.

As with the SBA Express program, lenders can approve unsecured lines of credit of up to $25,000. Rates, loan terms, fees, and conditions parallel the 7A program, making this the Microloan Program for designated areas.

In addition to its targeted nature, the 7A Community Express program also adds technical and management assistance, provided by the lender to help borrowers be more successful in both their applications and their use of the proceeds.

7A CAPLine Export Working Capital

The final variation of CAPLine is the Export Working Capital loan, which provides up to $2 million for labor and material to manufacture goods for export or develop services for export.

SBICs and SSBICs

Small business investment companies (SBICs) and specialized small business investment companies (SSBICs) were established in 1958 to help bridge the gap between venture capital and start-up businesses.

SBICs are privately owned, profit-making companies that are regulated and licensed by the SBA. They invest their own capital and can also borrow from an SBA trust fund at low interest to leverage that capital. SBICs pro-

SBICs are privately owned, profit-making companies that are regulated and licensed by the SBA.

vide long-term lending, equity investments, debt-to-equity conversion funding, and management and technical assistance to companies that may not have access to unregulated venture capital pools.

SSBICs are SBICs that provide loans and investment opportunities primarily to companies owned by economically disadvantaged entrepreneurs, such as women and minorities, and to businesses in economically depressed neighborhoods in inner cities and rural areas.

In fiscal year 2005, the program invested $2.9 billion in 2,299 small U.S. companies. More than 40 percent of all SBIC investment dollars in FY 2005 went to companies that had been in business only three years or less at the time of the investments. At the end of FY 2005, there were 418 SBICs of all types operating in 46 states, the District of Columbia, and Puerto Rico. They held $23.5 billion in capital resources—$12.3 billion of private capital and $11.2 billion of SBA-guaranteed capital or commitments. Most funds are smaller than private VC companies: they usually have less than $100 million available at any time.

Companies receiving investments from SBICs or SSBICs must meet the criteria for 7A loans in terms of business type and size. Typically, SBICs invest between $150,000 and $5 million in a company. Part may be as a loan and part as an equity purchase or a debt-to-equity conversion.

Many SBICs specialize in making investments in a small group of industries and almost all focus within a particular region.

To convince an SBIC to become involved, a company must show ability to repay a loan. Early-stage companies must exhibit good sales and earnings. Start-ups must have a dynamic idea that can get off the ground quickly.

SBDCs

SBDCs provide assistance to small businesses in the areas of financing, marketing, production, organization, engineering and technical problems, and feasibility studies.

Small business development centers (SBDCs) provide assistance to small businesses in the areas of financing, marketing, production, organization, engineering and technical problems, and feasibility studies. There are over 1,000 SBDCs throughout the 50 states, the District of Columbia, Puerto Rico, the U.S. Virgin Islands, American Samoa, and Guam. In each state, a lead organization, such as a state government office or a university, sponsors the SBDC and manages the programs at all locations. (A listing of sponsors is available at *www.sba.gov/opc/pubs/fs43.*)

SBDCs have full- and part-time staff and also can put the owner of a small business in touch with volunteers from professional and trade associations, attorneys, lenders, academics, and members of the Service Corps of Retired Executives (SCORE), a group that works with entrepreneurs. SBDCs also provide paid consultants to help clients with special needs.

SBDCs also help small businesspeople to assemble a loan application package that will be approved for an SBA guarantee and then help locate an appropriate bank to underwrite the loan.

SBIRs

In addition to the loan, investment, and technical assistance opportunities provided through SBA-guaranteed loans, SBICs, SSBICs, and SBDCs, the SBA also provides small business innovation research grants (SBIRs) for researching and developing technical innovations.

SBIRs provide $20,000 to $50,000 in Phase I funding for six months of basic research into a technical innovation and up to $500,000 in Phase II funding for further development of the innovation. Private sector investment funds must follow the two rounds of SBIR funding.

Equipment Leasing: Free up Cash for Intellectual Capital

The SBA's sole mission is to help small businesses. For information about the many SBA programs, you can visit the agency's Web site, www.sba.gov. You can also call the SBA Answer Desk at 1-800-U-ASK-SBA for answers to specific questions. Local SBA offices are listed in the telephone book blue pages.

Entrepreneurs have long been leasing equipment to reduce their cash outlays for many of the high-cost items necessary to run a business, such as real estate and other equipment. The lease is a simple transaction: a party that owns an asset such as a building or piece of equipment (a lessor) offers to rent the use of that asset to a party that needs it (a lessee) for a specific period of time.

The transaction itself is simple; the decision on whether to lease or purchase (either outright with cash or financed via a commercial loan) is complex. Imaginative people in the last 50 years have constructed many variations on simple leases that offer financial and tax advantages to the lessor, the lessee, and third parties.

Your decision about whether to lease or buy is one you should discuss with your financial and tax advisors. You should also have representation in negotiating such a transaction. This chapter will deal with leasing equipment rather than real estate. Although the basic concepts are the same, real estate leases are usually entered into for a longer period of time and there are important extra advantages often attached to equipment leasing.

Leasing Advantages

Entrepreneurs enjoy four major advantages in leasing equipment rather than purchasing it.

▶ **Leases can be entered into quickly.** Leasing arrangements are constructed so that lessors don't need to perform the same kind of analysis of your financial condition or subject you to the restrictions and covenants that banks and other lenders do when making an equipment loan.

▶ **You avoid the risk of technological obsolescence.** Because you do not own the property being leased, you avoid the problem of holding systems that are becoming obsolete. You can write leases for varying periods of time, depending on how quickly the technology involved becomes obsolete.

▶ **You can lease goods as you need them, without making large capital investments.** As your needs for space and equipment increase, you can lease more. You can also time new leases so they expire with old leases, allowing you to acquire an entire new generation of equipment at the same time.

▶ **Traditional leases are recorded as regular monthly expenses on your income statement**, rather than as assets and consequent loan liabilities on your balance sheet. This "off-balance-sheet financing" shows a more favorable view of your financial condition to other potential lenders or investors.

A lease can be created for used equipment.

The Operating Lease

The *operating lease*, sometimes called a *true lease*, gives the lessee the advantages of use without ownership and gives the lessor the advantages (and risks) of ownership. The lease can be written in such a way that the lessor and lessee share responsibility for some elements of the item's upkeep, reducing the risk of ownership to the lessor.

An operating lease provides a lessee with a single monthly payment that covers the cost of the rental plus any risk of ownership it is covering. For instance, the lease may include payment by the lessee of some portion of property taxes and general maintenance. On the other hand, this may be covered completely by the lessor.

As owner of the property, the lessor benefits from tax deductions for property taxes paid on the leased item and for depreciation and reaps any actual appreciation in market value. In the case of real estate, the lessor may also receive tax credits available for rehabilitation of property.

The Finance Lease

Over the years, sophisticated lessors have created modifications of traditional leases that benefit lessees and lessors alike. For example, there are now leases that look more like collateralized loans, with the item being leased acting as collateral for the loan.

These modified leases are called *finance leases* or *capital leases*. Some of the modifications were driven by tax-law changes enacted in 1986, which reduced deductions available for "passive investors" of real estate and equipment. Others were driven by the increasingly short life cycles of typically leased equipment, such as computer and telecommunications equipment.

The major modifications that create a capital or finance lease include:

> ▶ **Leases for the economic life of the item** instead of a fixed length of time, or for a fixed time with an option or series of options to extend the lease through the item's economic life.

> ▶ **Lease-to-purchase provisions.** These can be an option to purchase at the end of the lease term or a requirement to purchase at the end of the lease term for a fixed amount or for fair market value or the difference between the fair market value and the purchase price stipulated at the beginning of the lease term.

> ▶ **Variable monthly rental payments.** They can be gauged to volume factors, such as use (number of copies for a photocopier) or sales of goods produced with the machine. They can have an interest rate that floats in relation to some index, like any other variable-rate business loan. They can increase over the term of the loan so you pay less while your company is younger and then more, to account for inflation. Or they can be reduced later to allow you a better cash flow.

Capital leases make it easier for the lessor to repossess the property if you default. But capital leases with options to renew allow you to use a piece of equipment for its true useful life, not just for the life of the original lease. If the property becomes obsolete quickly, you don't have to renew; if it has a longer useful life, you can exercise your options.

Some capital leases are written so the lessor maintains the equipment and provides automatic upgrades as items become obsolete. Telecommunications and computer equipment companies have become masters at writing leases that provide growth opportunities for entrepreneurs while protecting the equipment manufacturers.

A large corporation with old equipment may lease it to you for a fraction of a regular lease in order to generate some income from an otherwise idle piece of equipment.

With a use lease, available for some equipment (e.g., photocopiers), your lease fee depends on how much you use the equipment each month. If you lease old equipment from another company, try to get a use lease.

29

Chapter 3

Getting Started/Need More Money, Part 1

ENTREPRENEURS WHO NEED MORE THAN $100,000 TO START THEIR business are beyond being able to use the "bootstrapping" techniques discussed in Chapter 1. While some of the players who may be able to provide financing are the same—family and friends, banks and commercial finance companies, etc.—they will often want to have a different kind of relationship with a company that is looking for between $100,000 and $1 million than with a company looking for less than $100,000.

Specifically, the need to raise over $100,000 forces entrepreneurs to think about not just borrowing money, but selling equity in the company to investors willing to put cash into the venture.

This chapter and the next two focus on equity investments. We also discuss briefly a number of government programs other than those provided by the SBA.

The Equity-Investor Universe: Different Investors Meet Different Needs

Unless you are incredibly wealthy, it is nearly impossible to grow a large company using only your own capital and loan proceeds. Most businesses that grow large enough to become publicly owned have to find private equity financing at some point in their growth cycle.

To be sure, if you are going to start a business, you must invest some money in it. Any professional investor in private equity deals will want an entrepreneur to have some of his or her own money at risk—commonly known as "skin in the game."

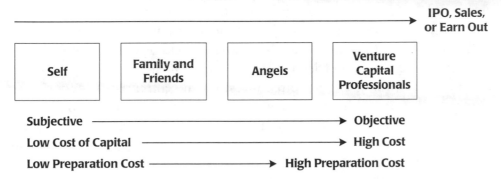

Figure 3-1. Progression of equity funding sources showing characteristics of funding decisions

Equity Investors

For growth financing that is beyond your own means, you will generally turn to one of four classes of equity investors:

1. Family members and friends
2. Wealthy angel investors
3. Professional venture capital (VC) firms
4. Investors in business development companies (BDCs) and other venture-oriented mutual funds.

We'll discuss family members and friends in this chapter, angel investors in Chapter 4, business development companies in Chapter 5, and venture capital firms in Chapters 6 and 10.

To fully understand the differences among these classes of investors, it is also important to know the life cycle of a new venture and its need for cash.

Remember: all of these investors want an equity position in your company. That means that in order to get access to their money, you will have to sell a piece of the company to them. This is an important point. As you go out and search for capital, be mindful of the trade-offs involved in raising capital and maintaining operating and ownership control of your company. (In reality, professional venture capitalists and even angel investors usually structure a deal in a complex fashion in which they take a special class of stock that gives them special rights in the event your company fails. They convert this *preferred* stock to *common* stock over time.)

Family and Friends

Family members and friends are the easiest investors to find, approach, and persuade to invest.

By far the largest pool of outside investors in new and young companies is the founder's family and close friends. This is especially true for entrepreneurs who do not have dreams of grandeur of an initial public offering (IPO), who want their companies to always be held privately.

Family members and friends are the easiest investors to find, approach, and persuade to invest. They often invest on the entrepreneur's conviction about the venture, rather than on a rigorous analysis of a business plan.

That is not to say that family and friends cannot be a powerful source of early-stage financing for entrepreneurs who want to grow their companies and yet stay out of the clutches of the large VC firms.

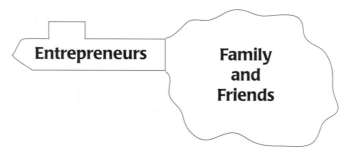

Figure 3-2. Entrepreneurs' relationship to family and friends investors (casting the net)

Angels

Entrepreneurs also turn to angels for seed funding, which is usually for amounts under $1 million.

Angels are wealthy individuals who invest in companies even though they have little or no personal relationship with the entrepreneur before making the deal. Angels are semiprofessional venture capitalists. They generally invest on their own, although they may team up in informal groups to fund a particular venture.

Some angels are entrepreneurs themselves, people who have started, operated, and then cashed out of lucrative businesses. They may use their investment as a way to nurture a new company and mentor an aspiring entrepreneur, without having to live the new venture from day to day.

It's harder to estimate the exact size of the angel community than it is the VC community, since VC firms have some level of regulatory paperwork they have to do. But estimates are that each year angels put as much money into new and growing businesses as venture capitalists do.

At any time, there are about a half million angels actively looking to invest in entrepreneurial businesses, out of between two and three million angels who have made an investment at some point. Angels invest in some 50,000 deals a year, about ten times as many investments as the funds operated by VC firms, and 80 percent or more of angel investments are made in start-up or seed-stage deals.

Professional Venture Capitalists

Professional venture capitalists are the managers of VC funds. A VC fund is a pool of money raised from a small number of wealthy individuals and institutions such as pension funds, universities, or foundations. Once the desired amount of money is raised, no more investors can get into it. The fund has a finite lifetime.

A VC firm may operate a number of funds, opening a new one to a new group of investors as soon as the previous one has been fully subscribed. Funds are typically $50 to $500 million, although some funds are over $1 billion. Each fund maintains a manageable portfolio of investments to monitor and to cash out of when it comes time to disburse proceeds to investors.

Venture-Oriented Mutual Fund Investors

Investing in a VC fund used to be for the very rich only. The Securities and Exchange Commission (SEC) allows VC firms to market their closed funds only to "sophisticated investors," whom the SEC defines as those with over $1 million in individual (not family) net worth or over $200,000 per year in income. But many mutual fund companies have in the past few years established mutual funds that invest in venture capital funds, allowing investors with as little as $10,000 to invest in venture capital pools.

At any time, there are about a half million angels actively looking to invest in entrepreneurial businesses, out of between two and three million angels who have made an investment at some

Business Analysis: From Subjective to Objective

Your analysis of your venture is purely subjective. If you didn't believe in your business concept, you wouldn't invest your time and money in it. But that doesn't mean your idea will make a successful business.

Your family and friends can't be expected to be objective either. Their relationship to you makes it difficult or even impossible for them to analyze the merits of your idea objectively.

Angels are theoretically objective. But even they are in a position where their personal preferences (such as the kind of business in which they've been involved) and their psychological makeup draw them toward certain kinds of investments over other kinds. For instance, Paul Allen, one of the founders of Microsoft, who cashed out of that company and is currently an angel investor, naturally gravitates toward software. There may be a far better opportunity with a biotech company, but he's a software guy.

The most objective analysis will come from professional venture capitalists. How they conduct their analysis of potential investments is part of the discussion of what venture capitalists want from you.

Equity Cost of Capital

You may have had to borrow the money to start the company. But you have 100 percent of the equity

In equity terms, financing your new venture out of your own pocket costs nothing. You don't have to give any of the company's equity away to get the funds.

Your cost of capital is not free. You may have had to borrow the money to start the company. But you have 100 percent of the equity (i.e., you own 100 percent of the company).

Your family and friends may not want much equity either. But angels will want a significant stake in your company—and venture capital pros aren't called vulture capitalists for nothing. The discussions over how much of a company the entrepreneur has to give up are often the most knotty in the relationship between funders and entrepreneurs.

It's also important to remember that if you give away too much equity too early, there may not be enough left to get the last round of funding necessary to take the company to the final stage before going public, if that is your ultimate goal.

That's why it is so important to think about the end of the funding process before taking the first step. As you plot your company's first five years, try to match the staging of equity investments to the milestones you hope to reach. Each milestone you reach successfully should reduce your cost of raising more equity capital.

Preparation Costs

Another variable in equity sales by entrepreneurs to investors is the preparation costs involved. If you are providing the funding, you obviously don't need any contract with yourself, so your preparation costs for getting equity from your own pocket are little beyond those of setting up an S corporation or an LLC (limited liablity company) and setting up a set of business accounting books. As you seek investments from outsiders, however, there can be significant costs in legal fees to draw up the appropriate documentation for the investments.

Depending on what route you choose—unregulated agreements with individuals or regulated agreements with a limited number of investors whom you solicit—you will need to have prepared one of the following:

- ▶ individual term sheets
- ▶ an investment memorandum (known as a *private placement memorandum*)
- ▶ a prospectus

The cost of negotiating terms can go into the thousands of dollars. (Lawyers are expensive.) But this is a fraction of the cost of preparing an IPO, which involves legal and investment banking fees that can be as much as 10 percent of the amount being raised (most of which goes to the investment bank that underwrites the offering).

Investor Fit

Whomever you select as an investor, that person or a person representing that company will be with you for a long time. When looking for investors, you need to use a screening process, just as if you were hiring a key employee. A key investor may merely wish to touch base every week or two or may be on the phone with you constantly and in the office two or three times a week, haranguing you over every little matter.

If your initial impression of a potential investor is that you can't work with that person, don't take the money. You should not be willing to take capital from someone who will be nothing but grief in the future.

In addition to getting a sense of a personal fit, it is important to determine what an investor can contribute to your company in addition to capital. Does the investor have contacts with suppliers, marketing support, a network of others who might provide future financing, or some other important capability? If you can't determine this before the person invests, there is little likelihood you will find out later.

The "Fit" Analysis

Before accepting an investment, do a fit analysis of the investor. This enables you to select investors who are most compatible with you and your business. The fit analysis has four elements.

1. *The potential investor must be compatible with the nature of the business.* This means being familiar with the business model and the technological universe the business is working in (e.g., a potential investor with a background in computer hardware may not be the best fit for an e-business company that focuses on distributing health care products).
2. *The potential investor must be capable of executing in the desired position and enjoy it.* When speaking with investors who would like some involvement in the company's operations, look for people who could fill gaps in the current management or operating structure.
3. *You should be able to interact with the investor apart from business.* If you can't have dinner with the potential investor and talk about your family and hobbies, find someone else. You will be working 18-hour days, but you should still be able to disengage for a few moments.
4. *The potential investor must be able to get along with the senior managers and operating staff.* If this person is going to be an integral part of the organization, he or she has to be able to talk with others besides you.

The bottom line is that a potential investor has to become a part of the team, in a capacity that is consistent with the business functioning well. If not, here's an example of what can happen. In one business, an entrepreneur needed capital and the one person who was willing to invest would not budge from having a 50 percent vote in major decisions. The investor was a full-time professional in another company in a completely unrelated field and was not involved in the entrepreneurial company's day-to-day operations. Yet he persisted in overriding the entrepreneur's judgment in critical business decisions. The company eventually bogged down and was unable to find future capital investments.

You should never allow yourself to be handcuffed with oppressive stipulations made by investors. Such stipulations are more frequently problems with angel investors and friends and family than with professional venture capitalists.

Some of these issues are intangibles of a personal relationship. Others are issues to be negotiated during the formalization of the business relationship.

Even with Family and Friends, Create a Business Relationship

To minimize the potential for confusion and misunderstandings and future problems in your relationship with a family member or a friend who is able and willing to be a source of capital, it is imperative that you use a business approach in dealing with such an investor. This approach goes beyond defining and committing to writing the terms of your financial agreement. It means that you treat any friend or family member who is a potential investor as you would a purely business contact.

Many entrepreneurs immediately think, "I can't do that, I've known Mike for years" or "It will turn Aunt Sadie off if I do that." But you need to change both your mindset and the mindset of your friend or family member the potential investor.

When money comes into play, the relationship will change, whether you want it to or not.

When money comes into play, the relationship will change, whether you want it to or not. By being explicit at the outset that the business aspect of the relationship is separate from the personal, you are able to move the relationship in a positive direction, rather than simply letting it just develop naturally and then reacting to harsh feelings later.

To ensure good and healthy interactions with friends and relatives who invest in your business, you must lay the groundwork. The first step is to tell any prospective investor that this matter is separate from the other aspects of your current relationship. For you it is important that your potential investor consider the investment on its merits. You want him or her to judge you as a potential entrepreneur on those merits, not simply on your current relationship.

Of course, we all know that friends and family members won't be able to completely ignore their current relationship with you. And that's OK. As you'll see in the discussion about angel investors, many of them are willing to invest in entrepreneurial companies for reasons that are not purely financial, such as to help their local or regional economy, to invest in alumni from their university, or to foster entrepreneurship among women or minorities. If someone wants to give you "an extra five points" or a "gold star" for being a friend or a family member, that's OK. But your friendship or kinship should not be the sole basis for the investment decision.

You should set up a meeting with the potential investor, just as you would with any other investor, to present and discuss the investment opportunity. Prepare for that meeting by analyzing the friend or family member as you would any potential third-party investor. Consider the kinds of business-related conversations you have had with the person, the person's level of financial and investing sophistication, and other factors. Make the presentation simple and straightforward.

The meeting should be held when it is convenient for the prospect. Make it separate from any event that is not business, such as a family dinner. Dress in appropriate business attire. If the prospective investor works outside the home, try to meet during a workday when it is convenient for him or her (e.g., early morning, lunch, or immediately after work) at his or her place of business. Dress appropriately for your prospect's work (e.g., business casual if the prospect owns a small retail business or manages a production plant; suit and tie for men, or suit, pantsuit, or skirt and blouse for women if the prospect is a corporate executive or a professional).

Prepare appropriate documents for the family or friend prospect to review, including a business plan or prospectus and basic agreements and a term sheet. (A term sheet is essentially an expression of interest. It is a document outlining the terms of an investment opportunity. It is a negotiating document to which the parties must jointly agree before a definitive investment agreement can be drafted. It does not constitute a legal obligation for either party.)

For example, if the prospect has expressed possible interest in making a loan, you should come to the meeting with a written loan agreement that states the loan amount, interest rate, repayment terms, and the lender's rights should you not fulfill your obligations. You should negotiate the terms, just as with any other lender.

A relative may decide to give you money as a gift. This does not lessen your responsibility to conduct yourself as a businessperson and have the same type of meeting as you would with a potential friend or family lender or equity investor, to make your presentation and state your business case. Should the gift materialize, write a formal thank-you letter that restates how you are using the money. (People who give gifts often like to know how they've helped advance a cause.)

If you are receiving an equity capital infusion, create a term sheet just as you would for an angel investor with whom you have no previous relationship. During the meeting, the investor and you will discuss the terms and possibly negotiate. The term sheet should state clearly such things as the equity investor's rights in terms of the company's operations and the level of involvement, which may include a position on the board of directors or an advisory committee.

A key part of the meeting should be discussing risk. Be clear that there is no guarantee the investor will get his or her money back, let alone get a return on the investment. Before accepting money on any terms from a friend or family member, explain as clearly as possible, both orally and in writing in the documentation you provide, the level of risk to the capital that they are investing in your business. Make sure your benefactor has the financial ability to put this money at risk. You should again make this risk clear before signing and perhaps even a third time.

Family and friends are a valuable and vital source of funding for entrepreneurs, yet they are often underrated. Entrepreneurs do not tend to address this universe of potential financial support methodically. They think of several people and approach them willy-nilly. However, if entrepreneurs do not take an organized approach, two things are likely to happen:

> *As you speak with friends, family, and angels, it is a good idea to determine their particular backgrounds and affiliations and leverage their connections into opportunities to meet others.*

- ▶ The entrepreneur fails to identify some potential friends-and-family investors, so he or she does not consider and approach them.

- ▶ Relatives and friends become alienated and relationships become strained or even ruptured, either because the entrepreneur neglects to invite someone to participate or because an investor feels that the entrepreneur did not warn him or her adequately of the risks of investing.

Many friends and especially family members will say, in effect, "You don't need to go through the whole song and dance for me." However, they will respect you for acting like a businessperson and appreciate your treating them as serious, sophisticated investors and not just like dear old Uncle Mike or Cousin Janet.

What Do Family and Friends Want from You?

"Whatever you give me is OK."

"I know you'll be fair."

"I trust you."

You may hear any one of these comments or a variation of one, two, or possibly even all three from a family member or friend when you begin discussing the equity share you will give him or her in exchange for investing in your company.

*F*amily members and close friends invest in your company because they like you, think you're bright, or want to give "one of their own" a helping hand.

Family members and close friends invest in your company because they like you, think you're bright, or want to give "one of their own" a helping hand. Although some may see an opportunity to get in on the ground floor of something that could be big, return on investment is not the primary motivation for investing in your company. This is true even for your family members or friends who may also invest in other companies as arm's-length angels. (The term "arm's-length" refers to a transaction between two or more unrelated companies or individuals acting in their own interests. Relatives—persons connected by a blood relationship, marriage or common-law partnership, or adoption [legal or in fact]—are not considered to deal with each other at arm's-length.)

Generally family or friends will accept your documentation for a stock offering made to a small group of select people—which is known as a *private placement memorandum* (PPM)—as presented without much question. A PPM is a simple version of the full prospectus that must be issued with a public sale of stock. A PPM or a stock prospectus states the cost per share to the investor and specifies the rights of the investor as a stockholder. The PPM also discloses the company's current financial state, outlines its plan for the future, and states the risks involved in the investment.

If you are going to sell stock to a number of family and friends, you must give each prospective investor the same offer and the offer must be exempt from registration with the Securities and Exchange Commission (SEC). A lawyer must draft the PPM and it must be marketed to investors in such a way that it falls into one of the exemptions for stock offerings under securities laws.

Some family and friends will not want to bother reading disclosure documents and may even say they do not need or want a formal agreement. It's up to you to make sure they read the disclosure and understand the risks involved in investing in your company. It's your obligation to provide a formal written agreement and to make sure that it is signed and notarized to make it legal and binding.

Differences in Motivation

Let's look at the differences in motivation between family members and friends who invest in your company.

Family

Family members usually want to help and they want to see someone in their family succeed. In most cases, entrepreneurs come to family members with an investment opportunity; family members don't often approach entrepreneurs looking for a way to invest their money. Family members expect that their entrepreneur relative will give them as good a deal as he or she would give an unrelated investor—or possibly a better deal. Of course, this is not possible, since friends and family who are approached in the same time frame about investing must be allowed to do so under the terms of the same private placement memorandum.

Most relatives will accept the terms offered. Their thinking is that the entrepreneur would not take advantage of them. The basis for their investment is trust and family loyalty.

Most relatives will accept the terms offered. Their thinking is that the entrepreneur would not take advantage of them. The basis for their investment is trust and family loyalty.

The entire deal can usually be closed in a few phone calls or over a meal. A formal presentation is rarely needed, although it's a good idea to make one. There are two reasons to give your family members a presentation. First, it helps them understand the risks involved in the investment. Second, it's good to practice in front of a friendly audience; their questions, including the silly, naive ones they ask because they feel close to you, may well point to holes in your presentation or even in your business plan.

Friends

Friends are more likely to treat an investment in your company as an arm's-length transaction. They may want an attorney or business counsel to review your documentation and provide advice. You have a relationship of trust with them, but unless they are your closest friends, they will probably use the old Reagan-administration adage about nuclear weapons, "Trust but verify."

Terms

Family and friends most often help fund a business that is either a rank start-up or very close to that stage. You may have done some work and spent some money on equipment and/or business services, but your business probably has little if any real value.

In all likelihood you have no prototype of your product (although you may have drawings or specifications), you have not clearly defined your market, and you have no prospective customers. So how do your price your shares? How do you determine what percentage of the equity in your company a family member or friend should get for an investment of, say, $10,000 or $25,000?

Any valuation benchmark you set will be arbitrary. Get advice from an accountant or an attorney who has worked with small businesses that have received outside financing. That experienced professional can help you value the business realistically so you do not give away too large an equity stake or constrain your ability to make business decisions.

Before taking on your first outside investors, it is important to establish milestones the company has to reach in order to achieve higher valuations for future sales of equity. One common approach is to structure the PPM as a debt-equity arrangement, with the debt at a high interest rate and the investor having an option to convert the debt to equity during a finite period.

For instance, an interest-only $25,000 loan could be written for a three-year term, with an annual interest rate of 15 percent ($3,750), with the interest deferred for two years and the entire principal due after three years. At any time during the three years, the lender could convert the loan to equity and refund all interest payments received. This allows the lender to decide over a period of time if he or she feels the company has long-term viability and wants to become an equity owner.

Closing a loan or sale of equity with a family member usually takes two to four weeks; for a friend it can take two to eight weeks. This is a lot less time than it takes to close a similar arrangement with an angel or a professional VC.

Approaching Family and Friends

You should not approach friends and family casually. You need to treat them with the same care, concern, consideration, and attention as you would any other potential investor.

Friends are more likely to treat an investment in your company as an arm's-length transaction.

Have a prospectus of your business (a business plan or a summary, minus the marketing hype) and a PPM ready. This is especially important with friends and family, many of whom would not be considered "sophisticated investors" under SEC rules. Sophisticated investors can be expected to cut through the usual hype and understand a business plan and perform enough *due diligence* (thorough research) to understand all of the business risks involved. Friends and family, given their relationship with you and the level of trust, will not always do that.

Documentation must be consistent with the securities regulations in the state in which the PPM is being offered (laws passed to protect the public against securities fraud, commonly known as *blue sky laws*). If you are pitching your offer to people in different states, your lawyer needs to check the PPM against each state's regulations.

After All, What Are Friends For?

In the early 1960s, a recent medical school graduate wanted to start a pharmaceutical company. He asked a group of classmates to invest $5,000 each in his venture. Some of his investors had to borrow money from their own families to make the investment. But he was bright and a good scientist, and they trusted him to be a good businessman.

After some years of struggling, his company became successful enough that a publicly traded drug company purchased it. Those who stuck with the investment were rewarded with common stock in the major company. Through the 1970s and 1980s, this company became increasingly successful and the stock split a number of times.

Through a series of mergers and acquisitions in the 1980s and 1990s, investors who held their stock were rewarded with holdings in ever larger and more successful companies. In 1999, the company of which the small drug company was a part was bought by a global drug company based in Europe. Since individual foreigners were not allowed to own stock traded on that country's market, the last of the initial investors were forced to cash out of their position, for well over $2 million each.

Your offering memorandum must include a statement of risks. You must also give each investor, including friends and family members, an accredited investor form to complete. (This is a document by which an investor certifies that he or she is an "accredited investor" as defined in rule 501(a) of Regulation D promulgated under the Securities Act of 1933 by the SEC.) If you don't have such forms when an investor hands you a check, that money should be placed in escrow until you get the form signed by the investor. Finally, each investor has 60 days in which to request that you return his or her investment.

In some instances, your legal counsel may decide that all money raised must be held in escrow until you reach your fundraising goal for that particular round of financing. You may structure your memorandum as an "all or nothing" round of financing or leave out this clause and be free to use money as it is raised, regardless of how much is ultimately raised.

Guidelines

When it comes to business, your relationship with friends or family needs to be different from what it is for backyard barbecues. If a friend or family member wishes to invest in your company, you must treat the transaction in a businesslike way. Your future relationship, not only with the investor but with all of his or her peers, is at stake. Try to follow these five guidelines:

1. From the first discussion about a possible investment, make it clear to the potential investor that this is a business relationship, not merely an extension of the family relationship. Your relatives and some friends will tell you that is not necessary; tell them it is. Blame formalities and legalities on your lawyer if necessary. Tell your potential family or friend investor that your attorney said unless investments are handled strictly as business, you can get in trouble down the line.

2. Provide a family member or friend who's a potential investor with all of the same documentation as you would provide an arm's-length angel or a professional venture capitalist. Ideally, you should give the person a full verbal presentation that sets forth the vision for the company and the particulars of the investment.

   The investor may not read the documents now or may just browse through them, but he or she will have them for future reference. And who knows? The investor may show them to someone he or she knows who is an angel who might want to get in on your next round of financing.

3. Put all agreements into writing. Again, many family members and some friends will suggest that written agreements are not necessary among people with a relationship of trust. Untrue. Written agreements are always necessary; in a relationship of trust they can be completed quickly and neither party needs to spend any time or legal energy trying to create an unfair advantage through the agreement. But there should be a written document that sets out the parameters of the business relationship. Again, when all else fails, blame your lawyer.

4. Tell the potential investor to exercise the same caution and due diligence as he or she would exercise if making an arm's-length arrangement. Encourage the investor to talk to his or her attorney and/or accountant before committing to the investment. Some people will change their minds during the course of these discussions; assure your potential investors upfront that if they change their minds about the investment, the personal relationship will not be harmed.

5. Find out if the investor wants to be involved in the company's operations and, if so, how. Everyone has expectations. Many angel investors want an active role in the company. So do many friends and family.

Many family members and some friends will suggest that written agreements are not necessary among people with a relationship of trust. Untrue.

With family or friend investors, you need to be especially careful about matching your expectations of an investor's role with theirs. Never allow any role they take in the company's operations to jeopardize the personal business aspects of your relationship.

Put their expectations in perspective and ask them to do the same. They may not want to hear you say you do not want a family member or a friend looking over your shoulder all the time, but they need to hear it. If you can't come to terms about the role the investor wants to play, you may have to say, "Thank you, but no thank you" to the investment.

*   *   *

The next chapter will discuss the second of the four classes of equity investors—angels.

Chapter 4

Getting Started/Need More Money, Part 2

A S MENTIONED IN CHAPTER 3, ENTREPRENEURS SOMETIMES TURN TO angels for seed funding, which is usually for amounts under $1 million. Angels are semiprofessional venture capitalists, individuals who invest in companies as business ventures, with little or no prior personal relationship with the entrepreneur.

Angels: Heaven-Sent Cash Can Jump-Start a Business

When angel investors are described as wealthy individuals willing and able to put capital at risk in other people's ventures, most people get the wrong idea, misled by the adjective "wealthy." The "capital at risk" can be any amount, as low as $1,000 in some instances.

Don't think of angels in terms of the amount of money they are willing to invest in a venture; think of them in terms of their relationship to the entrepreneur. Angel investors have a less personal relationship with the entrepreneur than do friends and family but may be closer than professional venture capitalists.

For instance, one group of entrepreneurs needed $500,000 to take a new medical device to the prototype stage. They were professionals in the field in which the device would be used. Through a combination of family, friends, professional contacts, and others they raised the entire sum through investments of $5,000 or $10,000 per investor.

The investors who were "once removed" from the entrepreneurs—friends of friends or professional acquaintances of professional acquaintances—meet the definition of angels. This is not the typical story you read about angel investors. It is far less glamorous than the one about the entrepreneur who cashed out his company's stock and began backing other entrepreneurs at $250,000 per investment or the story of the retired corporate executive who started an angels club that makes investments of at least $500,000 in each company and has three or four members who also act as company advisors and board members. (Such people certainly do exist.)

All evidence suggests that angels will be more important in the future. You may meet some angel prospects because they have personal or professional relationships with individuals you know, such as your lawyer, accountant, or banker. Others may express an interest because they have some affinity for you as an entrepreneur; for instance, you live in the same metropolitan area, you attended the same college or graduate school, or your business is in an industry in which the angel has worked or is currently working.

Not all angel investors are alike. They are scattered throughout society. There may be some angels among your relatives, friends, business associates, advisors, and social acquaintances. Remember: the line between these two classes of equity investors—angels and friends and family members—can sometimes be blurry. You may know some angels personally as family members or friends and thus are able to reach them without intervention. To other entrepreneurs they are angels.

Do you remember the movie *Six Degrees of Separation*? Angel investors form a community somewhat akin to the chain of characters in that movie—everyone is connected to someone who is connected to someone else. You must find out how you can use your contacts to bridge those degrees of separation and get to investors. We'll discuss ways to go about finding angels shortly.

Angels as Informal Investors

Angels are often considered—especially by academics who study them—as "informal investors." In 1981, William Wetzel, a professor at the University of New Hampshire's business school, and his colleagues began studying

When you create a chart of either friends and family or angels, put all of them on one chart and color code those who are in one category and those who are in more than one.

A Real Angel

Ed, a vice president of business development and contracts for a medium-size aerospace company, received a settlement from an injury claim when he was 48. His salary and that of his wife were enough for the family to live on, so Ed decided to use his windfall as risk capital.

A few months later, a business associate suggested that he and Ed invest in a start-up company that manufactured industrial products. Each man invested $50,000. They set 15 percent as their target annual rate of return, compounded, and agreed that the exit strategy should be to sell to a larger company within five years.

Since making that investment in 1997, Ed has tried to make one angel investment each year. He usually invests $40,000 to $50,000 in each deal, but once invested $100,000 in a company he found especially promising. He often invests with one or two other angels, especially in very risky ventures in which he wishes to invest a smaller sum.

Ed considers only deals that come from quality referrals, have a unique product advantage, are with an entrepreneur who has made a significant cash investment, and allow him a sense of personal satisfaction in knowing that his investment did some good for the entrepreneur. He prefers to invest in businesses that he understands and where he can help the entrepreneur by providing business contacts and marketing leads.

informal investors throughout New England. Their research helped define the key differences between angels and professional venture capitalists.

During the mid- and late 1980s, capital from informal investors helped fuel the wave of East Coast technology. Professional venture capitalists across the country were pulling back from investing after getting burned by failures during the early 1980s and because of changes in tax rates that drastically reduced the top income tax rate and thus caused venture capital to lose some of its allure as a tax shelter.

Angels operate less formally than professional venture capitalists. Although they want their investments to generate above-average returns, they don't always focus exclusively on the bottom line when deciding where to invest.

Angels get into venture investing in a variety of ways, from being asked to partner with someone in a small business to answering a newspaper classified advertisement seeking investors. Their knowledge of analyzing investment opportunities is often rudimentary; they tend to be self-taught. They often view any investment opportunity through the particular situation that brought them to risk-capital investing.

Angels are usually more receptive than professionally managed VC funds to investing early in start-up and young businesses. This may be because of the size of the investment they are willing and/or able to make, because professional venture capitalists have shied away from such investments in which the risk/reward balance is notoriously difficult to quantify, or because risk/reward ratio may be unacceptable.

Many angels are willing and even desire to contribute directly to the venture by taking on roles, including hands-on participation in management. Those angels who take on a management role—paid, unpaid, or as a condition of their investment—are often called *value-added investors*.

Another characteristic of angel investors is that they are sometimes willing to accept a smaller financial return on their investment in order to obtain some return of another kind. That return might simply be the opportunity to help young entrepreneurs in their geographic region or minority or women entrepreneurs or to contribute to the development of a socially useful technology.

Angels are usually more receptive than professionally managed VC funds to investing early in start-up and young businesses.

Angels as Risk-Capital Investors

Angels occupy an important position on the spectrum of capital providers for entrepreneurial businesses. In addition to providing more early-stage capital for young and growing companies than most entrepreneurs can gather from friends and family, angels also act as a "stamp of approval" for a young business, causing venture capitalists to consider it more seriously.

Commercial banks and other large lenders rarely if ever lend funds to companies with few assets, with no salable product, or a small customer base. And few professional venture capitalists typically invest in such "concept businesses" either, especially after the dotcom bust of 2000–2001.

Family members and friends, credit cards, and second mortgages are often used to start a business. However, this funding is rarely enough to sustain a business for the months or even years it can take to create and market a product or bring an invention through the necessary rigorous commercial development process. Angels provide a capital bridge to help an entrepreneurial business move from the high-risk, still speculative phase to a lower-risk, more substantive status that can attract professional venture capital.

Angel investors are generally willing to invest larger amounts of money than friends or family. They are more sophisticated investors who fill the niche for substantive capital infusions into "in-between" entrepreneurial efforts.

Dealing with an Angel

Working with an angel can sometimes be difficult. Although they more frequently work in tandem with other angels or even professionally managed VC funds, they often invest individually and demand unique terms for their investments. Angels can be as insistent as venture capitalists on having a solid exit strategy. They also tend to be tough negotiators, requiring a large portion of equity, management control, or both in order get them to come on board.

Where Do Angels Come From?

The concept of the angel investor was born on Broadway about 100 years ago. The first angels were wealthy theatergoers from whom playwrights solicited money to bring their plays to the stage or to keep their failing theatrical productions afloat. These generous financial benefactors were like angels who descended from heaven to support a worthy piece of art.

In the 20th century, the capital markets became more professional and liquid with the growth of regional and national stock exchanges, and institutional investors grew more prominent.

Over the years, that system became more professional. Today theatrical production companies and individual producers regularly spin their Rolodex in order to round up funding from corporations and wealthy individuals to finance a play.

Wealthy individuals have invested in other business ventures as well. In the 19th century, private investors risked their wealth in mines, railroads, and other ventures. In the 20th century, the capital markets became more professional and liquid with the growth of regional and national stock exchanges, and institutional investors grew more prominent. Individual financial backers of entrepreneurial efforts faded somewhat into the background.

In the first part of the 20th century, corporate investments in technological innovation were consolidated in a few enormous laboratories, such as IBM's Watson Laboratory in New York, Bell Labs in New Jersey (which remained with AT&T after its divestiture into a long-distance company and seven local "Baby Bell" operating companies and is now part of Lucent Technology), and Xerox's Palo Alto Research Center (PARC) near the Stanford University campus in Palo Alto, California. Government research grants for technological innovation, which began around World War II, went to major universities such as Massachusetts Institute of Technology, Carnegie Mellon University, and California Institute of Technology.

In the 1950s, some of these labs started to spin out civilian uses of their technologies into dozens of entrepreneurial companies, most of which were located within a few hours' drive of the university or major corporations.

Silicon Valley is the culmination of the Stanford and PARC effect and the Massachusetts high-tech belt east of I-495 around Boston is the outgrowth of four or five generations of MIT spin-offs and spin-offs of those spin-offs.

Although angel investors continued to operate throughout the century, they did so quietly. They began to come to the surface with the advent of the "garage entrepreneurs" of the 1950s and 1960s. Such entrepreneurs as David Packard and William Hewlett, who started Hewlett-Packard, and Ken Olson, who founded Digital Computer, had help from deep-pocketed investors.

Angels became a fixture in the popular culture of business in the late 1970s and early 1980s when they began funding a generation of "garage start-ups" in the personal computer hardware industry, such as Apple and Compaq, and in the software world, such as Lotus and Microsoft and Software Arts. Angels also were involved in many start-ups in the biotech industry.

During the dotcom gold rush of the late 1990s, angels were somewhat pushed out of the picture as venture capitalists threw more and more money at start-up companies that promised new, Internet-based business models. These companies burned through billions of VC dollars as they tried to prove that business was about attracting visitors to Web sites rather than making profits.

It is almost ironic that one of the Web-based markets that have held up in the dotcom meltdown is the one for services that match angels looking for deals with entrepreneurs seeking funding. Once again, as venture capitalists have pulled back, angels are again finding their role in providing seed- and early-stage financing.

It is almost ironic that one of the Web-based markets that have held up in the dotcom meltdown is the one for services that match angels looking for deals with entrepreneurs seeking funding.

Key Characteristics of Angels

Although each angel is unique, it is possible to draw six broad general characteristics of these investors.

1. Angel investors have discretionary wealth. They must meet the SEC guidelines for "sophisticated investors." These individuals are considered "sophisticated" (qualified) by virtue of having a net worth of over $1 million and/or an annual income of over $300,000 for a couple or $200,000 for an individual. In the United States, the area around New York City, including the suburbs in northern New Jersey and Fairfield County, Connecticut, has the highest concentration of households that meet these criteria.

Because of their status, angels can be approached about investment

51

opportunities not fit for ordinary investors concerned about the risk of failure and loss of capital. Entrepreneurs and their brokers or agents are free to market unlisted securities to angels. Angels usually have much more wealth than the entrepreneurs they fund, a disparity that can have implications for the relationship.

2. Angel investors travel increasingly in flocks. Over the past 20 years, angel clubs, networks, and other organizations have flourished. They provide opportunities for angels to meet entrepreneurs, obtain business plans, and explore investment possibilities. In Silicon Valley, an entrepreneur can reach 50 to 100 angels with a single presentation to such a group. Many of these groups have been organized by university business schools or satellite organizations, such as the MIT Enterprise Forum.

3. Angel investors go solo. They may gather to survey the entrepreneurial field, but when it comes to making investments, angels tend to go it alone. If they wanted to be members of investment pools, they would just plunk their money into a VC fund and not put the time and effort into sizing up investment opportunities.

4. Angel investors tend to invest close to home. The vast majority of angel organizations are geographically based. Many started out as local networks of entrepreneurs, angels, and managers and professionals looking for job opportunities with entrepreneurial companies. Since many angels like to stay intimately involved with their investments, they tend to invest in companies within driving distance.

5. Angel investors are Internet savvy. The Internet has opened up vast, new worlds for both angels and entrepreneurs to move beyond their local area and find opportunities across the country and even overseas. A number of Web sites cater to angels and entrepreneurs in need.

6. Angel investors differ regionally. In the Silicon Valley and around Boston, angels are disproportionately technology-oriented and often willing to put money into new concepts. In the New York area, angels primarily come from a finance background and are more risk-averse and therefore less likely to invest in unproved technology.

Finding Angels

Finding angels is relatively easy. Finding the right angel and making a deal is far more difficult. Remember: many angels are entrepreneurs who wish to invest in businesses, technologies, and innovations that dovetail with their own backgrounds and/or current businesses. Some women angels may wish to limit their investments to female entrepreneurs and minority angels may work only with minority entrepreneurs.

Aside from looking for angels who mesh tightly with your unique characteristics or those of your business, you should also look for angels by conducting a targeted search. You want to reach angels through personal contacts, to minimize the distance you need to cast your net by leveraging your relationships with friends, family, business associates, and professional advisors in order to reach any potential angels they know. First try those closest to you, then people with whom you have a more tangential connection.

These various degrees of connection are like the concentric circles on a shooting target, each circle a universe of more distant relationships.

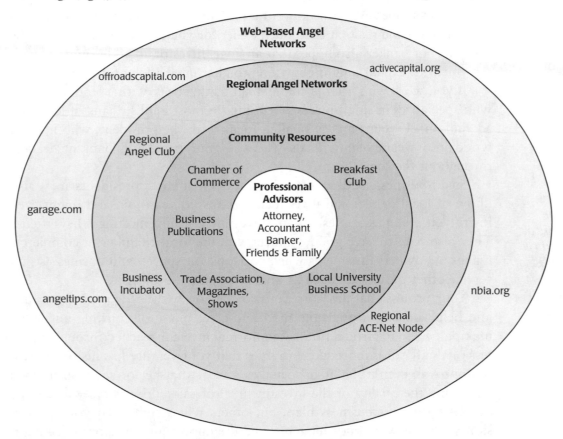

Figure 4-1. Targeted search for angel investor

The Inner Circle: Professional Advisors

In the bull's-eye of the target are your professional advisors—especially your accountant, attorney, and banker—and your friends and family. Any of these people may know somebody with the wealth and desire to make private-equity investments.

Many people who have risk capital available ask their accountant and/or lawyer to alert to investment opportunities. Your professional advisors know your personality and business-operating style, as well as the particulars of your business, and can often help match you with an angel of the appropriate temperament and personal style.

Bankers are another good source of referrals for angel investors. They are often eager to help new and young companies secure equity capital from an angel they know and trust; they want you to prosper and become a more valuable customer. Also this kind of a relationship can help raise the bank's comfort level and make it that much easier for you to get a bank loan in the future. Your banker also hopes that an angel investor, in addition to providing you with capital, might be willing to guarantee a loan for you.

If you work with a large commercial bank, speak with a lending officer who specializes in small-business lending (in most banks, loans of less than $1 million). If your bank is smaller, speak with the president, who is often wired into wealthy individuals who use your bank and banking leaders throughout the community.

Your professional advisors can provide you with leads, make referrals, and help you cut through the meet-and-greet phase of courting angels by making personal introductions.

Small-business lending specialists and small-bank presidents may also know of local or regional investment groups you can join and might even invite you along as a guest to any investment group meetings they attend. They also tend to have good contacts with the local chamber of commerce, real estate owners (this helps when you look for space), and businesses that service other businesses, such as office-equipment dealers.

Your professional advisors can provide you with leads, make referrals, and help you cut through the meet-and-greet phase of courting angels by making personal introductions. An informal investor reached through a professional advisor is more likely to infer that your venture has his or her seal of approval, even if the advisor makes it clear that her or she is in no way validating the quality of the investment. Professional investors will do due diligence on your business plan, but others will assume that your professional advisor would not have referred the opportunity without thinking it appropriate.

The Second Circle: Community Resources

In the second circle are what we call "community resources," people in your local and business communities. Members of this circle may introduce you to individuals interested in investing.

If you live in a metropolitan area, check out the chamber(s) of commerce. Many sponsor venture investment groups; if they don't, they should know which chambers do. Don't assume that the largest city in the area has the best chamber for finding potential investors. Also, chambers vary in the networks they support. If a venture group has a focus other than your area, ask about more appropriate groups. You can also check out any business breakfast clubs in your area.

Small business development center (SBDC) executive directors are also often tied into the angel and venture capital network. A call to the local SBDC is well worth the effort. The Small Business Administration (SBA) Web site, *www.sba.gov*, lists SBDCs around the country.

Your state or regional economic development agency can also help, as can the Secretary of State's office. The dean of the local business school and faculty members who teach entrepreneurship and finance should be wired into any venture investing networks in the area.

Leads to angel networks may be obtained from a local university's business school, a VC firm, the state economic development office, or a local government. Since you are not asking any of these sources for money, most should be willing to help.

Contact the editor of the local business newspaper; newspapers love to compile lists and business newspapers are heavily oriented toward service articles. There may have been a "best of the angels" article that the editor will send you or that you can access on the paper's Web site. Who knows? The editor may want to do a story about your company.

If any local companies have floated initial public offerings (IPOs) of their stock, you should get a copy of the prospectus and read it. It will include a list of principal shareholders. These are the angels and venture capital funds that invested early and cashed out by selling their stock at the time of the IPO. If they've cashed out recently, they may have money available to invest with you.

Your business community is an important resource. Your industry's trade association, trade magazines that cover your industry and the markets you're targeting, and trade shows that you attend or where you exhibit are all vehicles for meeting potential angel investors.

Remember the "millionaires next door." They live like you. Do not cross anyone off your list of potential angels because "they do not act like they have money."

Finally, there are resources for the angel community. *Angel Advisor* is a bimonthly magazine and Angel Forum is a conference and trade-show series. Both are operated by Angel Society, *www.angelsociety.com*.

The Millionaire at the Keyboard

A man in blue jeans and a cotton shirt walked into a piano store. The senior salesman, seeing how the man was dressed, asked a new, young salesman to handle the customer. The young salesman asked the man what he wanted. The man said he wanted a Bösendorfer grand piano. So the salesman took him to the $85,000 floor-model Bösendorfer.

The man played it for a few minutes and said, "I want to buy it." The salesman said there were none in stock and it would take a month to get another delivered. The customer said, "I'll take this one." The salesman asked what credit card the man would like to use to charge the piano and the man pulled out a roll of bills and said, "I don't like credit cards."

The Third Circle: Regional Angel Networks

The third circle consists of regional angel networks. There are dozens, maybe hundreds of such networks around the country, generally clustered around major metropolitan areas and/or universities, especially those known for producing entrepreneurs and business ideas.

Regional angel networks are often more formal than a chamber of commerce subcommittee or an angel investor breakfast club. Many are sponsored by centers on entrepreneurship that are affiliated with a university's business school.

Regional networks are also forming through an Internet network called Active Capital (formerly Angel Capital Electronic Network, ACE-Net), which can be accessed at *activecapital.org*. Although Active Capital is a tool for entrepreneurs to list their proposals and for individuals to search for possible investments, the site is a resource for finding angel groups across the United States.

Angels also often flock to business incubators, companies (either non-profit or for-profit) that offer spaces and services to small new companies. Many have office and laboratory facilities of various sizes in their building, so if a company grows it can move from one area to another within the incubator. Incubator services often include a central copy center for large printing jobs; an auditorium with state-of-the-art presentation media for gatherings of investors, business partners, and others; conference rooms; and even a caterer. Some incubators have a law, accounting, and/or marketing firm on-site, although tenants are not obliged to use these services.

The National Business Incubation Association (NBIA) has over 550 members. Its Web site, *www.nbia.org*, provides contact information on the members. Over half the member incubators provide formal or informal access to early-stage financing, according to the association.

The Fourth Circle: Web-Based Angel Networks

Internet-based investor networks form the fourth circle, the outermost, because through them you can reach potential investors far and wide. In addition to ACE-net, there are a number of Internet-based angel networks, as well as Internet-based matching sites.

Perhaps the best-known Internet-based sites for entrepreneurs looking to match up with angels are OffRoad Capital, at *offroadcapital.com,* and Garage Technology Ventures, at *garage.com.* The two go beyond mere networking to facilitate relationships. But they differ in the model they use.

OffRoad is a hybrid angel/professional venture capital site, where wealthy angels often piggyback their investments with those made by professionally managed VC funds. OffRoad operates on an underwriting model. It accepts a deal from an entrepreneur and then opens the deal up to its network of investors, who bid on it (how much they will invest for how little equity). Before the offer closes, potential investors can view the company's financial results and engage in Web-cast question-and-answer sessions with company executives. The entrepreneur pays for the underwriting service. Membership fees to investors are minimal.

Garage Technology Ventures uses a blind matching service model. Investors pay an annual fee to enter a password-protected area of the Web site called "Heaven," where entrepreneurs have posted business plans. If an investor is interested in the proposal, Garage forwards the investor's information to the entrepreneur. If the entrepreneur is interested, Garage gets the parties together for a handshake.

Brokers and Finders

Brokers and finders are intermediaries who help entrepreneurs raise capital. They promote themselves as having a broad range of contacts in the financial community and industry, which they use to find you funding.

This is a broad category. We distinguish brokers and finders from friends, family, professional advisors, and other acquaintances by the fact that a broker or finder wants compensation—either cash or a stake in the company—in exchange for helping you find capital.

How Do Brokers and Finders Differ?

Brokers usually advertise their services and have a set business model on which they operate: they expect predetermined compensation for performing particular services. For instance, they may charge a small cash fee for each referral they bring you and then a larger fee (all cash, cash and equity, or all equity) for every referral who actually makes an investment.

Brokers usually work with small businesses in several ways. They often find buyers for small companies and business owners looking to sell for potential buyers. They also assist in mergers of like businesses. In the course of these activities, they create a network of individuals with capital to invest, such as people who have sold a business and want to become more passive investors or possibly consultants to another business.

In some states, brokers need to be licensed with the Secretary of State. You should check out with the Better Business Bureau all brokers who operate under a corporate or "doing business as (DBA)" name.

Finders are a more elusive group. They may be business consultants, stock brokers or other investment advisors, or angel investors who have access to a network of other risk investors. Finders are not licensed and often negotiate different terms and conditions for each arrangement they make with an entrepreneur.

Accelerators may also perform the "finder" tasks as part of their more complete role. Accelerators are one-stop shops for business services for entrepreneurs; they may help find capital, personnel, and facilities (offices, labs, and/or product-development space), and provide consulting services of various kinds. Some accelerator organizations even have a physical location in which to incubate their entrepreneurial clients.

Sometimes it may be necessary to convert a member of your inner circle into a paid finder. You will have to sense whether someone is providing you a referral on a "friendly" basis or expects some kind of compensation if the referral works out. It's important to determine this early and to be very upfront about it. If the person wants compensation, negotiate seriously. Down the road, when your company is successful, you don't want that person to be complaining to everyone about helping you succeed and then getting nothing from you.

Family members and friends sometimes become angry and occasionally even sue if they feel they deserve compensation for providing successful referrals, even if nothing was ever put in writing. Oral agreements are often upheld in court, and the state of mind of the parties who allegedly agreed is

If someone offers to do something for you, ask how he or she would like to be compensated. If someone is in a position to help but you are uncomfortable asking, start by saying you would like to ask for help, but you want to compensate the person appropriately. Often people will help without compensation; your offer shows them that you are serious.

a key factor in court decisions. So, if you are going to create a "finder" relationship with someone from your informal network, pay a lawyer to draw up a proper, formal contract. The agreement can and probably should be short and simple, but it must be done correctly.

Professional finders always want a written agreement that outlines their compensation. Many want to be compensated for "expenses." This is often the trickiest part of the contract, since it can be difficult defining project expenses as separate from the finder's normal operating expenses. Others ask for unspecified "charges," which you must have defined clearly. Your contract should always state explicitly what expenses you are paying for.

Professional finders always want a written agreement that outlines their compensation.

Compensating a Broker or Finder

Compensation for brokers or finders generally has three elements:

▶ Fees for searching for capital. Most brokers or finders want an upfront fee for searching; they will not work purely on a contingency.

▶ Expenses incurred in the search. These should be defined clearly to distinguish them from normal operating expenses and to allocate any expenses that involve other clients. (For example, if the broker has four clients and he travels to another city to meet with potential funders, he should charge each client for one-fourth of the trip expenses.)

▶ A "success fee" if the search generates capital. This fee can be either a fixed amount or, more commonly, a percentage of the capital generated.

In some states, only brokers who are registered with the Secretary of State are allowed to take a success fee in either cash or an equity stake in the company (in the form of stock, warrants that allow for purchasing stock later, or a combination), while finders must be paid success fees in equity.

One common success fee formula is 5 percent for the first $1 million raised, 4 percent for the second million, 3 percent for the third, 2 percent for the fourth, and 1 percent for anything over $4 million. Other brokers and finders work on a straight 3 percent commission.

When the deal involves allocation of funds for several purposes or by different parties, the fee issue is more complex. For instance, an investor may agree to provide funding for particular activities but not others or may release portions of the funding over time as particular milestones are reached. In such a case, you should pay the broker or finder at the time you actually take control of the funds, not when the funding agreement is made. However, you might put the full fee in escrow. If you are paying cash, this puts it out of reach for other purposes. And if you are paying in equity, this ensures that it is issued at its value when the deal is signed, not at a variable value.

What Do Angels Want from You? Money on Wings Comes with Strings

What an angel wants out of investing depends on his or her motivation for becoming a risk-capital investor. What makes angels so difficult to capture is that each one is different. They all want an acceptable rate of return, but what's "acceptable" will vary. Motivations other than money may greatly influence their investment decisions: they are often willing to take less return or assume more risk if motivated appropriately. Therefore, you must customize your presentation and offer toward each angel's perspective and interests.

Understanding what a particular angel wants is no different than understanding what a particular customer or type of customer wants. Just as you should try to sell a customer on benefits, not features, you should try to sell an angel on investment opportunity in terms of how attributes of your company mesh with the attributes that he or she finds most important when making investment decisions.

The Angel and the Early-Stage Company

There are four principal types of benefits a potential angel may seek through investing in a company:

- A job.
- An opportunity to "run" an entrepreneurial business from outside, to exert some control by serving on the board of directors or an advisory committee or as a consultant.
- Diversification of an investment portfolio through high-risk passive investment.
- A means of doing some kind of social good.

If you agree that an angel will take a position in your company, work out a job description and compensation plan at the outset.

No matter which of these benefits a potential investor is seeking, part of the motivation is always a desire for "action." Just as some people bet on the horses or at casinos and others day-trade the stock markets, some individuals like to try to pick the winners from the hundreds of thousands of businesses that start up each year.

A Job

Angels who want jobs have various reasons. You need to understand what a particular angel expects for working for your company.

Angels will often work for little or no pay at first. Then, when the company begins to find solid ground, they expect to be put on the payroll at a salary near what the founder earns and in a top executive position.

For the entrepreneur, such an individual can be the answer to a prayer. If your company goes through the early stages of growth and attracts significant VC funding on the way to an IPO of common stock, the venture capitalists may move to replace you and other founders with seasoned professional managers. If you have an angel on board with management skills who is willing to continue working with you, you can keep some level of management control over your company as it enters adolescence, instead of being pushed out the door.

An Opportunity to "Run" an Entrepreneurial Business

Many angels are entrepreneurs themselves. They have started businesses, taken them through the early stages of growth, and maybe even cashed out in an IPO or a sale to a larger company.

As you know from running your own business, entrepreneurs want to be in control. And entrepreneur angels tend to demand a high level of control in the companies in which they invest. They usually do this from their position on the board of directors, a seat they demand in exchange for their investment. At the first sign of financial trouble, they may push for the board to install new management, possibly even themselves.

Such micromanagers can be a pain in the backside. However, they are sometimes willing to pay for the privilege by making investments larger than other angels might. While some micromanagement-style angels are serial entrepreneurs, others simply believe that they can buy power.

There can only be one boss but any number of advisors.

Diversification of an Investment Portfolio

High-net-worth individuals know that private equity investments usually produce a higher rate of return than publicly traded stocks and bonds. The very wealthy may have a portion of their investment portfolio in private equity opportunities such as real estate, leveraged buyout funds, hedge funds, and venture capital.

Many people who are angels solely to diversify their portfolios are not interested in active involvement in the company. However, there are two exceptions.

One is former entrepreneurs who believe they can help your company by sitting on the board of directors but have no interest in managing your company for you. These people can be true angels. They have a wealth of knowledge and experience, so they can advise you about how avoid problems, and substantial contacts who can help move your company forward.

The other exception is angels who invest in new businesses involved in areas with which they are intimately familiar. This happens a lot in the medical technology and biotechnology businesses, where doctors and scientists often put their investment capital. These angels usually don't want a seat on the board but may want some kind of scientific advisory position. If you keep them focused on their area of expertise, they can be a great help. But if they begin to meddle in management matters, they can be difficult, simply because they may not understand the normal early phases of a new company.

Means of Doing a Social Good

Since the mid-1990s, minority and women entrepreneurs have more means of bringing investments into their ventures.

Research on risk-capital investments has shown that most venture funding flows from white men to other white men. Since the mid-1990s, minority and women entrepreneurs have more means of bringing investments into their ventures.

Some angels interested in helping disadvantaged entrepreneurs are simply offering their own money, experience, and management talent to such entrepreneurs. Others have created focused angel clubs and even VC firms that direct investments solely toward minority or women entrepreneurs.

For instance, in 2000 Kay Koplovitz, the former CEO of USA Networks who would soon write *Bold Women, Big Ideas: Learning to Play the High-Risk Entrepreneurial Game*, created Springboard Enterprises. The idea behind this nonprofit organization "dedicated to accelerating women's access to the equity markets" is to train women entrepreneurs to better present their business plans to angels and venture capitalists.

Helping minority and women entrepreneurs is not the only social good of interest to angels. William Wetzel, a professor at the University of New Hampshire business school who has studied what he calls "informal risk-capital investors," has published studies of New England angels. One study showed that 45 percent of survey respondents were willing to accept less return or more risk in order to support entrepreneurs in their region, 39 percent to contribute to the development of socially useful technology, 37 percent to increase employment in their geographic area, 19 percent to aid urban-based entrepreneurs, 17 percent to support women entrepreneurs,

Socially Conscious Angels

There are angels who seek to invest in companies with particular environmental or worker-rights policies or with certain product attributes.

One national angel investor network is Investors' Circle (IC), a San Francisco group whose mission is *"to galvanize the flow of capital to entrepreneurial companies that enhance bioregional, cultural, and economic health and diversity."* IC tries to match its members with entrepreneurs seeking funds for companies with a combination of good financial outlook, environmentally friendly policies, and social consciousness.

Since its inception in 1992, IC members have invested about $75 million through the group, with investments currently running between $500,000 and $1.5 million. Each company that passes muster through the IC due diligence process is presented to members for their consideration. Groups of four members (a member can be an individual, an institution, or a pool of up to three individuals) invest in each deal as a syndicate.

One angel commented on his socially conscious funding: "This is a unique opportunity to create a legacy, an existence that will transcend my own."

and 14 percent to help minority entrepreneurs. And just as there are "green" mutual funds that hold stocks only in companies that are environmentally friendly, there are angels who invest in "green" ventures.

Qualifying the Prospective Angel

Given that it is difficult to generalize about what motivates angel investors, it is important for you to qualify any potential angel investor to make sure his or her motivations and desires mesh with your objectives and the role the angel may play. Understanding an angel's motivation is key to a successful relationship and possibly even to the success or failure of your business.

For example, one seed investor whose financial contribution entitled him to 20 percent of the company's equity demanded and received 50 percent of the voting authority on all major decisions (essentially a veto power). This investor saw himself as a capable manager and wanted to preserve the value of his investment. However, he did not know the industry in which the company was engaged. The investor often overrode company executives' decisions and effectively stymied the company's growth.

To qualify potential angel investors, ask the following nine questions and then do some background checking to see if their answers jibe with how others see them.

1. What is your business and professional background and how much of that experience is in my company's field?
2. Do you meet the SEC guidelines as a "sophisticated investor" ($200,000 annual income for an individual or $300,000 for a couple, or $1 million in household net worth)?
3. What is your experience investing in entrepreneurial businesses? (Ideally, you will not be getting much money, if any, from first-time angels.)
4. What type of business do you want to invest in? What products and services and what stage of a company's life cycle interest you?
5. What type of involvement do you want to have in the company's operations—active or passive, consultative, board, or management?
6. What investment range are you considering?
7. Do you want to be the single investor at this stage or a co-investor with people you know?
8. What are your financial criteria for making an investment—equity, debt, or debt-to-equity position, time frame for returns, minimum acceptable rate of return, and preferred exit strategy?
9. Do you have any other important criteria for investing?

Valuation must be reasonable because it is subjective and, just like expectations, personal. It must be agreed on, and it must take into account terms of the investment, whether or not the investor will be available for subsequent investments, and other circumstances.

Some angels, especially those new to private equity investing, may object to providing some of this information. You need to explain that you don't want to waste their time if the two of you are not a good match, especially since this would be a long-term relationship. Stress that if you two are a potential match, you want to be able to make a formal presentation that speaks to the specific benefits the investor might obtain by investing in your company. Also, tell the investor that you must be sure you are in compliance with securities laws. Just as with the discussions with friends and family prospects, blame the need to ask on your lawyer and the Securities and Exchange Commission.

What Angels Need

Unless you determine management control carefully, you may end up having a 50-50 partner. Know how much power you want any angel to have.

Because angels usually invest in the early stages of a company's lifecycle, most angels enter negotiations with an entrepreneur around five points, which vary in importance for each angel:

▶ More than just common stock
▶ A reasonable and realistic valuation of your company
▶ A seat on the board of directors
▶ Some degree of management control
▶ A clearly defined exit strategy

More than Just Common Stock

Most angels want a position in the investor hierarchy that gives them preferred rights above those held by common stockholders. They usually do this in one of two ways. Either they give the entrepreneur a loan that converts to stock if particular benchmarks are met or they take convertible preferred stock.

In the first option, if the company folds early on, you are on the hook to repay the loan. However, some angels invest on an interest-only basis and defer interest payments for one or two years. During those first years, as each performance milestone is reached, some of the loan and the deferred interest convert to stock. If the company hits all of its milestones over the defined period, the entire amount of the loan converts to an equity position for the angel. This conversion is usually to common stock, although some loans may be converted to preferred stock. Some angels retain their creditor status until there is a public offering.

In the second option, the angel usually waives payments of dividends due on the preferred stock for a period of time, possibly even until the company is profitable. As the company reaches performance milestones, some or all of the preferred stock and the waived dividends can be converted to a common-stock position. Or, the investor can wait to convert until there is a public offering of common stock or the company is sold to a publicly held company and the angel becomes a stockholder in that company.

The reason for taking preferred stock is to protect the investor if the company goes belly up. In that event, holders of preferred stock (the angels) get their money out before holders of common stock (usually the founders and early employees who have been paid with common stock in lieu of cash).

If an angel does accept common stock, he or she may want warrants that allow for the purchase of more common stock at the same price for a set period of time into the future. The angel may also ask for a clause that says the entrepreneur cannot initiate a buyback of shares from the angel with income from future rounds of private financing.

Reasonable and Rational Valuation of Your Company

Valuation is one of the trickiest parts of negotiations between an angel investor and an entrepreneur. An angel or a syndicate of angels usually wants between 20 and 30 percent of the company's equity. Because many angels or syndicates generally wish to invest between $500,000 and $1.5 million, they seek out companies with valuations between $1 million and $6 million. Of course, this is not a hard-and-fast rule, but it provides a good set of parameters.

If a company's valuation is less than $1 million, family and friends and other "bootstrap" funding is usually needed to boost that valuation above that level. If the company is valued at over $6 million, angels are rarely able to provide enough capital to reach the next stage of growth, so owners ought to be looking more to professional venture capitalists.

Matching the amount of funding needed to take the venture to the next level with the size of the equity stake the angel(s) wish to have and the valuation is an exercise in triangulation.

Matching the amount of funding needed to take the venture to the next level with the size of the equity stake the angel(s) wish to have and the valuation is an exercise in triangulation.

Early-stage companies usually lack hard data on sales, cost of goods sold, and margins on which to determine company valuation. Many not only have no revenues but also no prototype product or customer base. Some companies also have competitors that are further along on the same path they are, which limits their chances of success unless they can prove their technology or process superior.

There are various models angels can use to determine a rough valuation for your company. Some angels rely on a formal discounted cash-flow model, although this is difficult when the company history is short and it's necessary to rely on predictions about income and expenses. Others use less formal models. Some prefer to hold off on the valuation until after some performance milestones have been reached.

One long-time angel, John Ason, explains in an article posted on angelsociety.com how he values entrepreneurial companies when considering investing. He assigns the following valuations:

- ► A good idea: $1 million
- ► A working prototype: $1 million
- ► High-quality management: $1 million
- ► Meaningful revenues: $1 million
- ► Strong relationships in the company's industry and with potential clients: $1 million

With this down-and-dirty methodology, he comes up with a "positive valuation" for a company of between $1 and $5 million. Then he begins subtracting value for what he calls "valuation demerits," such as a lack of market focus, inability to forge alliances, bad deal negotiating, and poor attitude toward angel investors. Too many demerits can kill a potential deal, not just reduce its value.

Seat on the Board of Directors

About half of individual angel investors want to sit on your board of directors. An investor syndicate usually appoints one or two members to sit on the board.

From this perch, an angel can oversee how the company is progressing and determine if and when it will hit the performance milestones that trigger conversion of debt into equity or preferred stock into common, or other events, such as a need for more capital or a decision to seek a buyer.

A seat on the board also empowers the angel to influence major management decisions and effect changes, if needed. Because of this power, you should grant this position only for large investors or a representative of a group of smaller investors.

Also, make sure there is a personal fit between you and the investor or representative who will have a seat on the board. One CEO of a small company tested each prospective member of his company's board with a single question: "If I wanted to do something, how would you vote?"

Sophisticated investors know that getting a board seat depends on the size of the investment.

Unsophisticated angels may ask for a board seat because they have been told that investors are always appointed as directors. Sophisticated investors know that getting a board seat depends on the size of the investment. Seasoned angels also know that serving on the board exposes them to liability. Investors, vendors, and others who believe they have been misled by a company may take their grievances to the courts and try to hold officers and directors responsible in addition to managers. Most companies provide director and officer insurance. But this is expensive and does not cover instances of willful misconduct or misrepresentation.

The board should be composed of individuals who contribute substantially to the company's success—by their knowledge and experience as well as by their money. Entrepreneurs should view board seats as a premium not to be given lightly.

Degree of Management Control

Some angels demand a degree of management control (usually termed veto rights over particular issues) as a condition of their investment, even if they are on the board and don't take an active role in operational management. They might seek to control:

► Changes in compensation, especially stock options, for the company's top executives

► Executive hiring, including the CEO and chief financial officer

- ▶ Sale of the company or crucial or substantial assets
- ▶ Changes in the company's bylaws or articles of incorporation
- ▶ The annual business plan
- ▶ Contracts for over a particular amount (e.g., 25 percent of the amount the angel has invested)
- ▶ Borrowing over the amount of the angel's investment

The angel may also request other rights, such as:

- ▶ The right to countersign any checks over a particular amount (e.g., 10 percent of the amount the angel has invested).
- ▶ An antidilution clause, such that if stock in the company is sold within a certain period for less than the price the angel paid, the company will issue additional shares to the angel to maintain his or her percentage of the equity ownership.
- ▶ "Tagalong" rights, so that if a member of the management team receives an offer to sell or exchange any of his or her shares, that offer may be accepted only if the angel has the right to participate in the sale or exchange, on a pro rata (equal percentage) basis.
- ▶ The right to invest in further rounds of financing in order to maintain his or her percentage equity interest in the company, or even the right of first refusal to provide funds for any subsequent rounds of private financing.
- ▶ "Put" options on the stock he or she holds. A put is the option to force the company to buy back the stock at book value or at a set price at a specified time.
- ▶ An "unlocking" provision, whereby if there is a bona fide offer to purchase the company and the angel wishes to accept the offer but the entrepreneur does not, the company must purchase the angel's interest on the same terms as in the offer to buy the company.

An angel usually will seek to protect his or her investment by piggybacking rights onto those of the founders. For instance, if the entrepreneur wishes to sell more than 10 percent of his or her stake in the company, the angel would be able to piggyback an equal percentage of his or her stake in the sale at the same price. Likewise, if the company registers its common stock for sale to the public, the angel would want piggyback registration rights in order to sell some or all of his or her stake in order to cash out at the time of the IPO.

An Exit Strategy

Perhaps the most important issue angels and entrepreneurs face at the time of investment is defining the exit strategy. It is generally agreed that out of ten investments made by the savviest angel, three or four will go bust and the angel will be lucky to recover any of the initial investment. Another three or four will survive to earn mediocre results and the angel will probably recoup all of his or her investment but without much return. Only two or three will provide a profitable exit.

A thorough understanding of the various exit options and the likelihood of each is important at the beginning of the capital-raising process. Different exit mechanisms have an influence over what an angel investor can expect as a time frame and as the annual rate of return for the investment.

Contrary to popular mythology, an IPO is not usually the final outcome for a successful venture. Most companies are purchased by larger publicly traded companies before they can go public. Buying a privately held company is much easier than buying a publicly traded one.

Preferred stock, debt-to-equity conversions, nondilution clauses, and right-of-refusal clauses all provide angels with stronger assurance that they will exit with a profit—or at least won't lose everything—than a purchase of straight common stock. That's the golden rule of capitalism—those who have the gold get to make the rules.

These protective terms need not be given as a condition of investment. Negotiate them only if and when the investor requests any of them. Ideally, you will have a standard term sheet with a fair set of terms. The standard term sheet forms a barrier to anyone wishing special consideration. Once an exception is made, the venture may be stuck with making the same condition available to all investors, at least all future investors.

You need to create a plan with milestones and an exit strategy. The peak time for entrepreneurs to terminate their business is the fourth or fifth year. Better to plan for an unsuccessful end than to be caught by events.

69

Chapter 5

Getting Started/Need More Money, Part 3

NOW THAT WE'VE CONSIDERED THE INS AND OUTS AND ADVANTAGES and disadvantages of getting funding from family members, friends, and investor angels, in this chapter we'll consider financial strategies to try with professional service providers, benefiting from federal agencies and state and local governments, and using loan guarantees from individuals.

In the heady dotcom days of 1998–2000, everyone wanted to be either an entrepreneur or a venture capitalist. Even without an idea of their own or $1 million to invest, many became successful through a kind of venture bartering arrangement.

Professional Service Providers: Use Equity to Get Aligned with Your Service Providers

Instead of being paid in cash for services they provided to entrepreneurs, some professionals are sometimes willing to take some of their fees in the form of equity. Lawyers, accountants, marketing and public relations professionals, and management consultants are the most likely to agree to an equity stake. But even landlords have been known to take equity.

Some professional service providers are willing to take equity because they feel an equity stake will some day be worth more than the cash they could take today. They work on the notion that $1 in income today is only $1 of sales and far less than $1 in profit, but $1 taken as an equity stake in a company can some day be worth $5, $10, or more, with everything above the first $1 being pure profit.

Others take an equity stake because they have excess capacity in their businesses—more supply than demand—and prefer to gamble on getting some return from a deal rather than wait for cash-paying business to come through the door.

Most of those willing to take equity don't take their entire fee that way. They usually take enough in cash to cover their costs and then take the portion of their fee that would be their profit in the form of equity, gambling that their stake will increase in value over time. And they don't take an equity stake in any business, only in those they feel have a real potential for serious payback.

Service-providing professionals are usually in a position to do due diligence about a business while doing their work. Accountants and lawyers are privy to a company's intimate financial details. Management and operations consultants understand how the company actually does its business. Marketing and public relations consultants are able to see how the company is viewed by customers, suppliers, competitors, and other important outside groups. They all can develop some "gut feeling" about whether the business will flourish or flounder in the long run. If a service provider is willing to discuss taking a portion of fees in equity, that is a vote of confidence you should cherish.

Finders and Brokers

Finders and brokers who raise investment capital often like to take a portion of their compensation in equity, in states where they are allowed to do so. Most insist that the retainer portion of their fee and their expenses be paid in cash, but some are willing to take part or all of their "success fee" in the form of equity.

One formula that is often used in calculating success fees is 5 percent of the first $1 million raised, 4 percent for the next $1 million, 3 percent for the next $1 million, 2 percent for the next $1 million, and 1 percent for anything over $4 million. Thus, a broker or finder who raises $5 million would be due $150,000. If he or she were willing to take this in the form of equity, you would have enough cash to hire more employees.

Finders and brokers who raise investment capital often like to take a portion of their compensation in equity, in states where they are allowed to do so.

Watch out for Double Dippers

Accelera Concepts (not its real name) contracted with Software Systems Co. (SoSysCo) (not its real name) to secure any or all of the following:

► a strategic alliance
► additional financing
► a combination marketing-finance agreement

Accelera received a retainer to cover expenses and a success fee if it brought any arrangement to fruition.

Four months later, Accelera asked SoSysCo to sign a revised contract agreeing that it would move forward to create a strategic alliance with another of its clients and obtain financing from yet another client. Accelera also asked for a monthly fee of $5,000, larger than its current fee, and a substantial upward revision of the success fee.

It turned out that Accelera was already collecting fees from the other two parties as well. When SoSysCo discovered this clear conflict of interest in negotiations, it terminated the agreement.

Incubators and Accelerators

Incubators and accelerators are also often willing—or even request—to receive some of their fees in equity. What's the difference between an incubator and an accelerator? Incubators nurture new companies over time, while accelerators act to supercharge new companies.

Incubators

Incubators are essentially real estate that's loaded with extra services. They have always worked well for life science companies, which would have to invest heavily to build or retrofit space into laboratories.

A small company, instead of simply renting space, fitting it out as a lab, and hiring its own service providers and staff, can take space in an incubator that includes lab and office space, shared services such as marketing and accounting, and common spaces such as conference rooms, auditoriums, and a cafeteria or on-site restaurant.

During the dotcom frenzy, companies such as Idealab and CMGI sprouted and called themselves "incubators." They were essentially holding companies funded by VC money that invested in equity stakes in small dotcom businesses. To achieve their funders' goals, they were driven to try to help companies move from concept to initial public offering (IPO) in less than one year. However, most of the small companies and the incubators failed with the dotcom meltdown in 2000 and 2001.

Corporate incubators have been more successful than dotcom incubators. Paul Weaver, the former chairman of the global technology program at PricewaterhouseCoopers consulting, which has since become part of IBM technical services, argued a few years ago that there was more money being spent on incubating new ideas in large companies than in independent incubators. Today, incubators are even more out of fashion and large companies are setting up more elaborate mechanisms for partnering with and investing in start-up technology companies. (This will be discussed in more detail in Chapter 7.)

Corporate incubators work with outside entrepreneurs who have technology or products that dovetail with their own. Such companies as AT&T, Dow Chemical, and Sony have active incubator programs.

Corporate incubators have an advantage over independent incubators, Weaver believes, because corporations are inherently strategic in their thinking, incubating efforts that relate to their core businesses. The independents' business model is purely financial, essentially venture capital with added services.

Accelerators

Incubators have been around longer than accelerators. Accelerators were spawned by the same need for speed as touted by the for-profit incubators. With so many ideas—especially Internet-related ones—chasing venture capital and angel money, only those that got there early got funded.

Some accelerators are individuals; others are groups of independent professional service providers who team up to offer "one-stop shopping" for entrepreneurs in need of services. Some larger management consulting companies have also formed accelerator-type organizations to work with smaller, entrepreneurial companies.

An accelerator can add value in many ways. In addition to rounding up financing, accelerators can find real estate, provide legal and accounting assistance, and even mentor young entrepreneurs in the rudiments of running a business.

Some angels act as accelerators. These "value-added" angels often take an active role in a company's day-to-day management and put their network of contacts to work for the entrepreneurial company.

All incubators are not equal. Incubators run by profit-making companies have different terms and conditions than university or not-for-profit operations.

Some for-profit incubators take equity (e.g., 3 to 5 percent) because they select companies that have the promise to grow big and look for venture capital.

Equity for Service Providers

You should probably think of service providers as participants in earlier rounds of financing, either with family members and friends or with angels. This is important when determining how much equity to sacrifice. You always need to leave enough equity to attract enough funding for future rounds of financing.

If you find discrete service providers who will take some equity in the early stages of your business, don't let go of more than a total of 10 or 12 percent to them and the family and friends combined.

You probably don't have to throw around large amounts of equity to satisfy professional services providers. At this point, they know they are taking a big risk.

If you find an angel who is also acting as an accelerator, you need to factor that in when determining how much equity the angel will receive for his or her investment.

If you find an angel who is also acting as an accelerator, you need to factor that in when determining how much equity the angel will receive for his or her investment. Remember: the angel's investment of time may not be as valuable as his or her investment in capital.

For instance, suppose an angel wants to take 25 percent of the equity for a $500,000 investment and will provide personal services worth another $100,000 over the next year. A 25 percent stake for $500,000 assumes that the company's value is $2 million. Therefore, another $100,000 in professional services should be worth another 5 percent.

But you are taking a salary of $60,000 a year for a position that would pay $150,000 at an established company. You are assuming that your low pay will be compensated on the back end through additional value in your equity position when your company is bought or goes public.

In this case, you could ask the angel to consider taking 40 cents on the dollar in equity for his or her professional services, so another 2 percent, not 5, for $100,000 in services.

Federal Agencies Can Be Research Partners

In addition to the Small Business Administration (SBA), a number of federal agencies and departments provide funds for starting or operating small businesses. The three federal departments through which most of these funds are distributed are the Department of Housing and Urban Development (HUD), the Department of Commerce (DOC), and the Department of Agriculture (USDA).

Some of these funds are available in the form of loans; others are outright grants. Much of the money available from the federal government is passed through state or local governments in the form of block grants, with local officials making the decisions on whom to fund. Examples of such pass-through programs are Urban Development Action Grant (UDAG) funds and Community Development Block Grant (CDBG) funds.

The best way to determine what federal programs you might be eligible for is to check with your state's economic development office, which should be current on funds available throughout the state.

HUD

Loans and grants available through HUD are targeted mainly at urban areas. Many are aimed at businesses that employ people who live in HUD-financed public housing. UDAG and CDBG are both sponsored by HUD.

HUD has also been charged with administering most economic development programs under federal Enterprise Zone legislation. Through this legislation, local governments are provided with funds to help businesses locate in enterprise zones or in urban neighborhoods and rural/exurban communities in the most immediate need of economic development.

Enterprise zone funding includes direct loans, interest-rate subsidies, and loan guarantees for businesses that start in or move into the zone. Many federal enterprise zones overlap with areas that already had been designated state enterprise zones.

DOC

One of the responsibilities of the DOC is to promote American products overseas. It makes available loans, loan guarantees, grants, and other subsidies to American companies marketing or actively selling their products abroad.

The DOC houses an agency called the Economic Development Administration (EDA), which was created in 1965 to promote industrial development. The EDA makes money available through grants to state and local governments to help create the infrastructure that businesses need to grow and flourish.

If your business is one that helps other businesses or is starting or growing in an economically depressed area, or if you are a member of an economically disadvantaged class (i.e., African American, Latino, American Indian, Asian, Pacific Islander, or a woman), you may be eligible for money from one of these grants. You may also qualify for free technical assistance from an organization that gets money from the EDA.

The best way to determine what federal programs you might be eligible for is to check with your state's economic development office.

USDA

It may be surprising, but even people who are not farmers can receive assistance from USDA programs. The Farmers Home Administration (FmHA) is an agency within the USDA that makes direct loans and provides loan guarantees to all kinds of businesses that operate in rural areas. Priority for FmHA business programs is given to projects in rural communities and cities with fewer than 25,000 people.

Even in states that are considered highly urbanized, some areas are eligible for FmHA programs.

In addition to providing loans and loan guarantees for rural housing development and public facilities, and agricultural loans for family farms and family-farm cooperatives, the FmHA also provides loan guarantees through commercial lenders for the creation or expansion of industry in less populous areas.

Loan guarantees are available for acquisition of land, acquisition and renovation or construction of buildings, acquisition of machinery and equipment, and working capital for inventory and cash flow. Terms are up to 30 years for real estate, 15 years for machinery, and seven years for working capital loans. For loans of more than $1 million, FmHA requires a feasibility study. Your commitment must be at least 10 percent of the project cost and can be as high as 25 percent.

FmHA does not require that you be turned down for a conventional loan before applying for a loan guarantee, but it does require your personal guarantee on the loan. In many rural communities, FmHA has been a major player in economic development.

Small Business Innovation Research Program

The Small Business Innovation Research (SBIR) Program is administered by the SBA. The money for the research grants, however, comes from agencies and departments that participate in the program.

Part of the Small Business Innovation Development Act of 1982, the SBIR program is designed to include small businesses in federally supported research and development efforts by providing both grants and an opportunity for them to participate in government procurement of research services.

Each agency or department that participates in the SBIR program is responsible for committing a particular amount of its research and development funds to small businesses. Agencies establish their own criteria for obtaining grants or contracts. These are some of the departments and agencies that participate:

Government agencies have less well-known programs in areas such as environmental and energy resources, rural development, and technology. See if your business objectives are consistent with any program charter. Your local Small Business Development Center can usually help.

- ▶ Department of Health and Human Resources (HHS)
- ▶ Department of Defense (DOD)
- ▶ Environmental Protection Agency (EPA)
- ▶ Department of Transportation (DOT)
- ▶ National Aeronautics and Space Administration (NASA)

A full list of participating agencies and departments is available on the SBA Web site, *www.sba.gov*, or through the SBA's Office of Technology (formerly Office of Innovation, Research, and Technology) in Washington.

To be eligible for participation in the SBIR program, you must be a profit-making company with fewer than 500 employees. In addition to applying for an SBIR grant, you can have the SBA's Office of Technology place you on the list for its presolicitation announcements. These let you know which agencies and departments are issuing requests for proposals (RFPs) for procurement of research services or for distribution of grants to conduct research.

CRADAs

Another opportunity for small research-and-development-oriented businesses to obtain government assistance is through a Cooperative Research and Development Agreement (CRADA). A CRADA is a partnership between a government laboratory and an academic or industrial research organization.

Funding and staffing commitments are shared between the parties to the CRADA (just as in a strategic alliance), with the specifics of who performs what research detailed in the agreement. Any patents or inventions that come out of the joint work of the CRADA are owned by both parties.

The government then licenses its share of the ownership interest to the industrial company for the purpose of taking the fruits of the CRADA to market. If a small business is involved in the CRADA, both parties can license the product to another company to market and sell.

Federal government laboratories are constantly looking for partners to develop technology jointly and take the lab's work public, which brings in revenue and reduces the labs' dependence on taxes for its budget.

State and Local Funding Sources: Where You Locate Your Business Can Pay Off Big

If you sign the guest book at a local or regional VC fair, chances are within a few weeks your phone will be ringing with government officials trying to get you to locate your business in their city or state.

States and cities are all looking to attract new businesses. Not only does a business contribute state corporate income, sales, and local property taxes, but the employees of the business add to the local economy by living in the area and buying goods and services from other businesses in the area.

State Funding

States are increasingly rolling out the red carpet for businesses, through a combination of tax incentives, loans and loan guarantees, and other programs. Some are even sponsoring venture capital funds.

Tax Incentives

States don't usually create special tax rates for new or growing businesses. They do provide tax credits for particular activities that have public policy purposes. These credits offset corporate taxes owed by the company. Many credits are aimed at luring and keeping clean industries and technology-oriented companies.

Each state government has at least one office that can help you figure out which programs are best for you and help you apply for them. Your business provides future tax dollars that pay those staff salaries.

Loans, Loan Guarantees, and Interest Subsidies

As with the federal government, state and local agencies can help you in many ways, such as getting financial assistance, dealing with international trade issues, and addressing particular markets.

Many states provide loans and loan guarantees similar to those provided by federal agencies. The state department of economic development is the best place to check for availability of such funds. State financing is often provided as direct loans for fixed-asset purchases, construction or renovation, and infrastructure development. There are also some funds available for working capital loans. State agencies usually co-lend with a private-sector lender.

Loan guarantees are provided by state agencies in much the same way as the Small Business Administration (SBA), for a portion of a loan made by the private lender.

States also sometimes provide interest subsidies on loans. Under an interest-subsidy program, the state may pay for 30 to 50 percent of a loan's interest. For instance, if you borrow $250,000 at 12 percent interest ($30,000 interest) and the state subsidizes 30 percent of the interest ($9,000), your interest payment is really $21,000 and your effective interest rate is 8.4 percent.

Grants

State grants can be made directly to businesses, to municipalities to assist businesses in locating there, or to companies that help other companies. For instance, in some states, regulated electric companies have guaranteed that, in exchange for being allowed to earn a particular rate of return on their assets, they will provide a certain amount of money (say $250,000) to small businesses for market research and energy audits.

State departments of transportation sometimes provide grants directly to companies in which a certain percentage of employees take mass transit to work or participate in van pools.

Many states provide grants to businesses to locate daycare facilities within their walls, provided that a percentage of openings are made available to local residents.

States are increasingly piggybacking many of their grants (as well as loans) on federal enterprise zone legislation, providing businesses with additional reasons to locate or expand in these economically depressed areas. Some states provide matching grants to businesses that win federal grants.

Industrial Revenue Bonds (IRBs)

Industrial revenue bonds (IRBs) are issued by a state through a quasi-public agency to provide funding for acquiring and renovating or constructing industrial buildings and acquiring the equipment needed for those facilities.

In addition to loans and tax incentives, many states have annual competitive grant programs.

The bond is issued in the name of the corporation that will be buying and using the facility and machinery. However, the state and quasi-public agency underwrite the bond issue and the interest paid to the bond investors is free of federal income taxes (and state income tax for state residents). Because investors will pay less tax on interest from the bonds, they are willing to buy bonds that pay a lower interest rate, which means the cost of borrowing the funds is lower than if the company had issued the debt on its own.

Venture Capital Funding

Some states are becoming venture capitalists. Usually, these efforts are aimed at providing seed- and early-stage capital to companies within the state. The goals are to add jobs and tax revenue and to attract or keep innovative companies in the state.

Each state operates its program on a slightly different model:

- ▶ Some focus on funding and promoting industries that are traditional in that state; others attempt to create opportunities for technology-based entrepreneurial businesses to locate in the state.

- ▶ Some are concerned with making a traditional venture-capital rate of return on their investments, while for others profit is secondary to supporting local businesses.

- ▶ Some have funded these operations with cash, while others have provided tax credits that the venturing operation uses as leverage to borrow funds to invest.

- ▶ Some are going it alone, while others are joint-venturing their efforts with private venture capitalists.

Noncash Assistance Programs

States often provide education, job training, placement services, and market research for companies locating within their borders. Some also provide free or subsidized management consulting services to companies that are new or expanding, exporters, or operating in distressed industries.

Local Funding

Each state has an economic development Web site that lists a range of resources available to businesses in that state.

In addition to being the funding mechanism for Urban Development Action Grant (UDAG) and Community Development Block Grant (CDBG) funds from the federal Department of Housing and Urban Development (HUD), cities and towns can offer their own incentives to induce companies to locate there.

The most popular municipal incentive is a phase-in of local property taxes on real estate, machinery, fixtures, and other business equipment. Municipalities love business taxpayers: they provide a lot of tax income without using a lot of services. (Most of a municipal budget goes to pay for education.)

Cities and towns are often willing to allow businesses to phase in property taxes over five to ten years. As part of the deal, the municipality may require the business to remain in the town for five or more years after the tax advantage ends or to repay the taxes that it avoided. In addition, some cities require companies that get property tax phase-ins to create a particular number of jobs, sometimes even demanding that a specified percentage of those jobs go to city residents.

Municipalities may also add their own money into the federal and state pot for companies that locate or expand in federal enterprise zones.

Loan Guarantees Make Large Loans Available to Small Companies

In addition to federal agencies like the SBA and some state economic development agencies, individuals also sometimes provide loan guarantees for an entrepreneur.

A loan guarantee can be provided by a friend or family member or by an arm's-length third-party angel. In theory, anyone willing to make an equity investment in your company should also be willing to guarantee a loan. If the company fails, it doesn't matter whether the investor must pay off the loan or loses the value of his or her stock.

The advantage for a potential angel investor in guaranteeing a loan is that he or she does not actually have to provide you with the funds, but rather to put away the money as collateral against the loan guarantee (where that money maintains its value or increases in value). The angel loses the money only if your company can't pay back the loan. Some guarantors will also ask for a small percentage of the company's revenues going forward for the time the guaranteed loan is outstanding.

The downside for the individual in guaranteeing your loan is that there is no potential that the investment will turn to gold. However, the investor usually gets warrants to buy company stock at a deep discount as part of the guarantee deal.

Expenses of Privately Guaranteed Loans

There are a host of fees that come along with a privately guaranteed loan. Your bank will charge a loan origination fee. The bank providing the letter of credit for the guarantor to your bank will also charge a fee. If you work through a broker who finds wealthy people willing to guarantee loans for entrepreneurs, there is another fee. (If you're working with an angel you know or with a friend or family member, you can make your own deal.)

Since most banks that write such loans will demand that the interest payment for the first year be taken immediately out of the proceeds of the loan, a $1 million loan may yield only $800,000 to $850,000 in usable proceeds—an effective interest rate that can hit close to 20 percent.

Guarantees as Bridge Financing

A privately guaranteed loan is usually taken out as a short-term bridge to provide the company with a quick infusion of capital for immediate needs.

At the end of the term (usually one to two years), the company pays off the guaranteed loan with a new loan. It doesn't need a guarantor at that point because it has demonstrated its ability to pay off the new loan through cash flow or the proceeds of an equity sale.

If the guaranteed loan has been put to good use and the company is now producing steady revenue and has measurable assets, a capital investment by an angel or venture capitalist will not cost the company as much equity as it would have before it secured the guaranteed loan.

Chapter 6

Getting Started/Need a Lotta Money, Part 1

S TART-UP COMPANIES THAT NEED A LOT OF MONEY—MORE THAN $1 MIL-
lion to get going—often must go through more than one round of
financing to become fully operational. Very few entrepreneurs who
need more than $1 million to start a business can fund it fully on
their own. And few lenders will lend more than $1 million for a
start-up business unless the borrower has significant assets outside the business to pledge as collateral (for instance, a recently retired corporate executive with significant stock holdings or other assets). That means the
entrepreneur either needs to sell equity in the company or needs to be creative
about using suppliers, customers, a former employer, or joint-venture or
licensing partners to fund the start-up.

If the entrepreneur needs to raise the entire $1 million through selling
equity, it may be necessary to use a combination of family and friends, state-
run seed-capital funds, and angels. Few if any venture capitalists will work
with start-up companies, although there are a few that may see such promise in a business or technical concept that they are willing to make a first-
stage investment in the hopes of securing the relationship and keeping other
venture capitalists out.

This chapter will deal with venture capitalists only in passing. The major
part of our discussion on venture capital will come in Chapter 10. There we

will discuss the entrepreneurs who have a business with a proven concept and market and need more (often vastly more) than $1 million in later-stage financing in order to take the business to a national level or even beyond.

This chapter and the next focus primarily on three other ways of raising $1 million in start-up capital:

▶ spinning out a business from an employer

▶ creating a joint venture

▶ licensing a product or technology to another company to market and focusing on developing more products or technologies

Professional Venture Capitalists

Professional venture capitalists are the managers of VC funds. A VC fund is a pool of money raised from a small number of wealthy individuals and institutions such as pension funds, universities, or foundations. The fund is closed, meaning that once the desired amount of money has been raised, no more investors can get into it. The fund has a finite lifetime; when it ends, the value of the fund is disbursed to the investors.

VC funds are usually established as limited partnerships, with the passive investors being limited partners and the professional managers being general partners. The professional managers collect an annual fee for conducting the fund's business. They usually also own a portion of the fund and share in its gains or losses just like the passive investors. Professional managers of VC funds have a fiduciary responsibility to their passive investors and their primary—if not sole—motivation is the highest possible financial return they can obtain for their fund.

A VC firm may operate a number of funds, opening a new one to a new group of investors as soon as the previous one has been fully subscribed. Funds are typically $50 to $500 million per fund, although some funds are over $1 billion. Each fund maintains a manageable portfolio of investments to monitor and to cash out of when it comes time to disburse proceeds to investors.

Over a period of time—usually two to four years—the fund's managing partners invest the pool of money in a number of new or young and growing companies. In exchange for the cash the VC fund invests, it receives equity in the company. Many VC firms also take seats on the company's board of directors.

VC funds try to achieve cumulative annual returns of 25 to 30 percent, although they usually do not pay out annually but rather when the fund is

> *VC funds are usually established as limited partnerships, with the passive investors being limited partners and the professional managers being general partners.*

dissolved. In order to achieve such returns, the fund's managers try to invest in companies that eventually will go public through an initial public offering (IPO), will be sold to a publicly traded corporation, or will go to a new player in the universe of equity partners for new and growing businesses—a private-equity fund.

Companies that are destined to attempt an IPO often go through three, four, or even five rounds of private financing before going public. Most VC firms do not provide start-up and seed-stage funding of $100,000 to $1 million, although there are an increasing number of venture funds that are declaring themselves to be "multi-stage funds" willing to stake out a position with a new company right from the seed-capital stage.

Professional venture capitalists generally don't invest in start-up companies because of the higher degree of risk. In addition, the amount of due diligence work involved is the same for a $500,000 investment as for a $5 million investment and the rewards are not as great.

With VC Firms, You're Playing in the Major Leagues

Over the past quarter century, VCs have developed a model for spurring the development of new ideas and providing the resources to develop those ideas into successful commercial ventures. Through exchanging large blocks of capital for significant equity in young, growing companies, venture capitalists have enabled entrepreneurs to see their ideas blossom and grow while maintaining significant control over those efforts.

Since the late 1970s, the flow of VC funds to small entrepreneurial companies has been higher and lower but has never stopped. Successful investments bring in more venture capitalists and more investors for their funds. This money then spreads out to a larger pool of entrepreneurs. Many of these investments are made hastily, with little due diligence, on ventures that should not be funded. Success rates drop and VC money slows to a trickle.

Since the late 1970s, the flow of VC funds to small entrepreneurial companies has been higher and lower but has never stopped.

After the excesses of the dotcom era and the resulting shakeout from 2000 to 2003, VC firms went "back to basics." The investment pace slowed. They rarely put money into start-ups. Since 2004 the VC money has been flowing strong again.

Venture capital as we know it today is a phenomenon of tax-law changes in 1976, which gave a great advantage to capital gains derived from investments over ordinary income. In 1978, about $3.5 billion was managed by firms in the embryonic VC industry (firms such as Venrock Associates, established by the Rockefeller family, and the Bessemer Trust). By 1983, this amount had more than tripled to $12.1 billion.

85

After 25 years the VC business as we know it has some characteristics of a mature industry combined with the traits of independent entrepreneurs. The established quality firms are conservative and follow evolved guidelines and processes, while those born in successful times go with trends.

New firms were joining the VC community. Rather than tapping into smaller amounts of old money, these firms began actively soliciting wealthy investors who were willing to put money into professionally managed pools for investment in risky private-equity ventures rather than the public stock markets. VC firms sprouted in what has become the East Coast version of northern California's Silicon Valley near Stanford University, around Boston near Harvard and MIT, and in New York City.

In the early 1980s, many VC investments turned out to be failures. Many went south because investors did not do enough due diligence and threw money at technological innovation that proved not to have a profit-making business model (not unlike the dotcom mania). Euphoria over this new scheme for making money diminished. VC firms started shifting their investments to entrepreneurs who could show progress in developing their products. By the mid-1980s, venture capital for seed and early-stage financing had been significantly reduced to only about 3 percent of total VC funding.

Another shake-out in the industry came in the early 1990s because VC investments made in the late 1980s were failing.

Large and well-publicized returns from successful VC investments made in the 1980s brought many more people into the VC field. Younger employees of VC firms struck out on their own, using their association with their former employers' track records to raise large amounts of capital for their funds. Some of these newer venture capitalists were good; others were not.

With each round of adversity, the VC industry has instituted new measures to improve its success rate and manage risk more effectively. The result is that companies funded by venture capitalists today have a higher probability of success than those funded 25 years ago.

A "tiering" effect occurred, both in the VC world and in the world of entrepreneurs. Senior managers from successful entrepreneurial companies were able to go off, start their own companies, and raise money from top-tier VC firms. Less well-known entrepreneurs sought money from firms with less prestige. As part of their contracts with investors in their funds, venture capitalists are obliged to put their money to work within a certain amount of time, so less prestigious firms were often compelled by the need to invest funds quickly even when high-quality opportunities were insufficient.

Again, as low-quality VC firms failed to perform enough due diligence on prospective investments and subsequently did not obtain high enough returns, they closed up or merged. By the early 1990s, due diligence in the VC industry had become more rigorous. More firms moved away from making seed-capital investments and toward investing in later-stage companies that had already proven their business model concept using their own money and the money provided by friends, family, and individual angels.

There was yet one more cycle. By the late 1990s, business plans touting new e-business revenue models were flooding VC firms. A few early dotcom "successes" opened the floodgates, as investment bankers and stock analysts touted early dotcom IPOs and as stock values for companies like Amazon.com, eBay, and Yahoo skyrocketed. By 1999, venture capitalists were throwing money at dotcom proposals, funding rank start-ups with $50 million or even $100 million.

The term "burn rate"—the rate at which a dotcom was burning through its venture capital cash—came into use. The Dilbert cartoon of January 15, 1999, shows an entrepreneur in a venture capitalist's office. The venture capitalist says, "Despite your cool ponytail, you seem to have squandered our investment. You'll get no more funding unless you mutter empty Internet words that make us swoon."

The entrepreneur says, "E-commerce," and the venture capitalist swoons.

By 2001, even empty Internet words could not make venture capitalists swoon. When publicly traded Internet stocks dove to the bottom and the IPO market dried up almost overnight, the venture capitalists cut off the flow of funds to many early-stage companies.

In this latest venture capital uptick, which began in 2004, VCs are back looking for technological breakthroughs—although they are still somewhat gun-shy of the Internet in general.

Employers: Don't Buy Out, Spinout

Let's say you are not running your own business. Instead, you are working for a large company.

You have a terrific idea for a product or an innovation that appears to work. Or, you manage a business process and find yourself saying, "I can do this better than the company is doing it. If I were freed from this corporate bureaucracy, I could make a profit."

What do you do?

You might try getting the corporate management to nurture your idea as a new internal corporate venture. Or, you might work a deal where your endeavor is "spun out" of the company and established as a new business, with the larger company participating in some way. The company could take an equity stake in your business (supply venture capital), work with you in a strategic alliance, or license your product.

Corporate Venture

Most larger companies have had internal development programs for many years. Some of these programs generate revenue by providing technologies, products, or processes.

While most companies simply add these efforts to already operating divisions, departments, or strategic business units, some establish major new revenue generators as independent ventures. Such ventures are generally different enough from the company's mainstream or even ancillary businesses that they don't fit neatly into its current product portfolio.

The Network Manager

A large telecommunications corporation tried to develop a network management system for itself and its clients. After spending $2 million, it abandoned the project.

The project manager thought the software had potential and was disappointed with the company's decision. Figuring he couldn't lose, he asked the company if he could take the project outside the company and pursue it independently.

He didn't have the cash to pay for the intellectual property, so the company agreed to take an equity stake in his new venture and to receive a modest percentage on all products sold using the technology for the first seven years.

Corporate venturing, a popular strategic tool in the 1980s, was created as a way for large corporations to stem the tide of entrepreneurial employees leaving the company and chasing after venture capital dollars.

These intrapreneurial efforts can be held within a portfolio and managed as a professional venture capital firm might manage a portfolio of companies it has a stake in. Some companies even establish a program to allow and encourage employees to bring forward their proposals outside the formal hierarchy. The process is designed to sort, screen, and evaluate these projects as potential new ventures to be funded.

Corporate venturing, a popular strategic tool in the 1980s, was created as a way for large corporations to stem the tide of entrepreneurial employees leaving the company and chasing after venture capital dollars. A number of companies had strong corporate venturing programs, including IBM, which created 37 new ventures under its Independent Business Unit program in the 1980s.

By 1990, more than 100 major American corporations had corporate venturing programs; some of the most successful ones were those at 3M, Merck, and Corning. But the majority faded away within a few years, due to a lack of enthusiasm on the part of major corporations and an inability to blend an entrepreneurial business model for corporate venturing with a more traditional model for running ongoing business units. (A business model for corporate venturing can be found in our book, *New Corporate Ventures: How to Make Them Work*, John Wiley & Sons, 1988.)

Three Operational Options

There are three ways a corporation can structure its relationship to employee-developed entrepreneurial ideas:

► *Create a small stand-alone unit that reports to a key executive and serves as the "holding company,"* which grows and nurtures entrepreneurial efforts. Establish a "board of directors" for this unit. Initially, the entrepreneurial effort is housed within this unit. Because it is "off-line" from traditional development efforts, it can cut through the need for projects to fight for resources with others in departments, divisions, or business units. If the entrepreneurial effort grows and acquires critical mass, it can be pushed out and reconstituted as a separate business unit within the corporation.

► *Create a 100-percent owned subsidiary of the corporation.*

► *Establish a spinout, an independent entity that transforms the intrapreneur into an entrepreneur.* The corporation receives an equity position in the new company in exchange for its prior investment and for transferring ownership of the technology, product, or process. It can also purchase more equity to give the entrepreneur financing for taking the company forward.

What's Behind Spinouts?

Corporations recognize their need for intrapreneurs. However, most have not learned how to manage such employees or innovation programs within the corporate structure. The truth is that venture capitalists make their investment decisions and manage their portfolios in a way that is totally foreign to corporate management.

Corporate executives are uncomfortable with creating different rules for employees whose endeavors are selected for internal venturing. Some of the issues that keep them from trying to operate entrepreneurial efforts within their company include:

► Milestone funding
► Sharing rewards
► Cutting losses

Corporate internal ventures have been difficult to start and few have been successful. However, for the entrepreneur the advantage of available resources is a prize not to be quickly dismissed. A good idea is worth the sweat it takes to get your employer interested. It could be just as tough on the outside, with greater risks.

Milestone Funding

Corporations are used to budgeting annually. They ask all employees with budget-making authority, "What do you need to operate next year?"

However, the appropriate question for an entrepreneurial business is rather "What do you need to get to the next milestone (e.g., idea to proto-type, prototype to finished product, product to market)?" And milestones don't fit neatly within years.

It is possible for companies to "escrow" enough funding to get the venture through its growing stages by drawing from the escrow account as mile-stones are reached. This is, to some degree, what venture capitalists and angels do when they make a deal for staged funding.

But the way corporate accounting is done, the entire amount committed is booked as an expense for the year in which it is committed, and many cor-porations are unwilling to show that big an upfront "loss" on their books for a venture.

Sharing Rewards

Corporations have difficulty believing that anyone who works for them deserves an equity stake in an individual venture. Sure, they want their employees to own company stock and "align their goals with those of the company." But corporate accounting makes it difficult for people to have a big piece of the action in one particular project or entrepreneurial effort.

Some corpora- tions have established pro- grams in which employees bring their ideas to an independent review panel to see whether they qualify for resources.

Again, this is completely opposite the thinking of venture capitalists. Venture capitalists want entrepreneurs to feel ownership of the effort. They insist that entrepreneurs put up some of their own money to fund the com-pany, a concept known as "having skin in the game." They want entrepre-neurs to get rich, because only then do venture capitalists become rich.

Cutting Losses

Once a corporation has put a lot of money into a project, it is often loath to stop funding the effort. The corporate default position is always to take the product to market and count on marketing efforts to create success, even if the technology has been overtaken or the perceived market for the product has dried up.

Not so with venture capitalists. Even if they don't pull their funding, they constantly analyze the entrepreneurial company to see if it is achieving milestones and creating a revenue-generating and profit-making enterprise that brings them their 30 percent compounded annual rate of return. If the company isn't progressing, the venture capitalist begins to look for ways to turn the situation around or to get out of the investment.

Culture of Money

These issues all have to do with the culture of money. Corporate money culture is driven by annual budgets, linked to cost-accounting methods, and inherently risk-averse. Venture capital money culture is driven by results, linked to return on investment, and inherently risk-taking.

In most corporations, the inevitable force of the traditional corporate culture of money eventually squashes any small efforts to run what is in effect a venture capital fund for internal innovation.

Spinout

Just because most major corporations are unable to operate an internal venture capital function doesn't mean they don't understand the value of risk-taking entrepreneurial efforts. They simply have determined that such efforts need to be taken outside the context of the corporation's day-to-day operations.

Rather than try to corral intrapreneurship and house it inside the corporation, more and more companies are helping employees take their innovative ideas outside and set them up as stand-alone entrepreneurial businesses. This way, the company becomes a passive stakeholder through an equity investment or some other means of staying close.

Some companies have large portfolios of such spinouts, sometimes referred to as corporate incubators. In a corporate incubator, the company sets up a deliberate program of nurturing and growing ideas or concepts to the point where they can stand alone, then spins them out as stand-alone companies and takes an equity stake in each one.

To foster spinouts, a corporation creates a venture capital pool from which it makes investments in companies started by employees. These companies are based on ideas, product concepts, new processes, or technological innovations developed by the employees that the company does not want to pursue to completion but believes are viable.

Management must consider two things before spinning out an internally developed technology or product. There must be:

▶ Substantive and sustainable reason for pursuing the effort.

▶ Potential for large incremental value to the corporation.

Any venture spun out of a company is set up as a separate legal entity

91

Most large corporations have research and development operations and facilities for bringing an idea to fruition and a demonstrable prototype.

rather than a corporate subsidiary. The individual who develops the idea—and therefore "founds" the new company—may be asked to make a token cash investment in exchange for an equity stake. (Some make substantial investments.) But the largest way he or she puts skin in the game is through the "law of no return" that most companies have set up: if the new company fails, the employee is not automatically rehired into the company. For an employee who has spent years or decades in corporate life, this is a huge risk.

Making the Business Case for a Spinout

An intrapreneur who has the potential to take his or her project outside the corporate walls begins developing the business case by listing the reasons the company should pursue the idea. He or she also uses each of these reasons to test and validate the idea. This is sometimes referred to as providing *proof of concept*. Of course, for each reason the intrapreneur makes for pursuing an idea, the company can make a counterclaim for not pursuing it.

The intrapreneur could argue that the corporation has already made a substantial investment, and this is the best way to obtain a return. The counter to this, of course, is that the corporation should cut its losses rather than sinking more capital into the idea as a stand-alone entity.

The intrapreneur needs to show that the reason the idea is not further along is not because it is bad, but because it was stifled in the corporate bureaucracy or funding was insufficient for it to reach the necessary milestones.

Also, in the corporate arena, development efforts are often taken very far before being examined against the size of the potential market. If the intrapreneur has done some market testing and can show the corporate VC fund's leaders that the market potential is larger than expected, this can free up funding.

The intrapreneur can also point out that the new company's managers, having been employees of the corporation, can relate well to corporate management. Their understanding of the corporation's goals and operating guidelines reduces the "getting to know you" time that an entrepreneur would take with professional VC funders or that a corporate VC team would need if it funded a company run by entrepreneurs with whom they had not worked before.

The intrapreneur can contend that if the company becomes a passive investor, corporate managers will be able to spend less time managing the venture than when it was within the company. However, they can remain close to the venture and offer direction. In addition, by taking an equity position, the corporation can effectively freeze competitors from taking a financial interest in the new company by placing restrictive language in its investment agreement.

The intrapreneur can also point out that, given the nature of the enterprise and its managers' relationship with the corporation, it would be easier to fold the new company back into the corporation at a later date (if appropriate) than it would be if the venture were being operated by individuals who had never been related to the corporation.

Unfortunately, real-life experience shows that most former employees who become entrepreneurs do not relish the idea of working for the corporation again. When such ventures are brought back in-house, the entrepreneurial employee often leaves. And, as with any entrepreneurial company, the departure of the founder may reduce the value of the venture.

If the effort has already reached some of its milestones, the intrapreneur could argue that the corporation would risk a lot less investing in the venture than in a start-up company.

Finally, the intrapreneur could make the point that the corporation, by investing in the effort, is investing directly in a technology it believes is promising (or else it would not have approved the development effort in its earliest form).

Taking the Spinout to the Next Level

Once a spinout has been effected, the entrepreneur may need to raise more capital to get the company to the next level. (If the corporation were providing all of the new company's capital needs, the managers probably would have set it up as a subsidiary.)

There are a few ways to raise capital in this situation. Friends and family funding is not appropriate and, even if it were, it could not be adequate.

Once a spinout has been effected, the entrepreneur may need to raise more capital to get the company to the next level.

The primary means of raising the next infusion of capital is through angels or, better yet, professionally managed venture capital. This is complicated by the fact that the new company already has a significant corporate equity investor, which may scare off some venture capitalists. Corporations in general have different objectives than venture capitalists, and VC firms are reluctant to work with corporations on corporate-sponsored ventures. Many corporate minds do not understand VC thinking. The conflicts between return on equity and micro-managing technology development may be too much to reconcile.

Financial institutions may be inclined to consider the opportunity. Because a major corporation is involved, the new company has some implicit validity. An equity investment by an insurance company or a major loan from a bank or other financial services company, such as GE Capital, is not out of the question. Also, the relationship with a major corporation could make it easier for the new company to borrow in the public credit market or issue stock to the public. The former parent company could even guarantee a loan.

The new company may solicit other corporations that could benefit from the technology, product, or process or that simply want to make VC investments. Of course, those who could benefit include competitors of the corporate benefactor, which would have to approve any approaches made to other corporations.

Another corporation with complementary technology and outside the corporate benefactor's market and industry may be willing to establish a partnering relationship. (See Chapter 7.)

Finally, the technology, product, or process could be licensed to other companies, with the advances against future license royalties being used to complete work on the effort.

An internal venture may become the basis for a later strategic alliance between your company and your old employer.

Spinouts and Other Investors

Having corporate involvement may make it easier to find other funding. While some venture capitalists believe large corporations will try to interfere with a spinout's operations and therefore dislike co-investing with them, other venture capitalists and many angels like such co-investment opportunities.

They often consider that the corporation's internal investment and spinning off of the entity is analogous to the seed- and first-round financing that

---

Take This Product Line

A medium-size company had been supplying components to a large corporation for one of its assemblies. The large corporation was the only customer for this particular product and was moving into other product areas.

The owner of the supplying company approached the line supervisor for the product, knowing that he wished to go into business for himself. He offered to help the man start a company that would produce and sell these components. The owner of the supplying company would sell the equipment to manufacture the product and take an equity position in the new company but would have no day-to-day operational control.

entrepreneurs have to obtain. Therefore, a venture spun out from a corporation has already demonstrated the level of viability investors look for when analyzing potential investments.

The corporation may represent a waiting market for the company's technology, product, or process. There is a strong possibility the corporation will further strengthen its ties to the spun-out company, either by licensing any final product or process or by entering into a strategic alliance. This may include providing technical support. All in all, an angel or venture capitalist has to believe that the corporation has not spun the company out as an orphan to simply fend for itself.

The corporation might be willing to reacquire the company in the future, which helps the venture capitalists create a viable exit strategy. The venture capitalist may engage in discussions with the corporation to obtain a guarantee that it will reacquire the company if it meets certain milestones.

If the corporation actively solicits investments, the entrepreneur has an easier job. He or she does not have to spend so much time rounding up money, and the corporation's goodwill in taking this effort makes it easier to "sell" the venture to independent investors.

Both a Buyer and a Seller Be

A department within a large corporation had been working on a contract for another major corporation for four years. The customer questioned whether the scope of the work being performed was drifting beyond the original intent of the contract and might be inconsistent with the contract's mission. The customer didn't object to the work being performed, only that it had not contracted for the work.

In light of the prospect that the contract might be cancelled, the program manager proposed to both her organization (the selling company) and the buying company that a separate business be started to perform the work being done both under the contract and beyond its scope. She suggested that both companies take equity positions in the company, which they did.

Chapter 7

Getting Started/Need a Lotta Money, Part 2

T*HE PRECEDING CHAPTER DISCUSSED ONE WAY OF RAISING $1 MILLION* in start-up capital, by spinning out a business from a current employer. This chapter will consider two more ways: by creating a joint venture and by licensing a product or technology to another company to market.

Joint Ventures and Strategic Alliances: Make Your Company Valuable as a Partner

People often think joint ventures and strategic alliances are the same thing. In both cases, two or more companies join together to pursue a common objective. The difference is in the degree of the joining together.

In a strategic alliance, the parties join together to pursue a common and specific purpose such as marketing a product or developing a new technology. Generally, within such a collaboration, each company invests resources to support its own scope of work, carried out in its own facilities. If additional funds are necessary, they are financed by the company that needs them. Ownership of any outcome (i.e., a patent or a product) is usually shared.

A strategic alliance can be transparent to outsiders, such as customers, suppliers, and other business partners. They do not have to know about your relationship with your partner, since their relationship is with you, although any product can be designated as developed jointly.

In a joint venture, the companies that join together contribute tangible assets (i.e., people, hard goods, finances) to a separate legal entity, a company with its own facilities and administration.

Partnering: Strategic Alliance or Joint Venture?

Joint ventures are usually created by two or more large companies that want to create a platform on which all of them can gain.

Good examples of joint ventures are the industry-consortium model e-business marketplaces. These are buying and selling platforms in a particular industry created by a small group of large players that consolidate purchasing and sometimes collaborative design throughout the industry's value chain.

Such e-business marketplaces as Covisint in the automotive world and Transora in packaged goods are joint ventures made up of three to five large industry players and two or three technology companies. Each of these joint ventures is an independent business and does not provide any of the partners a trading advantage, although they do provide the partners a trading advantage over the suppliers, which are often being forced to use these marketplaces to work with the partners.

Small Company Value in a Strategic Alliance

Start-up and young companies are generally better candidates for strategic alliances than for joint ventures. The value of an entrepreneurial company in an alliance lies in the skills and talents of its employees, its intellectual property and proprietary know-how (sometimes called its technology), and its ability to make quick decisions and move projects quickly through its development pipeline.

A large company may need the proprietary technology for a new product, want to market the small company's product because it rounds out a product line, or be looking to diversify its product base, using the small company's technology as a springboard.

Here we'll assume that any strategic alliance is between one large corporate partner and a small entrepreneurial company. It is important for both parties in such an alliance to be clear about their motivations, the benefits they expect, and the other party's benefits.

Entrepreneurs are often excited when a large company expresses interest in their technology or company. As a result, they behave tentatively, may be intimidated, and accept any offer. Sometimes a large company enters into discussions on a potential deal in order to take an entrepreneur's product or technology off the market or to delay its entry into the market because its success there would adversely affect the company's own products.

Once you understand the reasons behind an alliance, it is essential to learn the proper steps for putting it together in such a way that it does not unravel. Dissolving an alliance costs more and takes longer than forming one.

Why Small Companies Enter Strategic Alliances

Small companies enter strategic alliances with larger companies for any of many reasons. Two of the most important are to develop a product without building an infrastructure and to market and sell a product without building a marketing and sales staff.

First, a larger company can provide a smaller company with facilities and personnel to take a new technology from the laboratory bench to the manufacturing floor without having to build the infrastructure.

Second, a large company can offer a small company access to specific markets it has established over time. Such a relationship can give a start-up or young company credibility that would be costly and time-consuming to develop on its own. The large company's access to markets also enables the small company to make sales and possibly even profits earlier than it might otherwise, making it a better candidate to receive further rounds of funding.

Preparing to Enter into an Alliance

If you are considering forming a strategic alliance, there are three major steps to take before entering into serious negotiations over the terms and structure of the alliance:

1. Understand your prospective partner's organization chart.
2. Determine the value of your product or technology to your prospective partner.
3. Understand your prospective partner's corporate bureaucracy and how a decision whether or not to partner will be made.

There are eight key elements to consider in forming a strategic alliance.

1. **Strategic fit.** Does the proposed alliance help both partners to implement their respective strategies?
2. **Advantage and benefit.** What are the benefits for each partner from the alliance? Will these benefits increase each partner's strategic advantage within its own competitive universe?
3. **Partner competence.** Does each partner have the competences and capabilities needed to achieve the alliance's objectives?
4. **Resource demands.** Do the parties have the funds, personnel, and other

resources the project requires? Are these resources sufficient to carry the project to the end? If either party does not have the resources today, will it be able to get them on a timely basis?

5. **Risks.** What are the risks involved in attempting to achieve the objective? What is the likelihood of any of these risks? What would its impact be?

6. **Corporate dominance.** Will one partner in the alliance try to dominate the other?

7. **Profit and loss impact.** Will focusing on satisfying the commitments to the alliance mean diverting resources from other efforts? This is more often a concern for the small partner. Small companies looking for resources and a quick route to achieving certain goals may enter into an alliance without thinking through the cost in resources and the impact on other projects.

8. **Image.** How would the relationship, if known to the outside world, reflect on the partners? Again, this is of prime concern to the small partner. Most entrepreneurs expect people to think their company and products must be worthwhile if a large corporation has teamed up with it. Unfortunately, there is some sensitivity, especially in the investment community, about small companies that are tightly interlinked with larger companies in alliances. Such an effort can hinder any future search for capital.

Understand the Organizational Chart

As soon as you begin discussions with a larger company about creating an alliance, you need to get a copy of the company's organization chart. Understanding the company's structure will give you a feel for the level of the people you are dealing with. Where in the organizational structure these people sit will, in turn, tell you something about the importance of this prospective alliance to the company. If a mid-level manager is in charge of the alliance, it may not be as important a relationship as if a vice president were in charge of it.

For example, one biotech company was excited by a large corporation's interest. The small company's top managers were called in for meetings with three departments over six months. But one of the small company's business advisors was not so impressed and asked the leaders to investigate how the three departments interrelated and how far along the corporation was in developing the alliance. Only then did the small company's managers find out that the large company's leaders simply couldn't decide which of the three departments should be responsible for the partnership.

As soon as you begin discussions with a larger company about creating an alliance, you need to get a copy of the company's organization chart.

A large corpora-tion may keep you on the hook with meetings and ongoing dis-cussions of your technology. The result is that you and your associ-ates disclose too many details of your technology and spend your time talking instead of devel-oping your busi-ness.

Nomenclature is not always helpful. It is sometimes difficult to ascertain the organizational level of a group, regardless of whether it is called a "depart-ment," a "branch," or a "division." Some companies call groups of more than two a "department," while others may call a small group a "branch."

Determine Your Value

Remember: large companies don't seek out small companies and strike up alliances because they are nice guys. They want something from you. That means you have some leverage.

Closely assess the importance of your product or technology to your prospective alliance partner. Is it a nice add-on to the company's current product line? Or does it fill out a strategic niche? Is it cornerstone technology for what could be a new product line needed to expand or even re-establish your prospective partner's business base?

You want to get as much information about where your product or tech-nology fits in without giving away too much sensitive or proprietary infor-mation. The more important your product or technology is to the prospective partner, the more negotiating leverage you have.

Understand the Decision-Making Process

Corporate bureaucracy can cause negotiations to take a long time. Decisions that you and your top managers would make in hours or days can take weeks or even months in a larger corporation. It is important in your early discussions about a potential alliance that you get a clear understanding of who makes decisions, what is needed from you to help that person reach a decision, and the time line for the decision.

Be candid about any other opportunities you may have to exploit the technology or market the product. But don't bully or establish ultimatums; just let it be known that you can't sit and wait forever. After all, your com-pany continues to exist and spend your financial resources.

Initial Conditions

Once you have received a positive response to creating an alliance from the larger company, begin negotiating the three basic conditions for the arrange-ment:

▶ Project plan
▶ Project budget
▶ Relationship managers from each company

Plan

The long-term project plan, complete with major activities, tasks, time lines, and milestones for both parties must be a part of the alliance agreement, even if your partner's lawyer says it can be worked out later. You need to make sure your activities mesh with your partner's in order to manage your company's resources and so everyone knows who will do what work and when.

Budget

A budget for implementing the project plan must be developed. Do not let the people representing your large corporate partner say they cannot tell how much money it is committing or they want to wait until everything else is funded. If they really want the alliance to work, they will commit to a dollar amount upfront.

Relationship Managers

It's important that the right person in the larger organization be assigned to manage your alliance relationship. If the person is too low down in the organization, he or she may not be able to get attention from the corporation's top executives. This may also be true of someone who is part of the technical organization. Also, that person may be able to communicate the technical aspects of the alliance but not the business aspects.

It's important that the right person in the larger organization be assigned to manage your alliance relationship.

If you don't determine these factors, you could end up stuck in a situation where the larger company is slow in making decisions and you are locked into the relationship.

For instance, a start-up in medical technology had an agreement with a large multinational corporation that called for a market launch of the smaller company's product within two years. But the corporation argued that it couldn't plan the launch because it still needed to perform in-house tests and then take the product to clinical trials, despite the fact that the smaller company had already obtained patents and FDA approval for the substance.

After a year the smaller company began asking the corporation to set a timetable for market launch. This was important to the smaller company, because its payments from the larger company were tied to various milestones leading up to the product launch. Every time the larger company postponed an activity or slipped a milestone, it meant that payments were delayed. In addition, the longer it took to get the product to market, the longer it would be before royalty income started flowing.

After two and a half years, the clinical testing was completed in Europe, but the multinational company said it wanted to do further clinical testing in the United States. The smaller company asked why this was necessary and it soon became apparent that the multinational company simply had not prepared a comprehensive product plan. The alliance eventually collapsed.

Giants Scour the Valley

In little-publicized efforts, IBM, Microsoft, and some other major companies have set up venture capital/joint venture offices that since the late 1990s have been scouring the Silicon Valley area of northern California looking to team up with and make investments in start-up technology companies. The software giants in particular have been taking equity positions in a dozen to two dozen companies a year since 2002 in an effort to extend their product lines of application programs. Yahoo, Google, and other providers are looking for start-ups with services that can be bundled with the larger offering.

These companies usually take a small equity stake in a start-up and support it with technical assistance in developing new products and services. Microsoft seeks partners that will use its proprietary technology while IBM works with companies that use IBM or open-source software.

The agreements usually include exclusive licensing arrangements or formal joint ventures. Successful companies are often purchased outright by their larger partners a few years after the initial investment is made.

According to a June 2006 article in *The Wall Street Journal,* Microsoft's venture capital staff of more than 20 completed 22 acquisitions in the year ended May 2006, while IBM, with a similar number in its VC operation, bought 16 companies in 2005.

The Partnership Deal

Establishing a relationship between two companies that will work toward a common goal takes more than simply describing the legal form of the relationship, the financial terms and conditions, and issues such as liability and property ownership. Most relationships don't falter in the organizing stage; they fall during implementation.

Many people entering alliances believe that "once we get the agreements signed, it's all downhill." Unfortunately, "downhill" may mean rocky times rather than easy sledding.

The key to doing a deal is for each party to go beyond defining the purpose and nature of the relationship. Both partners must be willing to state in concrete terms what they want to get out of the arrangement and each must agree that the other's objectives are important and realistic. They must also define tasks and achievements each partner organization will undertake and agree to a dispute-resolution mechanism.

Negotiating an agreement with a business partner can be emotional and traumatic for a number of reasons. Here is a list of negotiating points to help smooth the way:

1. Planning and Preparation

- ▶ Use people inside your company as well as outside specialists to create a team with the necessary skills.
- ▶ Do not change team members midcourse unless absolutely necessary.
- ▶ Include marketing, financial, and technical people and an attorney on the team.
- ▶ Know what you want out of the negotiations. Go in with a list of goals and objectives for the relationship.

2. Negotiating Behaviors

- ▶ Don't talk too much. Everything you say provides clues to the other party about your motivations.
- ▶ Don't fear silence. All negotiations need some "cooling off" time.
- ▶ Don't accept a deadline without thinking it through. Don't let artificial deadlines limit negotiating, force a quick deal, or cause a "rush to close."
- ▶ Don't negotiate when tired. Get enough rest and start negotiations after noon on Monday and end before noon on Friday.
- ▶ Use anger constructively. Getting angry at the right moment is great, as it can force the other party out of complacency. But don't get angry too often; this becomes an emotional button the other party can press to achieve its aims.
- ▶ Don't be critical without being reasonable. Constant criticism or ridicule of the other party's position can undermine yours.
- ▶ Everybody reads upside down. Don't think the other party's negotiating team isn't full of grade-A upside-down readers. Be careful not to expose documents you don't want them to see. Let them see only things you want them to see.

3. Negotiating Tactics

- ▶ Forgetting, bypassing, or neglecting your strategy and objectives means you have lost the focus of the negotiation.
- ▶ Don't give "free" concessions.
- ▶ Don't withdraw concessions.

> ▶ Calculate how you will respond "spontaneously" to a new term introduced in negotiations.

4. Negotiating "Musts"

> ▶ Always calculate the economic value of each term or condition.
> ▶ Always get it in writing.

Since the two organizations will be working closely together, they must understand each other's corporate culture and operating dynamics. Otherwise, they could be setting themselves up for the oft-repeated experience of one alliance.

An established East Coast corporation entered into an alliance with a growing West Coast technology company. The large corporation had a mature organization and a bound management handbook and it tended to operate by the numbers. The West Coast company was growing fast and, in real terms, becoming large, but still operated in a fairly loose, highly flexible manner—like a start-up.

It took six months to put the arrangement together and within a year the two companies wanted to break it up. Although they had negotiated all of the fine points of who would do and contribute what, the companies failed to define *how* they would operate together. The clashes of the two cultures were simply too much and they found they could not work together.

Using Business Advisors

Owners and executives of small and growing businesses who are thinking of forming an alliance with another company often turn to their attorney for help. Some, however, fear that their long-time attorney is too "small time" for such a task and seek out specialists in a larger law firm.

Neither of these options is the right path. Unfortunately, most attorneys don't think like businesspeople. They are trained to think in terms of contingencies—what-if's—and the documents they produce assume a worst-case scenario. Agreements negotiated and written by attorneys are based on a simple business model: company A works for company B and company B pays company A so much for its work. Such agreements are written so they can be enforced in court, assuming that one party will fail to perform its end of the bargain.

The partnering agreement is an important business document and a sensitive legal document. The following checklist will help you work through the process of creating a partnership agreement with another company. All

The corporate executives who negotiate with you probably have negotiated fewer deals than you have. Your ideas and considerations are as important as theirs. They believe that, with the large company behind them, they have more clout. However, remember that they want your technology as much as or more than you want an association with them.

but the final elements should be completed by business executives; the final section is to be performed by legal counsel.

1. Statement of Purpose: (Legal term: "Recitals")

2. Roles of the Partners and Scope of Work: partners' and participants' responsibilities for:

- ▶ development
- ▶ manufacturing
- ▶ testing
- ▶ marketing
- ▶ milestone schedule

3. Activities

- ▶ time lines
- ▶ milestone schedule
- ▶ completion and acceptable criteria

4. Financial Amount(s): what is paid by whom to whom, distribution ratios, and purpose:

- ▶ investment and form
- ▶ services
- ▶ advance payments and royalties

    payees—commitment
    - – extent
    - – duration
    - – consequences of defaults

    proceeds
    - – payments
    - – royalties
    - – allocation

5. Organization and Structure

6. Rights to Intellectual Property

- ▶ ownership
- ▶ reversions
- ▶ licensing
- ▶ exclusivity
- ▶ assignment
- ▶ extent of use
- ▶ right of first refusal regarding other developments
- ▶ escrow requirements

7. Equity
- ▶ earning basis and amounts
- ▶ basis for changes—financial and other milestones
- ▶ public stock issues (e.g., price, registration)
- ▶ incentives
- ▶ warrants

8. Indemnification
- ▶ patent infringement
- ▶ allocation

9. Confidentiality and Disclosure Conditions

10. Major Exposures and Consequences

11. Conflict Resolution Formula

12. Termination and Exit
- ▶ during development phase
- ▶ during full-scale operation
- ▶ penalties
- ▶ dissolution formula

13. Requirements (agreements contingent on completion of)
- ▶ delivery of "know-how"
- ▶ examination of invention disclosures, papers, and patent disclosures
- ▶ definition of "know-how"—sometimes called "application technology" and "intellectual property," this refers to all information and anything that represents or describes the invention or innovation, including, without limitation:
    - all inventions covered by the patent
    - designs
    - drawings
    - photographs
    - instructions
    - prototypes and models
    - technical information
    - specifications for materials and production
    - special tools and equipment
    - data concerning development
    - testing and evaluation of inventions covered by patent
    - laboratory records and reports
    - other data that have been developed, acquired, owned, controlled by

the developer, and are useful in the manufacturing and installation of inventions and/or maintaining and inspecting the same

14. Legal Aspects (performed by legal counsel)

- ▶ compliance with laws of all jurisdictions
- ▶ legal due diligence
- ▶ contract enforcement
- ▶ equipment patents and trademarks
- ▶ patent infringement
- ▶ contract/agreement drafting and review
- ▶ key personnel agreements
- ▶ tax planning
- ▶ entity structure and plan (if separate entity is formed)
- ▶ examination of records:
- ▶ articles of incorporation
- ▶ financial statements
- ▶ by-laws
- ▶ review of existing contracts and lawsuits
- ▶ lien search
- ▶ draft and review opinion of counsel

When two companies leave it to their attorneys to work out a deal, it often takes too long to negotiate, costs too much in attorneys' fees, and comes out tying the hands of both parties into performing their roles in narrowly defined, often ritualistic ways. The contracts themselves create an adversarial relationship between the two parties.

An alliance is by nature not adversarial. Rather, it is a relationship based on trust.

But an alliance is by nature not adversarial. Rather, it is a relationship based on trust. You, in contrast with your lawyer, go into negotiations to set up an alliance in an optimistic frame of mind. You realize that, in order to achieve your goals, you need to allow your alliance partner to achieve its goals as well. Sometimes this means you need to back off on reaching all of your goals in a particular area and agree to reach all of your goals in another area where your partner is willing to back off a little.

You also understand that businesses are organic and dynamic. You want to reach an agreement that allows both you and your partner some flexibility in how you reach the goals, if not in the goals themselves. You want your agreement to bend with changes in business conditions and not have to be constantly amended.

Large companies understand this. When they begin talking to another company about a relationship, be it for rights to a patent, a license to market a product, or even a merger or acquisition, their business people take the lead in the negotiations and their attorneys are present as part of the team.

Depending on the type of relationship, a particular businessperson will take the lead in negotiations. For a product license, for example, a marketing executive will take the lead, with a finance person crunching the numbers to see if the basic parameters of a deal work financially to the company's benefit.

Once the business and operational conditions of the relationship have been defined and agreed to, the lawyers can step in to take the structured relationship and write it up in language that conforms to the etiquette of a legal agreement.

In a small company, you may not have the depth of expertise on staff to conduct such negotiations. That's the time to call in a business consultant, especially one who helps companies establish strategic alliances, joint ventures, and other partnering arrangements. Such a person understands the gestalt of business partnering, not merely the formalities of a legal agreement.

A specialist in business partnering agreements brings a number of special skills to the negotiating table:

> *Once the business and operational conditions of the relationship have been defined and agreed to, the lawyers can step in to take the structured relationship and write it up in language that conforms to the etiquette of a legal agreement.*

- ▶ A business approach rather than a legal mindset
- ▶ Business knowledge born of involvement in business operations
- ▶ Technical familiarity with the particulars of the specific products or technologies under discussion
- ▶ A working familiarity with a range of financial alternatives for structuring a partnering relationship
- ▶ Negotiating skills that focus on formulating win-win arrangements rather than contingency planning for nonperformance

A business consultant focuses on sections of the agreement that explain the scope of the work. Items discussed include the following:

- ▶ which party will perform what portion of the work
- ▶ timetables and milestone schedules
- ▶ resources each party will contribute to the partnership
- ▶ rights of each party to the intellectual property developed through the partnership
- ▶ how the organizations will work together to reach their common goals

---

A Good Reference

One company with a new technology and a well-defined market, but little money to market its idea, created an effective technique to reach its audience. It demonstrated the value of its technology to a nonprofit association that represented many of its potential customers.

The association endorsed the company's technology to its members. One member company gave the start-up an order large enough to begin production.

Licensing Your Technology, Product, or Process: Let Another Company Make and/or Sell Your Product

For a start-up or growing business, licensing is a viable approach for raising capital without giving away equity or incurring debt that has to be repaid with interest. The difficulty is finding a company willing to license your technology, product, or process and also able to take it to market.

Licensing is conventionally thought of in connection with a sports or entertainment celebrity who licenses his or her image or name to be used in connection with a branded good or service. You may also be familiar with the use of licensing in art, collegiate activities, or designer clothing.

But licensing is a way to take a large variety of technologies, products, or processes to market. In fact, it has long been used by game designers and inventors who are purely creative individuals with no desire to become involved in the business aspects of their activities. In fact, publishing a book is essentially a license granted by the author(s) to the publisher to conduct the business elements involved in bringing the result of a creative process to market.

Licensing, simply put, is the act of giving someone permission to use your intellectual property in exchange for a fee.

What Is Licensing?

Licensing, simply put, is the act of giving someone permission to use your intellectual property in exchange for a fee. (For the rest of this discussion, we are going to focus on licensing intellectual property, rather than a name or a likeness, as celebrities do.) Intellectual property is, according to law, the fruits of creativity that the creator has a right to claim as his or hers alone. In order to have a valid claim that a particular technology, product, process, or creative work is yours and yours alone, you must have registered it and acquired intellectual property protection.

Intellectual property is protected in the United States by a patent, a trademark, a service mark, or a copyright. Once you have obtained protection for your intellectual property, whenever it is used, the user by law must pay you a fee.

Once you agree to let someone exploit the value of your intellectual property, the licensee can use it in a product or make it if it is a stand-alone product or can contract with someone else to make it or a product that uses it.

Licensing is complex. You'll need a qualified professional to help you develop a licensing plan and/or agreement.

This permission is defined in an agreement, called *rights*, which describes the extent to which the licensee uses the intellectual property of the licensor. Anything you own you can use yourself, lease (rent), or sell. Granting a license for intellectual property is analogous to owning a physical asset (such as a building or machinery) and leasing it to another party. However, while only one party can lease a physical asset, many parties can obtain licenses to intellectual property.

Within the agreement that spells out rights, you define limitations and constraints on how the intellectual property can be used. You (the licensor) and the user (the licensee) negotiate the terms and conditions under which the licensee can use the property. Issues to be negotiated include:

▶ how long the license is for or how many units of the product the licensee may produce;

▶ in what geographic area the licensee has the right to sell (e.g., you may license a product for sale in the Americas to one company and in Asia to another company);

▶ in which products the licensee is permitted to implant your technology (if you are licensing something that is not a stand-alone product);

▶ in how many facilities the licensee may implement your process (if you are licensing a process);

▶ whether the licensee may assign the rights it is licensing to another party.

The second part of the negotiation is around the method and payment you will receive for the license. Will payment be based on the period of time for which the licensee uses the technology, product, or process or rather on the level of usage (i.e., volume of units produced)?

If payment is volume-based, will there be points at which the payment per unit increases or decreases (e.g., $2 per unit for the first 500,000, $1.50 for the next 1,000,000 units, and $1 for any unit above 1,500,000)? If the license is granted for more than one year, will staged payments be cumulative over the life of the license or will they begin anew each year?

Using Licensing to Raise Capital

Licensing can be a viable way for you to raise capital. Here are some examples.

You are operating in a leading-edge industry and have developed technology that takes a particular device to the next stage of effectiveness.

One entrepreneur started a company on the basis of a new communications development he had invented and patented. He did not have a facility, staff, or production capacity to build these subassemblies and sell them to communications equipment manufacturers to use in their devices. Yet he found a customer willing to pay in advance for exclusive rights to buy the subassemblies. On the strength of that customer contract, he found another company willing to license the development and build it.

You have created a design that can help companies make a product less expensively.

One company patented the design of a new type of cardboard box. Box manufacturers (corrugators) then negotiated licenses to use that design. It reduces their manufacturing costs, so they are willing to pay for it. So ...

You develop a process that allows another process to work faster, such as a computer algorithm for testing chemical compounds used by pharmaceutical companies to fast-track drug development.

You create a small computer program that a maker of a larger software package licenses and imbeds into its program as a bonus.

These examples are of technologies, designs, processes, and products that other companies want to use. You may even be willing to license your property knowing that the licensee will not use it.

For instance, perhaps it would address a niche market. Another company operating in the industry in which this niche exists has a product similar to yours and access to the market. However, it knows that your product's features are superior. Rather than allow competition in the niche market, the company wishes to license your product, incorporate some of its features into its product, and eliminate you as a competitor. For "appropriate consideration" (a legal term that means what you get out of the deal) you may be willing to license your product, knowing that it will be cannibalized and never reach the market.

Why License?

This all leads to the question of why you would want to license instead of exploiting the technology, product, or process yourself.

111

First, if you have a technology or process, licensing works well because the technology or process is, in effect, your product. You are producing a behind-the-scenes element that can foster the production of goods. While you don't make outright sales of the technology or process, licensing it has two advantages:

- By creating a stream of license-fee payments (royalties) you are in effect setting up an annuity for yourself or your business.
- You do not transfer ownership of the technology or process to the licensee, so that party cannot turn around and sell it. You prevent uses of your process or technology by people with whom you do not agree or for purposes of which you do not approve (assuming that no one transfers the technology illegally).

If you have developed a product, licensing also has a number of advantages, especially for a small business.

- If there's already a demand for your product, licensing it to a large producer can get it to the marketplace far faster than if you had to ramp up production on your own.
- If you are in an industry with short product life cycle, such as fashion or software, and therefore must produce and sell goods quickly, before they fall out of favor, licensing allows you to pass off some of the risk to a goods producer while exploiting the opportunity.
- If the product is something unrelated to your company's core product line and you do not want to produce it, licensing it allows you to use your production facilities for more important products.
- If you decide you want to be a product design company, licensing allows you to maintain a lean operation, since you eliminate the need to produce and market the products you design and licensing provides you with income to continue designing more products.

Financial Issues in Licensing

So where does the money come from in a licensing deal?

The "appropriate consideration" you get in return for licensing your product is usually financial. There are other considerations you can get, such as access to the licensee's established markets for your other products, or cross licensing, in which case the parties exchange licenses that help each of them. If you receive a fee or an advance payment against royalties, you can use that as you would any other capital infusion.

Some companies are started and operated strictly for the purpose of developing and licensing intellectual property, with no intention of ever manufacturing any product. Other companies are established to manufacture, but license out all product marketing and selling.

Reverse Licensing

Some companies that need cash but wish to exploit their technology in the long term choose to sell the technology then license it back from the new owner. A company thus receives a jolt of cash from the sale and is freed from committing resources to exploit the technology in the marketplace immediately, enabling it to focus on developing new technology or new uses for the technology. Also, the company that purchases the technology may enjoy some tax advantages from owning the technology.

Paying for Licensing

Payment schemes for licensing are usually determined by historical business practices in the specific industry. There are five basic license fee payment models:

- ▶ A one-time payment when the agreement is signed for use of the technology, product, or process for a specified period of time. This method is far more common in licensing processes or technology licensing than for products.
- ▶ Royalty payments. This is the method most frequently used for product licensing. The licensee pays a certain percentage of either the gross or the net sales price (gross minus expenses) of the product. In high technology, for instance, royalties run anywhere from 2 to 7 percent of gross sales. The royalty rate and the basis for calculation are determined by the nature of the product. The royalty on a component, for instance, could be based on the percentage of the price represented by that component.
- ▶ An annual license fee, either fixed or based on sales volume. This can take the place of a royalty when it is difficult to compute a basis for the royalty or when the licensor does not want the burden of auditing the licensee's books.
- ▶ A royalty with an advance payment against future royalties. This method has two advantages for the licensor.

Marketing a license means determining who will benefit if they have rights to your intellectual property.

113

- It provides a capital infusion up front, although it is smaller than a one-time payment.
- It puts the licensee at some degree of risk and motivates it to push the product hard in order to recoup the advance.

▶ It provides a hybrid one-time fee plus royalties. The fee is not an advance and is not credited against future royalties.

A problem with a straight royalty deal, as many licensors have learned, is that the licensee may not prioritize the product and market it aggressively or use the technology to its fullest, so the licensor may not receive any royalty income for a long time. Sometimes licensors also put clauses into the agreement that force the licensee to begin using the technology or process or to take the product to market, within a certain time. If it fails to do so, the licensee can be subject to paying a penalty fee or it can lose the license.

Valuation of Intellectual Property

Royalty rates for different kinds of products, processes, or technology generally fall within certain ranges.

Licensing fees and royalties are determined based on the value of the intellectual property being licensed. You should therefore not set a particular fee or royalty rate just because that fee or rate has been used for another product. Royalty rates for different kinds of products, processes, or technology generally fall within certain ranges, and the royalty for a particular piece of intellectual property or likeness generally falls somewhere within that range.

For instance, while 75 percent of all royalties are for rates less than 5 percent, rates for art generally fall between 5 and 8 percent, for entertainment property between 8 and 12 percent, and for events between 10 and 15 percent.

Valuing intellectual property can be difficult. Although many methods have been identified, not all of them may be usable in any given situation. In addition, there are many intangible considerations in the marketing and technical areas.

In marketing, intangibles include corporate name and logo, promotion activities, and advertising. For instance, the name Stephen King automatically sells one million copies of a book, while the names Ralph Alterowitz and Jon Zonderman do not; hence the authors of this book have far less leverage in negotiating a royalty deal with their publisher than does Stephen King with his. Most of the time, a start-up or young business does not have much brand recognition and thus cannot command a high royalty rate.

In the technical area, intangibles include packaging technology or process, technology updates, and production techniques. There is no limit to the number of such enhancements that can be added to the license. The technological intangibles that go along with one license will not necessarily be the same as those for another granted by the same licensor.

As a licensor, you should be cautious not to demand compensation for intangibles that can't be supported. However, you should consider whether supporting the licensed technology, product, or process through technological intangibles adds value to the license without draining efforts from your core business. This might mean creating new intellectual property for license or products for your company to actually produce and sell.

Negotiating the Licensing Agreement

Every negotiation starts the same way. You as the licensor should have established guidelines for licensing the technology, product, or process.

Have an intellectual property attorney prepare a standard licensing agreement for you to present to the prospective licensee. Guidelines for use of the intellectual property, such as specifying the industries to which the licensee may market, should be submitted in draft form for the other party to review.

Several conditions affect the negotiating protocol. For instance, as a start-up or young company, you may have been identified by a larger company as one that is developing innovative and potentially useful technology, products, or processes. The opportunity to license may have therefore come about because of another company's interest in your intellectual property, rather than through any effort on your part to license that intellectual property. If a potential licensee comes to you, you are in a stronger negotiating position than if you were scrambling for funding and decided to cash in on some intellectual property.

The following 11 sections must be included in any licensing agreement:

1. Definition and description of the intellectual property being licensed.
2. Type of rights granted (exclusive or nonexclusive).
3. Description of the geographic territory in which the licensee is allowed to use or sell the intellectual property.
4. Applications for which the intellectual property may be used.
5. Financial (sometimes referred to as compensation), specifying the applicable payments: fees and/or royalties.
6. Representations and warranties, in which the licensor states things such as that he or she is the owner of the intellectual property and has the right to execute the license.

You need to determine the value to users of your licensed technology or product in order to decide on the right compensation plan. Unless your intellectual property is completely new or in an industry that does not routinely use licensing, there are standard payment ranges.

115

7. Confidentiality agreement stating that the licensee must not divulge any proprietary information that it obtains while working with the licensor.

8. Proprietary rights, including who maintains the intellectual property rights, etc.

9. Infringement, describing what happens if someone copies the product or uses the technology or process without a license.

10. Term or period during which the license is in force.

11. Termination, describing what happens at the end of the agreement period and under what conditions the agreement can be terminated early.

A number of other issues need to be laid out in the agreement, such as accounting, auditing, and taxation. The best person to write the agreement is an attorney familiar with both intellectual property and licensing arrangements. Not every patent attorney is competent to write a licensing agreement or to pursue an infringement action.

Sometimes a licensing agreement is preceded by a letter of intent, which lays out the proposal in broad terms. Most, if not all, of the elements in the letter are then formalized in the final agreement.

Part Two

Growing Businesses

B USINESS IS PERKING ALONG. EVERYTHING IS WORKING SMOOTHLY. Sales are picking up and the business owner realizes that fairly soon he or she will have to increase his capacity in order to produce more product.

The first challenge is to get more money to purchase equipment, to hire more people, and to increase the inventory of raw materials and other supplies. That means that the owner will have to raise more money than expected. Finding a funding source is always a substantial challenge, but there are several other significant tasks to be accomplished so the business can grow successfully.

Growing the business means scaling up the operations. The owner currently has processes in place for producing a given volume. Personnel, equipment, and supplies are in balance to yield this output. Increasing the production of goods means the owner must do the following.

The owner must revamp the infrastructure. This means determining the changes necessary for ensuring that the desired level of product can be produced. How many more people will be needed and does the company need to replace any equipment or bring in additional equipment?

The owner must upgrade marketing and distribution, to increase sales and sustain that increase. More people and materials may be needed for the marketing. Furthermore, the outlets currently distributing the product may be too limited. The owner may need to consider adding new outlets or shifting the business completely to larger outlets and possibly changing the financial terms to ensure a profit.

The owner must control overhead. A large operation will usually demand more managers and staff as well as other indirect costs. The owner must be attentive to this aspect of the operation. Poor supervision hurts output, as does having too many layers of decision making between those in contact with the customer and the company's leaders. It is very easy to add people and facilities in advance of achieving expected revenue levels and then find that the operation was expanded too quickly or was too large, which meant a significant cash outflow.

Business owners like to be optimistic and often think in larger terms before it is warranted. The same caution that existed at start-up must be exercised throughout the growth phases as well. Investors and lenders want to see reasonable growth and good support for expansions.

Chapter 8

Getting Bigger/
Need Money Again

NOW IS THE TIME TO LOOK TO NEW SOURCES OF CASH IN ORDER
to grow your business and possibly take out some of the cash
you put into your start-up to replenish your personal savings.
We have all heard stories about entrepreneurs who emptied
their piggy banks to start their companies, plowed every
penny earned back into their companies, and then had nothing in reserve
when the companies fell on hard times.

Of course, you shouldn't expect that your company will encounter difficulties. But you should be ready for that eventuality. Reclaiming some of
your initial investment is a way to cushion yourself and your family against
any business downturn. Recapitalizing your company and restructuring
your company's balance sheet is an important step when growing a business.

Once you have established a track record as a viable business, it is possible to borrow from a bank or finance company on better credit terms than
you could have received as a start-up. All of the rules discussed in earlier
chapters about dealing with banks and commercial credit companies apply,
as do the discussions on programs available through the Small Business
Administration and state or local economic development offices.

In this chapter, however, we want to focus on a couple of avenues open
to growing businesses that are not generally open to start-ups. These are

working with suppliers to minimize the cash you have to put out to buy production-oriented as well as non-production goods, and working with customers to make sure they adhere to your credit and collection terms.

Suppliers: Good Cash-Flow Management Is Money in the Bank

Suppliers (or vendors) provide you with the materials, components, and other production-oriented goods that go into your product, as well as the goods and services you need to run your business. So, why do they belong in a chapter about financing growth?

Suppliers don't normally provide capital for your business in the form of a cash investment in exchange for equity. However, they do offer credit to their customers. Working closely with your suppliers can help you capitalize your business by better managing your cash flow.

If you produce, distribute, or retail products, there are three ways suppliers can help you manage cash flow and reduce the need for working capital in the form of cash:

▶ Buying on credit

▶ Buying on consignment

▶ Supplier-managed inventory

Buying on Credit

Most suppliers of goods (and some suppliers of services) are willing to provide favorable credit terms to capture new business.

Most suppliers of goods (and some suppliers of services) are willing to provide favorable credit terms to capture new business. Of course, the best credit terms are usually extended to companies with the best credit history.

Suppliers are often willing to work closely with a customer that is a young and growing company, since there is a good chance the customer will return the kindness when it becomes larger and better established. Filling small orders, extending no-interest payment from 30 to 60 days for a few years, and providing favorable credit terms are all ways in which suppliers can build relationships with their customers.

As your company grows and after you have established a credit history, it is a good idea to revisit the issue of credit terms with each of your current suppliers. A common way to begin is by checking with competing suppliers to see if they will offer better terms. You can use an offer of better terms to try to get your current supplier to match those terms in order to keep you as a customer. Of course, your current supplier may refuse to match the credit terms offered by the competitor. Then you have to decide whether to switch on the basis of price or to stay in the supplier relationship you have built over time.

Most suppliers do not charge interest on payments made within 30 days (and sometimes 60 days) of the date of purchase. This means that if you have a quick production process or a distribution or retail business that moves goods quickly to your customers, you may have a lag between the time you receive payment for your sales and the time you must pay your suppliers for those goods. In this case, you can earn interest on the money in your possession during that lag, a situation known as "playing the float."

That is how supermarket and fast-food outlets keep their prices and profit margins low and still make money for their owners. The profit margin on a fast-food meal, for example, is essentially 0 percent. That means it costs the franchise owner of a Burger King or Wimpy's or Dunkin' Donuts as much to buy the food and paper goods, lease the space, hire the help, and take a salary every month as the store takes in from customers.

Yet the franchisee still earns a profit if suppliers allow 30 or 60 days to pay with no interest charge, the rent comes due only monthly, and paychecks are cut every week. Every night the day's cash goes into a cash-management account at the bank where it earns interest until the bills fall due. For a company with a large daily turnover, the daily float can generate sizable yearly profits.

Remember: in the case of fast-food outlets, whoever owns the franchise (a franchisee or the company) also owns the real estate on which the store

Relationships can be established with your supplier that range from very favorable transaction terms to outright investment in your company.

CBS and iWon

Occasionally, a supplier will actually invest in a company by providing goods or services in exchange for equity.

In 1999, CBS invested $85 million in the Web portal company iWon. CBS put up $15 million in cash and provided iWon with $70 million in services in the form of advertising time.

iWon's unique offering in the crowded Web portal space was to give away a chance at $25 million worth of cash sweepstakes prizes every time a user clicked onto the portal. The company's ads, which ran on CBS from 1999 to 2001, were catchy and garnered iWon a following.

The company kept its operations lean, remained privately held, and survived the Internet bubble implosion. In November 2001, tiny iWon purchased the Excite portal from Excite@home, which was liquidating through a bankruptcy proceeding, for only $10 million.

sits. The greatest profit for a long-time owner of such an outlet is the real estate when it is sold.

Even if your throughput time (the time your inventory is in your facility, be it production, distribution, or retail) is such that you must pay your suppliers before your customers have paid you, most suppliers will extend you credit at a rate lower than you would pay for an unsecured bank loan and certainly lower than for your credit card.

Buying on Consignment

Some suppliers may be willing to sell you production materials on consignment, meaning that you pay only for what you use and can return unused materials over a specified period of time. Consignment raw material inventory is usually offered by companies that deal in products with an infinite life, such as steel or plastic resin. If you return the unused inventory six months after you take possession of it, the supplier can usually find another customer.

Consignment buying is based on the honor system; you write a check to the supplier every month for the amount of material you have actually used.

Sometimes a supplier will sell you a standard amount of material every month based on your best estimate of production and provide you with more material (safety stock) on consignment in case you have higher demand than predicted.

The objective of conserving capital forces you to explore every avenue for delaying cash outflows. You have to pay your bills, but later is better.

Many suppliers also sell to retail outlets on consignment. This is typical in the clothing industry, where the financial risk has always been on the brand-label companies rather than the retailer. If an item falls out of fashion between the time it is designed and the time it appears on retail store racks, the brand-label company is stuck with a lot of unsellable goods.

Supplier-Managed Inventory

Supplier-managed inventory is a technique used in manufacturing. A supplier accepts a large order for a certain amount of raw materials, components, or sub-assemblies that the customer will use over a long period of time. Then, the supplier delivers to the customer only the amount of goods needed for a week or a day of production, holding the remaining inventory in its own facilities. A supplier that manages your inventory may also store parts or components from other suppliers and then kit materials from many suppliers for delivery to you.

Suppliers charge a premium to manage your inventory for you, but it is often cheaper to pay the supplier to do it than to finance and build a facility for your production-oriented inventory. Whether you hold the inventory or the supplier does, the payment for the goods themselves will be the same.

Maintaining good supplier relations and managing inventories with your suppliers are only two aspects of sound cash management. Another two are timely collecting of accounts receivable and daily posting of income into your cash-management account.

Good cash management can win you the respect of banks and other lenders, which in turn can enable you to borrow early in your company's growth cycle and at favorable terms. In addition, banks will often consider references from suppliers (sometimes called *trade creditors*) when considering a loan request.

Inventory management and other transactions with suppliers demand careful record-keeping to avoid errors in either party's accounts.

Customers: If Possible, Piggyback on a Big Customer's Technology

Customers can help you finance your company in two major ways:

- ▶ They can adhere to your credit terms.
- ▶ They can provide you with services through a Web-based enterprise portal.

Customers are much more likely to invest in your company than are suppliers, especially if you provide them with critical components, software, or knowledge.

Large technology and pharmaceutical companies have for many years invested in start-up companies that can potentially provide the larger company's customers with complementary products. Sometimes this is done through some sort of a strategic alliance and sometimes it's done through providing capital and taking an equity position, as discussed in Chapter 7.

Adhering to Your Credit Terms

For a young and growing company, the flip side of working with suppliers to stretch your payments and obtain the best possible credit terms is getting your customers to pay you promptly.

It is often more difficult to work with customers than with suppliers. Remember: whatever advantages you try to work out with your suppliers, your customers will try to work out with you. Many, if not most of them, have more leverage with you than you have with your suppliers. While you are hunting for suppliers who offer the best terms and conditions, so too are your potential customers.

Before you open your doors for business, you need to define a payment policy that brings in cash in a timely fashion yet doesn't turn off potential customers. One of the most frequently cited reasons for small businesses closing is excessive accounts receivable, as the need to pay their suppliers drains operating cash.

As your business begins to grow, you may be tempted to relax your credit terms in an effort to grow faster. Don't do it. One of the biggest problems for small businesses in a growth mode is a cash-flow squeeze because they need to purchase more materials and hire more people, yet have trouble collecting on customer accounts.

If you are operating a retail store, managing incoming cash is little or no problem. Customers will pay by cash, credit card, or check. But if you operate in the business-to-business realm and have to sell on credit, whether to other companies in a product's production chain or retailers as a distributor, you need to manage incoming cash flow closely. Always take the following four steps before you sell on credit:

▶ Determine the grace period for payment without interest (30, 60, or 90 days).

▶ Determine the interest rate for payments made after the grace period.

▶ Create a set of standard collection documents (first letter, second letter, demand letter, etc.).

▶ Set a policy for when you will send an account to a collection agency or an attorney.

Enterprise Portal Access

One of the hottest things in the world of business-to-business e-business is the use of enterprise portal software by large companies. Even after the dot-com bust, companies have continued to install enterprise portal software and make it more useful by extending portal access beyond the company's employees to other companies throughout the value chain.

An enterprise portal is front-end software (the software with which a computer user interacts). It uses Web-browser technology and allows the user to access a host of software applications, information sources, and services that the hosting company packages. Like a consumer portal, it allows the user to move back and forth among applications, information sources, or service components quickly without having to log on separately for each use.

By extending the use of its enterprise portal to its business partners, a

As your business begins to grow, you may be tempted to relax your credit terms in an effort to grow faster. Don't do it.

Gregg Gloor: Turning Wood into Millions Through Advance and Progress Payments

Advance, partial, milestone, and periodic payments are fairly standard in professional practices. Dentists require periodic or milestone payments when undertaking long-term and complex procedures, such as implants and dental reconstruction. Usually, when a client orders something from a craftsperson or custom builder, the agreement includes a deposit of 10 to 15 percent, to pay for the materials needed to begin the job, with periodic payments throughout the project.

This system usually works out, although there is always some level of anxiety. For the client, the question is whether the person providing the service will do so as agreed on time and at the agreed-upon price. For the person performing the service, the issue is how to maintain enough working capital for all the projects in process, which may need different sorts of supplies and even special-purpose equipment.

In their hippie days in the late 1960s, Greg Gloor and a friend became pretty good at building things for friends out of wood. They decided to go into business together making simple platform- and loft-style beds. They rented a basement apartment (borrowing money for the rent) and set up business with a belt sander, a circular saw, a drill, and a router.

Short on cash to buy materials and more sophisticated equipment, Gloor and his friend asked for deposits of 50 percent. Over time, they continually expanded both their space and their catalog, using their reputation for quality goods (they guarantee their furniture for life) to maintain their 50 percent deposit policy and thus always having enough cash flow to keep their business steadily growing. Today, Hardwood Artisans does $6 million in business annually and employs 60 craftspeople.

company that hosts a portal can streamline the information flow up and down the product value chain and reduce costs for itself and for its business partners. Increasingly, sophisticated software allows designers at different companies to work together to design end-user products and their components simultaneously.

As a small company, you don't have the resources to implement an enterprise portal. But much of the software you use can be "plugged into" other companies' enterprise portals.

Large companies are beginning to use their enterprise portals to cement relationships with suppliers and B2B customers. They are offering more and more software applications, business information, and Web-based services to their business partners. While "plugging in" may seem to make you a captive partner (and in some ways it does), it can provide you with computer power that you simply can't afford on your own.

There are two ways to utilize a customer's or supplier's enterprise portal to your advantage.

As a Supplier

Suppose you have created an electrical component that uses new technology you developed. Your product has uses in all kinds of controls, from avionics for planes and helicopters to devices for automobile dashboards, boats, elevators, and lawn tractors. Your company will not manufacture these components but does the design engineering for them so they can be integrated into larger systems and used in products.

Piggybacking on corporate customer programs gives your company visibility and credibility, in addition to enabling you to stretch your dollars.

DaimlerChrysler issues a request for proposals (RFP) for a new dashboard system for a car that will become available to consumers in two years. You receive a call from a major developer and manufacturer of systems for cars (called a tier-1 supplier), such as Johnson Controls or Honeywell. The company wants to incorporate your technology into its proposal.

Such a company is big enough to implement an enterprise portal. This portal provides employees (and select business partners) with access to a variety of corporate information, software applications, and Web-based services.

You receive a code that allows you to get into the portion of the company's enterprise portal on which collaborative design takes place. Using this platform, the proposal's project manager downloads to you a copy of the RFP, with the parameters for your component highlighted.

You tinker with the basic design of your component to get it to meet the design specifications and then upload your design to all the other designers and engineers working on this project, both at the tier-1 company and the other subcontractors.

Unfortunately, engineers at another company have designed their piece of the major system so it is incompatible with your component. The sophisticated design-management software on the tier-1 company's in-house computer system (to which all project participants have access) points out the incompatibility. Before this kind of software, such an incompatibility might not have been discovered until the final system went into testing.

This problem is discussed during the regular Tuesday conference call with all of the engineers from all the partner companies. Instead of having to paw through piles of design documents, each person uses a computer screen to display the items being discussed. The problem is ironed out and you go away to work on the redesign.

Toward the end of the three-month design project, the project manager calls for a face-to-face meeting. (In the past, you may have been at meetings every two weeks.) All project partners are given access to the company's travel service through the enterprise portal to make arrangements for planes, hotels, and rental cars.

By consolidating travel arrangements, the tier-1 company, which is responsible for travel costs, can reduce its processing expenses by simply paying its travel service rather than reimbursing individual project partners. In addition, by logging into the travel service, each project partner creates a permanent record of preferences for future travel he or she may do with the company.

The system you helped design is chosen. You are asked to fill an order for 400,000 units over the next two years, with the first delivery due in nine months.

As a design engineering firm, you have no manufacturing capabilities. However, that's not a problem. The tier-1 company puts you in touch with a contract manufacturer that has worked on sophisticated components in the past. You will work with the manufacturer to build a production line for the component, source the raw materials and parts, design and implement a quality-control process, and fulfill the order.

All of this, as well as coordination with the production management team for the entire system at the tier-1 supplier, will be done through the enterprise portal. The contract manufacturer's internal computer systems have already been integrated into the portal, so you can have access to production and inventory information through your computer at your facility. Third-party logistics providers are already on board and their computer systems have been tied in, so you can track delivery of components to the tier-1 supplier.

You will invoice the tier-1 supplier electronically at the time of delivery. You will receive electronic payment and be responsible for electronic payment to the contract manufacturer, which is technically your subcontractor.

All this will be done through the enterprise portal.

Oh, and by the way, since you are now a fully integrated business partner, you can continue to have access to travel services and the same volume discounts that apply to the tier-1 company, because you are a "sub-account." You will receive bills and make payments for your travel electronically.

As a Customer

Let's say your business is automotive repair and maintenance. You have a dealership agreement with a particular brand of tire (e.g., Bridgestone), meaning you only sell that company's tires and third-party tires that company wholesales.

The tire company is large enough to have an enterprise portal available to its employees and business partners. These partners include suppliers of materials for tire manufacturer (steel belts, rubber, white-wall material, plastic air stems, etc.) as well as its authorized dealerships, such as you.

Through the enterprise portal, you can place your orders for tires and tire equipment such as balancing hardware, replacement stems, repair kits, and patches. Ordering, billing, and payment can all be done electronically. You can track the status of your order and find out when to expect delivery.

Of course, none of this is very special; you could do it simply through a company's Web site. But an enterprise portal enables the company to increase its communication with you by "pushing" information so you don't always have to "pull" it (search for it) on a passive Web site.

Enterprise portal software allows a company to send out alerts and other important information to its portal users that is specifically tailored to them. For you, this can include new wholesale prices, special incentives to dealers and consumers, and shipping offers from the logistics carrier for orders placed at a certain time.

The enterprise portal can also save you money. Say the tire company makes a deal with a company that provides Web-based accounting software to set up a computer server dedicated to the company's distributors. Now you don't have to pay for accounting software or a computer with enough storage capacity to hold your accounting data. You simply log on to the enterprise portal, find the software, perform your accounting chores, and upload your data to the server. The company providing you with server access is responsible for keeping your records secure; this is often done by having a third party manage the enterprise-portal servers.

The company may also allow you to gain access through its enterprise portal to a third-party e-business marketplace where distributors of auto parts, mechanics tools, or computerized diagnostic equipment sell directly to businesses like yours.

Chapter 9

Getting Bigger/Need Even More Money

MANY SMALL, PRIVATELY OWNED COMPANIES FIND THEMSELVES poised for a growth spurt, yet needing cash to take them to the next level. They have exhausted their ability to borrow against company assets, yet need another $100,000 to $1 million or even more to hire staff, buy equipment, expand office space, or purchase materials to enable them to take on larger business deals.

Here are three fresh sources of funding for such companies that have tapped out their founder's ability to finance growth and can't go back to the bank for one more loan. Two involve borrowing and one involves providing an equity stake in the business to employees.

Mezzanine Financing

Mezzanine financing refers to lenders that provide funding for just this niche market, between secured debt and significant sale of equity. Mezzanine finance providers lend anywhere from $500,000 to $20 million, without taking any collateral. A few companies, such as Snowbird Capital in Reston, VA, specialize in what is known as "micro-mezzanine" financing, under $5 million.

Mezzanine finance companies generally charge 12 to 20 percent interest, because the loan is unsecured by any collateral. This makes the loan "subordinate" to any loans that are secured—hence another name, *subordinated debt*.

While mezzanine finance companies are not venture capitalist players, they usually include taking a small stake in the company in addition to the interest charge. Often, part or all of this stake is reversible over time. The entrepreneur can buy back the equity portion of the loan; this gives the mezzanine finance provider an extra layer of profit. Or the entrepreneur can allow the mezzanine finance provider to maintain its equity position.

Accounts Receivable Financing and Factoring

New and growing companies don't always get the best credit terms from their suppliers, so they often have to pay suppliers before their customers pay them. This can create cash-flow problems. In order to maintain cash flow, companies can pledge their accounts receivable as collateral on a loan or sell those receivables to a company known as a factor.

Using Receivables as Collateral

Many banks and finance companies that would be unwilling to provide you with an unsecured working capital loan will lend if you use your accounts receivable as collateral for the loan.

Many banks and finance companies that would be unwilling to provide you with an unsecured working capital loan will lend if you use your accounts receivable as collateral for the loan. They usually use a monthly borrowing-base calculation, which is based on historical averages. A lender will typically finance 80 percent of good-quality receivables (those that are not too old and are deemed collectable).

As you collect on your receivables, you pay the bank, which lowers the borrowing basis until you make the next round of sales.

This is a labor-intensive type of loan. Both you and the bank must keep voluminous records. Also, banks usually charge higher interest rates than for other loans, as well as more in service fees.

Factoring

In a factoring arrangement, a company uses its accounts receivable to raise cash. But rather than using receivables as collateral for a loan, the company actually sells its accounts receivable to a finance company, known as a *factor*. (Banks don't factor.)

Keep in mind the following points about factoring.

▶ Factoring is expensive.

▶ The factor does not pay the company 100 cents on the dollar. There are also charges and commissions for its collection services.

▶ There are advantages to using a factor. The company receives money almost immediately after the sale and it gets to limit its credit, collection, and bookkeeping expenses to a fixed percentage of its credit sales (the commission it pays to the factor). Many companies use factoring to avoid setting up a credit and collection department.

▶ Most factors also work with companies to help run credit checks on customers who wish to open accounts and to establish proper credit lines for those customers.

There are two types of factoring: *old-line* factoring and *maturity* factoring.

Factoring is used by companies large and small to cope with short-term cash-flow problems or long-term cash needs.

Old-Line Factoring

In an old-line factoring arrangement, the factor pays a certain percentage of each account receivable, known as an *advance payment*. It may trade advances for receivables monthly, weekly, or even daily. The rate of advances, which can vary from 70 to 90 percent of the total value of the receivables, is determined by subtracting for historic bad debt, slow paying, etc., from a base of 100, adding back 10 to 15 percent (or points), and then subtracting this number from 100 again. This final calculation is called the *dilution*. A *spread* is then added to the dilution to determine the final amount the factor will advance. For instance, if the factor calculates a dilution rate of 7 percent for your company and takes a 13 percent spread, it will advance you 80 percent against each receivable.

The factor is actually lending the company the advance payment at a rate of 1 to 3 percent over the prime rate. When the factor collects against an account receivable, the first 80 percent expunges the advance it has paid against the receivable. If the factor collects more than the 80 percent, it pays you cash, minus a "discount fee" of 2 to 6 percent, plus the interest you owe against the advance.

Some old-line factors also hold reserves against uncollectible accounts. If the factor works *without recourse*, any bad debt is the responsibility of the factor: it gets stuck with any deadbeat receivables or deficiencies below what it has advanced. (It will, however, use these deficiencies and no-pays to recalculate your dilution rate.) If the factor works *with recourse*, you are responsible for picking up deficiencies of receivables that age out.

Maturity Factoring

In maturity factoring, the factor purchases the receivables, assumes the credit risk, and advances cash to you as the invoices mature. You and the factor determine the credit limit for each account (the amount that the factor will pay you against that account) and the average collection period for all your accounts receivable. At the end of that period, the factor pays you the entire value of each customer's receivable (up to the specified limit), less its commission for collections, regardless of whether or not the customer has paid in full.

For instance, if your average collection period is 45 days and XYZ's credit limit is $25,000, 45 days after you make a sale to XYZ the factor will pay you the entire $25,000 (minus a commission of 2 to 6 percent for handling the collection), even if it has collected only $10,000. Many factors that work with maturity factoring will charge you interest on the difference between what they have collected and what they pay you, again at 1 to 3 percent over the prime rate.

While maturity factoring provides some protection against deadbeat customers, you end up paying interest on any advances the factor has made against accounts that turn out to be uncollectible.

Using Factoring Wisely

Factors have a stake in your customers' creditworthiness. Use their knowledge and expertise to perform credit checks and let them work with you to establish realistic credit terms for your customers.

It's important when establishing a relationship with a factor to understand the full extent of that relationship and create a strategy to use it to your advantage.

Factors have a stake in your customers' creditworthiness. Use their knowledge and expertise to perform credit checks and let them work with you to establish realistic credit terms for your customers.

Some factors specialize in working with companies in a particular industry. Try to find one that specializes in your industry.

There are also factors that specialize in working with companies of certain sizes. Many require you to have minimum monthly level of accounts receivable before they will work with you; this can be as low as $10,000 or as high as $250,000. Many also reduce their fees as the dollar volume of accounts receivables increases and raise their fees for receivables of lesser amounts. Try to find a factor that works with a lot of companies of your general size.

Take the factoring relationship into account when you establish prices and credit terms. Think of factoring the same way you think of credit-card selling, for which you pay a processing commission to the credit card company.

Use the proceeds from factoring to get the best terms possible from your suppliers. The savings you receive through discounts for timely payment can offset some of the costs of factoring.

Six Questions to Ask a Potential Factor

Remember: factoring is a service being provided to you. As with any other professional service provider, the agreement you sign with a factor should define the level of service being provided and the payments you will make for that service. Before you sign an agreement, find out the answers to the following important questions.

1. Do you require a minimum monthly dollar volume of receivables? If so, what is it?
2. What is your basic discount fee? Does it depend on the dollar volume or number of receivables? What other fees and charges are there?
3. What is your advance rate (dilution plus how many points)? How quickly do you pay the advance on new receivables (daily, weekly, monthly)? How frequently do you recalculate the dilution rate? Do you increase the advance rate for larger dollar volumes?
4. Do I have to sell you all of my receivables or a certain percentage or dollar volume?
5. What level of service do you guarantee? Do you perform credit checks on my accounts? If so, how frequently do you monitor the credit ratings of my accounts? How aggressively will you pursue a collection? What other services do you provide?
6. What is the length of the agreement? What are the terms under which I can get out of the agreement?

Merchant Cash Advances (Credit-Card-Receivable Financing)

Retail merchants that receive a lot of payments through credit cards can look to a small group of companies that provide cash advances against future credit card sales, collecting payment for those advances over time with credit card receipts. These are called *merchant cash advances* or *credit card receivable financing*.

In a merchant cash advance arrangement, the advances usually start within 14 days of signing a contract and are paid back over time as a specified percentage of each credit card sale is routed directly to the advance provider. Loans generally cost between 20 and 35 percent annually.

Check out www.thefactoringnetwork. com for an evaluation of whether factoring will work for you and for access to over 150 factors.

Advances can be short term (long enough to buy supplies to produce one major project that is repaid by credit card) or for long-term growth.

As with mezzanine financing, credit-card advances are unsecured by any collateral, and the industry is unregulated, so companies can charge whatever the market will accept.

One of the largest of these providers is AdvanceMe, of Kennesaw, GA, a subsidiary of Capital Access Network, Inc. These companies generally will make advances of as little as a few thousand dollars to more than $100,000 per location to a retailer that needs the cash to add staff, expand space, or take on new merchandise lines, but not generally to open a new location.

Employees: Stock Options and ESOPs Spread the Wealth

Employees can help finance your company by accepting an equity stake in exchange for less cash compensation.

*E*SOPs allow an owner to "cash out" all or a portion of his or her ownership over time in order to diversify her investment portfolio.

This usually means providing employees with a grant of stock options. But you can also create an *employee stock ownership plan* (ESOP), a vehicle that transfers all or part of your company's ownership to employees over time.

Stock options are valuable only if the company's stock will become publicly traded. ESOPs make sense if the company will remain privately held. They allow an owner to "cash out" all or a portion of his or her ownership over time in order to diversify her investment portfolio. ESOPs are especially useful for family-owned businesses if there are no members of the next generation who wish to own and operate the business or if there are family tensions that might cause the business to be sold upon the owner's death.

Stock Options

A stock option provides an individual with the right to buy a share of stock at a set price for a specified period of time. The use of stock options as an incentive for employees of young entrepreneurial companies became widespread in the 1990s.

Huge grants of stock options were used to hire, retain, or lure talented individuals away from other companies. Many management-level employees were hired for relatively low cash compensation in exchange for the chance to become wealthy through stock options.

Since most entrepreneurial companies either fail or are sold to larger companies, rather than to the public through an IPO, few people who receive stock options are actually able to exercise them. And since many of those companies that went public had a lock on their employees' stock, setting a time after the IPO during which employees could not sell their stock, many of those employees who exercised their stock options and became paper millionaires ended up going bust.

After the dotcom bust of 2000–2001, many prospective employees of entrepreneurial companies often said, "Forget the options, show me the money." But since the economic rebound began building speed in 2003, stock options have again become an arrow in entrepreneurial companies' quivers to lure talent.

Stock options in a start-up or young privately held company may give employees the right to purchase a share of stock for $2 or $3 any time within the next five years. The assumption is that the company will become publicly traded before then and the price at which the stock is sold to the public will be set above $2 or $3.

If, for instance, an employee is granted 40,000 options to buy stock at $2 in his first year of employment, the company's founder could argue that the employee is, in effect, receiving a deferred payment of $80,000. The employee hopes that the company will go public, stock will be issued at $10, $15, or even $20 a share, and the price will continue to climb. At any point until the option expires, the employee can exercise all or a portion of the options (i.e., purchase the share of stock on which the option is held) and recognize an immediate gain above the deferred payment.

There are some tricky accounting and tax implications for stock options. They are not taxed at the time the company issues them, but rather at the time the employee exercises them. The difference between the price at which the option is granted, known as the *strike price* (i.e., $2 or $3 a share), and the market price at the time the option is exercised is taxable as ordinary income for that year. This often drives an employee into a higher tax bracket than normal.

For instance, an employee is granted 100,000 options at $3 per share in exchange for taking a low salary with a start-up and the company goes public two years later in an IPO at $10 per share. The employee did not declare the options as income in the year they were issued—after all, they had no real value then since these was no market for the stock. The employee decides to exercise those options and purchase the 100,000 shares of stock for $300,000. The stock is worth $1 million. The $700,000 difference between the market value and the purchase price is taxable as ordinary earned income in the year in which the employee exercises the options.

To exercise stock options after a company goes public, most employees usually have to borrow the money from their stockbroker's firm. The prudent thing to do at this point is to immediately sell enough of the stock to pay back the loan and to set aside the cash necessary to pay the taxes the next year.

However, in the heady years of the late 1990s, a lot of brokers urged their clients who exercised stock options to keep the stock in a brokerage account and use it as leverage to maintain the loan they took out to buy the stock and then borrow more from the brokerage house to pay taxes. This is known as *maintaining a margin account*.

Margin accounts must have stock equal in value to at least two times the amount of the outstanding loan. During the market tumble of 2000, many people were wiped out when their stock holdings lost value and they had to sell off portions to pay off enough of their margin loan to maintain the margin account's ratio of value to loan amount.

More companies have lost valuable employees through inequitable treatment than any other way.

The Securities and Exchange Commission (SEC) has since taken a tough stand against brokers who don't explain these intricacies to their clients who exercise company stock options.

Of course, if the company goes belly-up or never achieves the necessary traction to be anything but a modest-size privately held company, the employee has received a deferred payment worth $0. He or she never has a chance to become a paper millionaire or to lose everything to margin calls.

In the case of entrepreneurial companies that get sold to larger publicly traded companies, it is possible for employees with stock options to make serious money. Usually they may exercise their options at any time until the sale closes. They buy their company's stock and then convert their shares into shares of the publicly traded company at whatever conversion rate founders, angels, and VC investors get.

Regardless of how well the employee makes out, the company has not had to pay $80,000 in cash for each year of employment.

Employee Stock Ownership Plans (ESOPs)

ESOPs are not that common in entrepreneurial companies today. They are much more frequently set up by established family-owned businesses. But they were somewhat popular even with start-ups from the 1980s until the middle of 1990s, when they fell out of favor.

ESOPs provide the owners of a privately held company a number of tax advantages over other kinds of employee retirement plans, such as profit sharing prior to the advent of 401(k) plans and SIMPLE plans for small businesses.

Profit-sharing plans, 401(k)s, SIMPLE plans, and ESOPs are all *defined contribution plans*. This means the amount put into the retirement plan is set, but the amount the employee will receive is not. Traditional pensions are *defined benefit plans*, meaning that the benefit is predetermined and based on a formula that combines years of service with pay. The employer must put in as much money as necessary to meet the defined benefit each year.

Small companies were never able to establish pension plans. Profit-sharing plans became popular in the 1970s. Under such a plan, the company would put a certain amount of money in each year, which would be divided up into individual employee accounts proportional to each employee's salary or wages. Any employee who stayed long enough to become vested in the plan would receive the amount in his or her profit-sharing account upon leaving.

Here's an example. A company makes a $400,000 contribution to a profit-sharing plan for employees. The $400,000 is deductible as compensation. But the company loses the productive use of that $400,000, since it is in a trust account for the benefit of employees. If the company instead establishes an ESOP, it can make the profit-sharing payment to the ESOP and the ESOP then buys shares in the company at an agreed-upon price. The shares are held in trust, the company gets the same tax deduction, and it has access to the $400,000, which means it has to borrow $400,000 less for operations and saves $40,000 or more in annual finance charges.

ESOPs can also be *leveraged*, meaning the company can borrow money to fund them and the ESOP increases its percentage of ownership in the company as the loan is paid down. Such leveraged ESOPs can be used by owners of privately held companies to cash out in a tax-advantaged way.

On the face of it, ESOPs look terrific. But what if the company fails? Employees are left with worthless stock as their retirement proceeds.

ESOPs must be structured carefully to make sure the interests of both the company owners and the employees who will become owners are all protected, to the extent possible. ESOPs have been used by groups of employees to save companies that owners wished to close as well as by owners looking to sell out but unable to find a buyer.

Chapter 10

Need a Lotta Money to Go Big Time, Part 1

S MENTIONED AT THE START OF CHAPTER 6, VENTURE CAPITALISTS generally are not interested in companies in the early stages. However, if your company has proven itself and now needs more (maybe much more) than $1 million to go big time, to rise to a national level or even beyond, then it's time for venture capitalists.

Finding Venture Capitalists

The best way to look for institutional venture capital is by conducting a targeted search, just like one you'd conduct for an angel investor. Remember: there many different kinds of VC funds, including the following:

- ▶ Private VC firms, small groups of individuals who invest money pooled from wealthy individuals, pension funds, university endowment funds, and/or foundations. Each fund managed by the VC firm has a limited number of investors and a set level of funding; it is closed when the capital raised reaches that level.

- ▶ Public VC funds, which operate like closed-end mutual funds, with a large number of people making investments in smaller amounts than investors in private firms.

- Small Business Investment Companies (SBICs) and Specialized Small Business Investment Companies (SSBICs), which are private VC funds that are registered with and regulated by the SBA and that can borrow at below-market rates to supplement the private capital they raise for investment.

- VC funds operated by investment banks that are responsible for underwriting initial public offerings of stock and often use their VC funds as ways to create relationships with entrepreneurial companies. Their goal is to get the IPO business, as well as ownership of a block of the pre-IPO stock.

- Corporate VC funds owned and managed by publicly held corporations, which often take equity positions in companies that are experimenting with innovative technology. This provides an inside track to that technology through a technology license, a technology purchase, or an outright purchase of the company at a later time.

- State governments and occasionally local governments that have developed VC funds to keep businesses in the state or cities or to attract businesses. These funds are usually managed by a professional VC firm. Cities and states use equity investments as one enticement for businesses—along with loans, grants, and tax breaks.

Your target should take into consideration four variables: geography, specialization, your company's current stage of maturity and growth, and the amount of funding you are seeking.

As when dealing with angel investors, you begin your search close to home, with people with whom you have the most intimate contact, and widen it using available tools and resources.

Inside the first circle are your company's professional advisors, especially your accountant, attorney, and banker. You can often leverage these people's contacts to reach professional venture capitalists, who might be their clients or might have funded their clients. Remember: venture capital is a world of relationships and venture capitalists love to invest in networks that have proven profitable in the past.

The second circle includes the same community resources you used to find angel investors. These could be chambers of commerce, local and regional business publications, local university business schools, breakfast clubs, and informal networks where angels and venture capitalists congregate. They also include your industry community—the trade magazines you read, associations you belong to, and conferences and shows you attend.

Your target should take into consideration four variables: geography, specialization, your company's current stage of maturity and growth, and the amount of funding you are seeking.

139

The third circle has local and regional VC funds. Many venture capitalists like to invest as close to home as possible, since this makes it easiest to stay in intimate contact with the company being funded and to monitor its progress.

In the final outside circle is the entire universe of other VC companies and the resources you can use to find them.

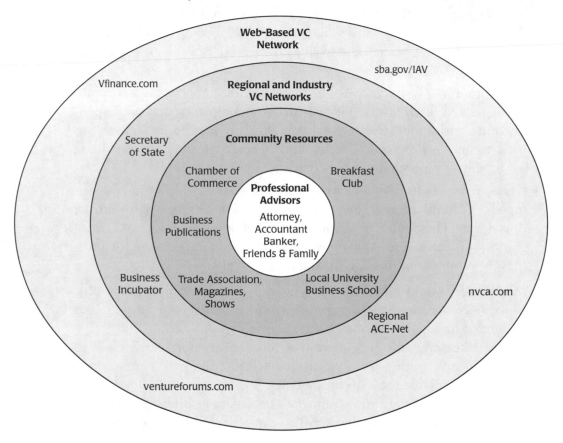

Figure 10-1. Targeted search for venture capital investors

Resources in the Outside Circle

A number of organizations provide directories and other resources to help you with your search for venture capital.

The National Venture Capital Association (NVCA) is the VC industry's trade association, with over 400 members. NVCA members represent the bulk of venture capital invested in all U.S. companies. The association Web site is *www.nvca.org*.

The National Association of Venture Forums runs conferences at which entrepreneurs make presentations to potential funders. It posts a calendar of upcoming venture forums and proposals by ventures looking for funding on its Web site, *ventureforums.org*.

The Small Business Administration has a complete list of SBICs at *sba.gov/inv*.

vFinance, Inc., features an online "search for capital" by dollar amount, industry, and state, with a choice between venture capital firms and angel investors, at *www.vfinance.com*.

The Thomson Corporation publishes the monthly *Venture Capital Journal* (*www.venturecapitaljournal.net*) and the annual *Pratt's Guide to Venture Capital Sources*, which lists over 1,400 firms.

The Venture Capital Road Show

It used to be that an entrepreneur would do a "road show": he or she would travel around for two or three weeks pitching his or her presentation to VC firms in order to line up investors.

More and more, however, an entrepreneur needs a referral. Today it is more common for venture capitalists to come to entrepreneurs. These meetings follow one of two distinct models:

1. The venture forum
2. The venture capital firm cattle call

Identifying venture capitalists is easy. But in the post-dotcom era, they're more cautious and require a stamp of credibility before they review a business plan. This means you need a reference.

Venture Forum

A venture forum is a meeting attended by a large number of venture capitalists and a large number of entrepreneurs looking for funding. Investors or their intermediaries (i.e., attorneys and accountants) are often in attendance. These forums generally include networking sessions and display halls, as well as an opportunity for a limited number of entrepreneurs to make their pitch to the assembled venture capitalists.

VC Firm Cattle Call

In a cattle call, a single VC firm advertises throughout the entrepreneurial community that it is looking for business plans. The model is similar to the one used by some angel clubs. Some cattle calls are supported by or accredited by a local organization.

Entrepreneurs pay a fee to make the presentation. Presentations can be done in one round or two. If done in one round, all entrepreneurs are given

VC Spooks

The Small Business Administration isn't the only place in the federal government to look for venture funding.

In 1999, the Central Intelligence Agency created a private, not-for-profit VC company called In-Q-Tel to make investments in companies developing technology that can be utilized in security, intelligence gathering, and counterintelligence work.

The terrorist attacks on September 11, 2001 made In-Q-Tel a hot VC-400 entrepreneurs inquired about funding in the final three months of 2001, four times the normal number of inquiries. Since its founding in 2003, the Department of Homeland Security has also entered the VC arena, as have some offices of the Department of Defense.

about five minutes (and five presentation slides) to make their case. With two rounds, entrepreneurs have only two minutes (and no slides) to make their case in the first round and then those who survive the cut and make it to round two are allowed more time and a half-dozen slides. Only a handful of entrepreneurs whose presentations are deemed best are asked to submit documentation.

Fees collected from entrepreneurs making presentations help the VC firm cover expenses for travel and rental of the facility in which the presentations are made. Some firms that run this kind of program provide counseling and assistance in shaping the presentations before they are made.

A viable alternative to venture capitalists is to talk with people in a corporate venture capital department or to the R&D department of a corporation that has parallel or complementary technology/products. If you show that your technology can advance its efforts and products, the company may fund you.

What Do Venture Capitalists Want from You? Be Prepared to Sing for Your Supper

Professional venture capitalists want a lot. But that's all right. They provide a lot, too.

Since the 1970s (save for the bursting of the dotcom bubble in 2000–2001), professional venture capitalists have consistently provided their clients (wealthy individual investors and institutions) with the highest rates of return of all investment vehicles.

These professional financiers have also finely honed skills and techniques that allow them to properly assess whether or not an individual entrepreneurial company will succeed over a five-year period. They have created a model for investing in those companies to the greatest advantage of their limited-partner investors.

They also have learned how to evaluate and quantify risk and to thus place a value on a closely held entrepreneurial business. This allows them to provide an appropriate level of funding in exchange for equity interest and to provide a *risk premium* (a higher rate of return for a more risky investment) for their investors.

These financiers have made their investors—and many entrepreneurs as well—very wealthy indeed.

In order to "do a deal," a professional venture capitalist has to be convinced that there is a good chance the investment in the new venture will create a compound annual return of 30 percent or better for a five-year period (in other words, a 250 to 400 percent cumulative return on the invested capital over five years). In order to achieve this return for their investors, venture capitalists must closely assess risk and invest in a portfolio of companies that offers opportunities for blockbuster economic growth and various ways to realize that economic gain. (This will be discussed under "Exit Strategy" later in this chapter.)

So what do these professional, institutional venture capitalists want from you?

In general, they want ten things, which are listed below. There are exceptions, which we'll take up as we go along. Some of these exceptions have to do with the particular structure of some VC firms, others with firms that are targeted to special types of entrepreneurs (i.e., women or minorities). But these differences are usually related to form, not substance.

The first five items that a professional venture capitalist wants are necessary to get you into serious discussions over the size and terms of an investment. We call these the "stage setters." The second five are the major terms around which the professional venture capitalist negotiates. We call these the "deal makers."

Venture capitalists demand integrity above all else.

The Stage Setters

Professional venture capitalists receive inquiries and business plans from hundreds of thousands of entrepreneurs each year, yet they make only about 5,000 new investments each year. Many of these are follow-on investments

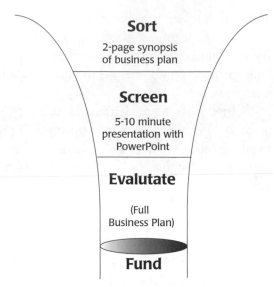

Figure 10-2. Funnel for VC evaluation

in companies they have already invested in and many are in new companies run by entrepreneurs they have dealt with before in other companies. So the odds of a new entrepreneur receiving an investment are lower still.

Each VC firm, no matter how it receives inquiries (venture fairs, business plans arriving "over the transom," or referrals), is in contact with hundreds of entrepreneurs, all seeking to be one of the handful of investments that the firm makes during the year.

Once you get a VC firm to consider a proposal, there are five key "stage setters" a professional venture capitalist needs in order to be interested in beginning serious negotiations about investing in your company:

1. A viable business, not just a dream
2. An experienced, professional management team
3. A set of polished presentations for each of the phases of the venture capitalist's analysis
4. Realistic projections
5. Good karma

Viable Business

Most institutional venture capitalists do not invest in pre-seed or seed rounds of financing. Of course, there are exceptions to this rule, especially among the smaller regional firms and SBICs.

For the most part, however, institutional venture capitalists want to come on board after you have proven your business model and product concept, developed any innovative product (at least in prototype), and done some significant amount of market testing regarding size and receptivity of market and sensitivity to pricing in the market. (An exception is in the area of biotechnology, where some venture capitalists are willing to come in during the early phases of new-drug research, after it has gone from the laboratory bench or computer models into animal testing.)

If your business is at the gleam-in-the-eye stage, you need to work on your own bootstrap capital: investments from friends, family, and/or business partners; and possibly an angel investor.

If your business is at the gleam-in-the-eye stage, you need to work on your own bootstrap capital: investments from friends, family, and/or business partners; and possibly an angel investor.

Management Team

Institutional VC investors invest primarily on the strength of the management team and the numbers. The difference is in how venture capitalists weight the two variables, with the primary variable being about twice as important as the secondary.

All institutional venture capitalists, whether they focus primarily on the management team or the numbers, want the team to be composed of professionals with a demonstrated track record in business management (especially as successful entrepreneurs), as opposed to technology. If the whole management team is technical, the venture capitalists may insist that any negotiations and ultimate investment be predicated on finding a suitable chief executive to run the company.

The great exception to this is start-ups founded by whiz kids right out of school, recent graduates from either a top-notch MBA program or a first-rate technical program. But even in these cases, the professional venture capitalist will want to make sure it has significant influence in the decisions made by the management team and the decision to change management at any time.

Polished Presentations

More venture capitalists are asking for three different and distinct forms of presentation. These presentations correspond to the three-stage analysis (sort, screen, evaluate) performed by venture capitalists.

Most no longer accept unsolicited full-blown business plans. If you send in a plan, they will send it back or put it in a "slush pile," to be read by a lower-level associate as time allows.

*M*anagement and business viability are the foundation of venture capital interest.

Rather, the first presentation they want is a succinct summary of your business plan—usually only two or three pages. This should be one or two pages stating the company's product, industry and market, competitive advantage (especially if it involves a proprietary technology or process), senior management team, major accomplishments since founding, and major goals and objectives for the immediate future for which financing is being sought. The final page is a profit-and-loss (P&L) spreadsheet that goes back two years in annual increments and projects forward for two years by fiscal quarters and another three years in annual increments.

The second presentation, if the first has piqued the venture capitalist's interest, will probably be a brief oral presentation. This might be at the firm's offices, at a regional gathering of presenters, or at a third-party-sponsored venture fair in which the firm is participating.

Some VC firms are running two- or three-day presentation festivals where they bring together dozens of entrepreneurs who have made the first cut (or sort cut) to compete against one another. Some of these firms provide coaching and mentoring ahead of these presentation festivals. Many charge entrepreneurs a fee if their proposal brief is accepted and they are asked to present; this fee offsets the firm's costs to host the event and to provide any upfront assistance to the presenters.

Such a presentation will usually be limited to five to ten minutes; some firms limit them to two minutes in a first round and then reduce the field again before a round of longer presentations. Most ask for a PowerPoint® presentation with the talk and for a specific number of hard copies of the slides for those in attendance. The number of slides is also limited by the firm. (Microsoft PowerPoint® is a simple graphics and text software program that creates presentation slides that can be projected onto a screen directly from a computer.)

The third presentation is a full-blown business plan, which is the basis for an in-depth evaluation. If your company passes this evaluation, the firm can use the business plan as the basis for a detailed due-diligence investigation of your company, should it decide to pursue the investment.

Due diligence involves not just picking apart the business plan but also doing a detailed investigation of the entrepreneurial team, including personal, financial, and even criminal background checks.

Realistic Projections

Remember: professional venture capitalists are in the business of picking business plans apart. They are sensitive and experienced enough to detect the slightest hint of exaggerations about attainable market share and pricing.

Venture capitalists also know there are no truly new ideas. If you claim there is no competition for your product, that probably means there is no viable marketplace for your product.

What venture capitalists want to see in a business plan is a product or service that exploits a market niche that large companies are ignoring or a problem in an industry that has until now been technologically unfeasible or too expensive to solve.

But even if you are developing the first real solution to a problem, that doesn't mean your solution will be the only one tried or even the only one that works adequately. You will never achieve 100 percent market penetration and you must achieve a balance between pricing and market penetration.

Venture capitalists demand realistic projections on the expense side as well as on the revenue side. How much time and money will it take to get your product or service concept to the market? How much will it cost to make the market aware of your product or service?

Venture capitalists like to make follow-on investments. But they also weigh each new investment on its own risk-reward scale. If you set a record of making bad projections—by being too aggressive on income projections or not fully accounting for the time and money required to reach each mile-

How Well Do You Struggle?

A start-up software and device company was referred to a VC firm. A member of the firm said he was interested in meeting with the management team. After the meeting and discussions with his partner, the venture capitalist told the entrepreneur the firm was extremely interested in the opportunity.

But the VC firm did not want to invest the full amount the company was seeking. The venture capitalist advised the entrepreneur to seek other investors and tell potential investors that one firm was willing to invest $500,000 of the $2 million needed.

In the meantime, the start-up was in danger of running out of money before it could arrange all of this funding. The entrepreneur called the VC firm to find out if his company could receive some of the funding to carry it until he found other investors.

But the VC would not put up any money at this point.

When asked why, the venture capitalist replied that he and his partners were testing the entrepreneur's creativity by seeing how well he operated in a crisis and how quickly he could marshal his resources to find the necessary additional funding.

stone—your investors will make sharp adjustments to your projections and possibly your capital stream.

The world of professional venture capitalism is small and all of the players talk to one another. A reputation for insisting on unrealistic projections will make it that much harder to find funding in other places.

Good Karma

Beyond the numbers and the qualifications of the management team, there is an intangible element—the relationship between an investor and an entrepreneurial business. They must be able to work together. Some people call it personal chemistry. We call it good karma.

The venture capitalist needs to feel that you are not just engaging in a fee-for-service relationship but that there is a basis for a deep level of trust and bonding.

Good karma is not as important for a professional venture capitalist as it is for an angel investor, who often allows these intangible relationship issues to have a greater influence on his or her decision to invest. But it does matter.

Think of it this way. With angels, the intangible is often a positive: they are more willing to invest because of a "good feeling" about the entrepreneur. For professional venture capitalists, the intangible can only be a negative: Despite good projections, professional management, and terrific presentations, "bad feelings" about the entrepreneur or the team can lead to a decision to pass on the investment opportunity.

Distressed ventures have an avenue for obtaining new funding because some VC firms search for companies with depressed valuations in which to make cheap investments of fresh money.

The Deal Makers

Once you've made it through the preliminaries and the institutional venture capitalist has established through due diligence that you and your company are worthy of investment, you are halfway home.

This may seem disappointing; after all that work you should be at least 80 percent of the way to getting a check. But before the paperwork can be signed, there is a lot of negotiation—which can be difficult, although it should never be testy.

Chapters 11 and 12 discuss the parts of the investment agreement and the specific issues surrounding negotiations. Here, we just want to touch on the five keys that venture capitalists look for to make the deal work for them—and, they hope, for you:

1. A reasonable valuation of your company

2. A deal structure that protects the venture capitalist
3. A major influence on the board of directors
4. A significant equity position to make the investment fruitful
5. A set of viable exit options (known as an *exit strategy*)

Reasonable Valuation

Valuating an entrepreneurial company is very difficult. A publicly traded company is valued every day, in the marketplace: the number of shares outstanding multiplied by the price of the stock provides the company's valuation. At the other end of the scale, a small business of long standing is also relatively easy to value: it has hard assets, regular predictable revenues and cash flow, and goodwill within its customer base.

But a rapidly growing entrepreneurial business, based on an innovative product or service (possibly even a technological breakthrough) is, by its very nature, a subjective valuation question.

While angels typically use informal valuation techniques (e.g., $1 million in valuation for each of five variables, up to a possible $5 million total value: good idea, working prototype, good management, meaningful revenues, and industry relationship), professional venture capitalists still depend more on valuation techniques used by investment bankers and taught in business schools. These include calculating the payback period and working through a series of discounted cash flows. The more innovative your technology, process, or product, the more difficult it is to make reasonable sales forecasts.

The benchmark for many financiers is to determine some expected multiple on their investment over a specific period of time (e.g., three times the investment in five years). This rate of return works out to be more than 30 percent per year, compounded. It is about what venture capitalists received who invested at the end of the 1970s (after tax-law changes). During the 1980s, the rate of failures increased and average compound rate of return declined. The rate of return increased steadily during the 1990s and went through the roof in the years 1997 to 1999, but then declined rapidly as the dotcom bubble burst and many investments failed.

The benchmark for many financiers is to determine some expected multiple on their investment over a specific period of time.

Some venture capitalists are beginning to use a tool known as *option pricing*, an economic model that helps value the price of a financial market option, based on an assessment of the probabilities of future uncertainties.

Whatever valuation techniques venture capitalists use, these negotiations are the starting point in any discussion about making an investment. Entrepreneurs usually begin with their valuation, which is usually a number plucked out of the air or one related to a prior valuation created during an angel investment. They also consider the equity they have already sold and other factors that determine the viability of the venture.

Only after the valuation is determined and the venture capitalist sees how much equity is owned by other parties (you and other founders, friends and family and angels), can he or she determine if there is a reasonable opportunity to make a meaningful investment and receive an equity position in exchange.

Assumptions Necessary to Value Start-Ups

In the early venture capital days, some VC firms had an orderly method for arriving at the valuation, while others arrived at the result haphazardly. It is fairly straightforward to value a company that is a viable entity and has revenues and even profits. Standard discounted cash-flow calculations and other methodologies help to create a valuation. Then the venture capitalist can simply say, "I will invest 25 percent of the current valuation in exchange for X percent of the total equity." This amount is always less than a straight percentage of the pre-investment amount, since the company will have a larger valuation with the new money invested.

For instance, if the venture capitalist values the company at $4 million and is willing to invest another $1 million, that's 25 percent of the current valuation, but only 20 percent of the post-investment (or "post-closing") valuation, which would be the percent of the company the venture capitalist is buying.

More recently, when venture capitalists were funding companies that were little more than an idea or even a dream, it became more difficult to reconcile venture capitalists' valuations with those of entrepreneurs. Without sales, analytical methods are based mainly on market definition and expected expenses until product launch and wrapped up in projections.

If a company is not operating or has been set up but is engaging in product development, creating a context for valuation requires answers to a host of questions, such as the following:

▶ Is the company entering an established industry or one that is relatively new?

▶ Is the product or technology new to the industry?

▶ How will people or companies in the customer universe accept the product or technology?

Yet another factor for the venture capitalist deciding whether to make an investment is the number of equity holders. If a venture capitalist is extremely interested in the venture, yet uncomfortable because there are many other investors, he or she may work with the entrepreneur to develop a plan for buying some other investors out of the venture.

Finding Common Ground in Forecasts

Venture capitalists today want to invest in companies that not only have good management, but can generate $100 million in annual revenue within five years.

While entrepreneurs often project such earnings, venture capitalists usually discount them by at least 50 percent.

While entrepreneurs often project such earnings, venture capitalists usually discount them by at least 50 percent on the assumption that entrepreneurs always overestimate both their product's market penetration and the price and gross margin the product can sustain.

The financial statements should show an ability to eventually generate revenues sufficient to return the venture capital investment compounded at 30 percent or more for his or her percentage of the equity. Cash flow is used rather than net profit from the profit-and-loss statement, because net profit can include depreciation, tax-loss carry forwards, and other reductions. Cash flow is a concrete measure for determining the return on an investor's share.

Even though the venture capitalist will not usually take out his or her earnings (we'll discuss this in more detail in the section on exit strategies), the cash flow shows whether the investment is earning the desired rate of return. Again, this measurement is taken only after the fifth or sixth year the investment is in place (unless the company has been sold or gone public before then). Through the early years, the company may actually be losing money even if it has revenues, due to the costs of developing products and bringing them to market.

Deal Structure

Today's venture capitalists are not inclined to make a simple purchase of common shares in exchange for their investments. They hope to take convertible preferred stock and then convert from preferred stock to common stock over time or just before an IPO.

Venture capitalists, like many angels and even some friends and family, will want this preferred stock investment because it both provides better downside protection than common stock and better potential for upside return than straight debt.

Founders, as well as friends and family and other early investors, retain their common stock. The venture capitalists thus receive returns ahead of founders and earlier investors, both if the business fails and if the company does well but not well enough to pay off everyone.

The venture capitalist also wants to determine the terms of the conversion to common stock (i.e., the events that will trigger the conversion), as well as any conditions that, should they occur, would allow him or her to get out of the deal.

Some of the other terms of the venture capitalist deal concern SEC registration rights once the company goes public (the ability to sell out of all or some of the equity position as part of the IPO at the same time as the company sells its new shares to the public). In addition, the venture capitalist will set other conditions.

Even though the venture capitalist will have one or more seats on the board (but usually not a majority), he or she will also have a number of veto rights provisions (e.g., the company can't incur debt without the investor's express permission, the investor must approve any changes in the company's charter and bylaws and any changes in the nature of the business).

Usually the amount of money a venture capitalist brings to the deal is sufficient to accomplish several milestones in the company's business plan.

As we have said before, venture capitalists prepare the term sheet. As an entrepreneur, you will be put in the position of negotiating the terms. However, the venture capitalist is at an advantage. You may be unwilling to pass on the deal—even if you don't like the terms—because you are desperate for the cash.

Usually the amount of money a venture capitalist brings to the deal is sufficient to accomplish several milestones in the company's business plan. This allows the company to achieve a higher valuation and have an easier time raising the next round of capital. It usually makes it more palatable for an entrepreneur to accept somewhat onerous conditions placed on the deal by the venture capitalist.

Board Influence

Venture capitalists also often seek to structure deals so they get substantial influence on the board of directors in order to protect their investment. For instance, if your company has a nine-person board, a venture capitalist may wish to have three seats, even though it has purchased only 20 or 25 percent of the company.

Significant Equity Position

In order to receive this disproportionately generous treatment, venture capitalists need to be able to acquire a large enough equity stake in the company. Even if 25 to 40 percent of the company has been sold off to friends and family and angels in prior financing rounds, it is not unusual for venture capitalists to purchase another significant portion of the company, leaving the founders with well less than a majority position.

The venture capitalist wants not only to make it possible to force out the founders, if necessary, but also to reduce the influence of all prior investors.

Exit Strategy

A properly defined exit strategy is perhaps the most important thing to a venture capitalist. The exit strategy allows the venture capitalist to get out of the investment position "whole" (including a premium rate of return) before the entrepreneur recognizes any profit.

A properly defined exit strategy is perhaps the most important thing to a venture capitalist.

While you may have the vision of becoming an instant billionaire through IPO, venture capitalists know that the IPO route is the least likely of all outcomes. Fewer than 10 percent of successful entrepreneurial companies issue an IPO within their first five years—the magic time horizon for a professional venture capitalist. (Since at least half of all new businesses fail within the first five years, according to SBA research, fewer than 5 percent—only one in 20 entrepreneurial businesses—will ever issue an IPO.)

So what are the other ways for a venture capitalist to exit its investment in your company?

1. Sale to a strategic buyer
2. Sale to a financial buyer
3. Earn-out (sale back to the company)

Sale to a Strategic Buyer

A strategic buyer will want to purchase the company in order to acquire something it doesn't have—most often technology but sometimes market presence or market share.

In fast-moving industries, such as telecommunications and pharmaceuticals, larger players are always taking equity positions in or buying outright small, nimble companies working on promising technologies.

Occasionally, a strategic merger will occur between two smaller companies joining forces to more effectively battle larger industry participants. The valuations provided in these "merger of equals" transactions are hardly ever as rich as when a smaller company is bought by one of the big players. They do, however, allow passive investors such as VC firms and angels to recognize a significant return on their investments.

A VC Firm for Slow-Growth Companies

The dotcom fizzle forced many VC firms to change their modus operandi, but few were willing to admit it. Here's an exception.

Ignition Corporation, a VC firm started in 2000 by former executives from McCaw Cellular and Microsoft, raised $285 million for investments in start-ups in wireless communications, business software, and Internet infrastructure.

In announcing the fund, Ignition said it would not try to bring public the companies it funds as quickly as possible. Rather, it would take a patient tack, mentoring the entrepreneurs and nurturing the companies in an effort to make them profitable before looking for an exit. All eight Ignition founders have operating experience in communications or software and work closely with the entrepreneurs of businesses in which the firm invests.

Sale to a Financial Buyer

Private equity firms have come into their own since 2000. Money from wealthy individuals, pension funds, and university and foundation endowments have poured into these companies, which typically seek to either buy and operate attractive companies or buy sagging companies, polish them up, then resell them.

Because of the stringent regulations on publicly traded companies put into effect by the U.S. Congress, the Securities and Exchange Commission, and other federal government agencies after the bankruptcies of some of America's highest-flying companies from 1999 to 2002, an IPO is no longer seen as the Holy Grail to all entrepreneurs. Many would prefer to be bought by a private equity company.

There are a number of private equity partnership firms that purchase companies that have established a track record. These include HM Capital Partners LLC (formerly Hicks, Muse, Tate & Furst Inc.), Kohlberg Kravitz Roberts, Forstmann Little, and The Blackstone Group. Many of the large investment banking firms, both in the United States and abroad, have also set up private equity units to get into the act.

Financial buyers sometimes purchase a number of smaller companies and combine them to achieve economies of scale in operations.

Sale to a financial buyer is a more likely outcome for a company that is not involved in cutting-edge technology but has capitalized on an opportunity to fill a profitable market niche that larger players in the industry do not want to try to exploit.

Earn-Out

An earn-out is when the entrepreneurs within a business gradually buy back the equity position taken by passive investors, paying a premium return on the investment.

Earn-outs do not occur frequently. They are most common in companies that are exploiting an industry niche rather than dealing in innovative technology.

They are most likely to occur after a period of time when it is determined that the business will produce steady, predictable, and generous revenues, but is not the kind of blockbuster company that can produce a public offering. A candidate for earn-out is also a candidate for purchase by a financial buyer, if there is one that deals with companies in that specific industry.

Chapter 11

Need a Lotta Money to Go Big Time, Part 2

I F YOU HAVE FOUND AN EQUITY INVESTOR, YOU MAY FEEL RELIEVED. BUT, AS we all know, "The job's not over until the paperwork is done." And that's the subject of this chapter and the next.

Equity-Investor Arrangements: Nitty-Gritty Legal Language Is Important

Any time you sell a portion of your corporation to an investor, you are engaging in the sale of *securities*. Sales of securities (stock shares or bonds) are highly regulated, both at the federal level through the Securities and Exchange Commission (SEC) and at the state level.

This high degree of regulation requires that the documentation laying out the terms and conditions of the arrangement between you and an investor incorporate specific legal language. There are four kinds of transactions for selling stock in exchange for an investment of capital:

- ▶ Private Placement
- ▶ Direct Public Offering (DPO)
- ▶ Initial Public Offering (IPO)
- ▶ Reverse Merger

Private Placement

There are two different forms of private placement—a term sheet or a private placement memorandum.

A *term sheet* is used when the investor is a professional venture capitalist or an angel who has been involved with private equity investing for a long time. A *private placement memorandum* (PPM) is used for investments by friends and family and by less sophisticated angels. The difference is basically that a PPM provides investors with more detailed disclosure about the nature and risks of the business than does a term sheet.

Term Sheet

A term sheet is a document created by a venture capitalist that lays out the terms of a capital investment by a single investor or a consortium of a small number of individual investors. The term sheet can be drawn up for a single investment or for multiple investments that will take place over a timeline or when predetermined milestones are reached. These pretimed or predetermined investments by the same investor(s) are called *tranches*.

The two most important things to remember about the term sheet are:

▶ It is prepared as a one-time document.

▶ It is subject to negotiation between the entrepreneur and the investor(s). But because term sheets are usually drawn up by the venture capitalist or angel, in reality the entrepreneur has little leverage to change the terms.

If the investor is an angel, the level of negotiation depends on how experienced the angel investor is (the more experienced, the more he or she will want and the more tightly he or she will want it spelled out in the term sheet) and how much has been negotiated prior to writing it down in the investor agreement. The relationship between the angel and the entrepreneur is closer to parity than the relationship between entrepreneur and professional venture capitalist, because the angel may have more than strictly financial motivation for making the investment than the venture capitalist.

Most of the required documentation in an investment offering can be found in the business plan.

When the investor is a professional venture capitalist, the VC firm prepares the term sheet and the entrepreneur must review it and comment on it. The entrepreneur enters any negotiations as the weaker party. In the venture capitalist-entrepreneur relationship, the venture capitalist clearly holds the power. Most venture capitalists are not at all shy about asserting the Golden Rule—"Whoever has the gold makes the rules": term sheets between venture capitalists and entrepreneurs are rigid documents.

157

Private Placement Memorandum (PPM)

A PPM is a document drawn up to solicit investors for a sale of stock that is exempt from registration with the SEC. This exemption cuts down drastically on the amount of paperwork that must be generated, as well as on the cost of preparation. The Small Business Investment Incentive Act of 1980 expanded the exemptions in the original Securities Act of 1933.

While private placements are exempt from the SEC's registration requirements, they are not exempt from registration under some states' securities laws or from the antifraud provisions of the Securities Act of 1933.

Securities Laws

The sale of securities is governed by both the federal securities laws and the securities laws of individual states.

The sale of securities is governed by both the federal securities laws and the securities laws of individual states (often known as "blue sky laws"). They describe the guidelines and methods for people marketing within each state financial securities that are not registered with the SEC. The two sets of regulations are tightly intertwined and state regulations do not supersede those of the SEC.

Federal Securities Laws

If you are offering your stock to the general public through either an initial public offering (IPO) or a direct public offering (DPO), you must register it with the SEC. But it is not necessary for a PPM. PPM's are issued under one of numerous exemptions to the Securities Act and the Securities Exchange Act. PPMs are written explicitly so they qualify for one or more of these exemptions.

The regulations for sales of stock to small groups of qualified investors are commonly called Regulation D offerings. Regulation D is an SEC regulation that was the outcome of interactions between the SEC and various state securities regulators. The three most often cited portions of Regulation D are Rules 504, 505, and 506.

Under Rule 504, known as the Small Business Exemption, nonpublic companies (those not subject to the reporting obligations of the Securities Exchange Act of 1934) can issue a private placement of up to $1 million in securities over a 12-month period and can sell the stock to an unlimited number of investors. Investors do not need to be "accredited."

Accredited investors include individuals who meet the SEC's criteria for being a "sophisticated investor" as well as institutional investors, private business development companies, tax-exempt organizations, trusts with more than $5 million in assets, or entities in which all of the equity owners are accredited investors. (Since the mid-1990s, many institutional investors, including universities and pension funds, have set aside a portion of their assets for investment in private placement offerings.)

The company issuing the stock cannot be an investment company (one that simply invests in other companies) or a "blank check" or "blind pool" company. (It must inform potential investors in the PPM what its operations are and how it will use the proceeds of the stock offering.)

Under Rule 505, a company that is not an investment company (but which may be a public company under the Securities Exchange Act of 1934) may issue up to $5 million of securities over a 12-month period to an unlimited number of accredited investors and up to 35 unaccredited investors.

Rule 506 is the most common rule under Regulation D that small companies use to prepare a PPM and issue a private placement of stock. Under Rule 506, a public or nonpublic company can sell an unlimited amount of securities to no more than 35 unaccredited investors and an unlimited number of accredited investors.

State Securities Laws

Every state has blue sky laws designed to keep frauds who would sell "the blue sky" to unwary investors from gaining a foothold in their state. Under blue sky laws, a company that wants to sell equity investments under a uniform set of terms to more than a few individuals in a particular state must register with that state's securities regulators (generally the state securities commission, attorney general, or secretary of state), unless the investment qualifies for an exemption.

If you are going to market your company to potential investors, you must check with the securities regulator in each state in which you will conduct the marketing effort to determine to which regulations your offering is subject.

You generally don't need to register an offer made to a venture capitalist, an individual angel or small group of angels, or to a small group of friends and family. However, private equity investments such as limited partnerships that are being marketed to a larger number of potential investors whom you do not know must be registered in every state where the offering is being made. (This falls under the SEC Regulation D.)

Most states allow unregistered stock to be sold only to investors who meet the SEC's definition of an "accredited" or "sophisticated" investor.

These are individuals who have either an annual income of $200,000 ($300,000 for a couple) or a household net worth of $1 million. These people are "accredited" to make risky financial investments because they have a financial cushion should a high-risk investment turn to dust. Because they are qualified and presumably knowledgeable in investing, companies don't have to provide in their prospectus the same detailed description of risk that is necessary for the general public in an IPO or DPO.

Create an equity distribution plan with a securities attorney in advance of raising capital.

Qualified investors receive a PPM, which provides limited information about the venture and its risks; this is essentially a business plan framed in proper regulatory language. A PPM is much less detailed than a full-blown prospectus, which must be produced for an IPO.

Dialing for Dollars

Some entrepreneurs use telemarketers to raise money from investors as part of a private placement. Such an effort needs to be undertaken with great care. Solicitations should be made only to a targeted list of prospective investors and not to the general public, which would nullify the exemption from the securities registrations. It is also important not to violate the provisions of any state's blue sky laws.

Telemarketers generate more than $200 billion in sales annually, including financial products and securities. They buy lists or other information from brokers and have access to various databases, which they use to construct lists of potential buyers of private placement investments. Some companies use telephone book white pages, combined with listings of automobile registrations and local and state government real estate records, to find homeowners who might fall into the right price range to buy a securities investment.

Brokerage houses are sometimes enlisted to sell these private placements to their clients. They usually sell in minimum investment blocks of $1,000, $5,000, $10,000, or even $25,000. Brokers are required to explain to their clients that these are unregistered, illiquid investments in high-risk ventures.

Some companies that sell only private placements use telemarketers armed with lists from market research firms, nonprofit organizations, and list-generation services. (List services are notorious for selling old lists or phonebook-type lists that have been "salted" with a few good names.)

Some ventures have successfully used telemarketing to raise money in small amounts from strangers. But it still makes many people queasy. If you are going to look for stranger-angels, it's probably better to use one of the Internet-based matching services, where at least the potential investors have chosen to be listed, than to have silver-tongued telemarketers call up names out of the blue.

Restrictions on Transferability

Whether it's issued through a term sheet or a private placement memorandum, there are restrictions on the resale or transfer of privately issued stock. Because the securities have been sold to a limited number of investors, there is no public market for them. Any resale or secondary transfer must comply with both the SEC regulations under the Securities Act of 1933 and any applicable state securities laws.

Direct Public Offering

A direct public offering (DPO) is the direct sale of shares in a company to individuals; it does not rely on an investment bank to underwrite the offering or market the shares. Shares issued through a DPO are subject to the same SEC registration requirements as shares issued through an IPO that has an investment bank as an underwriter.

A direct public offering (DPO) is the direct sale of shares in a company to individuals; it does not rely on an investment bank to underwrite the offering or market the shares.

Once the shares are in the hands of individual investors, they can be traded through brokerage houses. Depending on the number of shares issued and the volume of shares that trade on a daily basis, they may trade on an exchange, through NASDAQ, or in the thinly traded "over the counter" marketplace between brokers.

A DPO is a costly way to raise capital, but not as costly as an IPO since there is no underwriter taking a fee. The Internet has created a vehicle for many companies to undertake DPOs that were not previously possible. Much of the cost of a DPO comes from the regulatory burden placed on these offerings.

A DPO is sometimes used to raise capital prior to a larger public offering undertaken with the assistance of an underwriter and as an alternative to a private placement.

Initial Public Offering

An initial public offering (IPO) is the more traditional way of opening a company up to investment by the general public. It is usually the culmination of the process of growing a new company. Venture capitalists invest in young and growing companies with the express desire of liquidating their investment in four to seven years, either through an IPO or sale of the company to a larger, publicly traded company. In either case, with their assets

*U*nderstanding
securities law
restrictions is nec-
essary to prepare
a good strategy
for raising capital.

becoming liquid, they can exit the investment and return the cash to the investors in the fund, or reinvest it in other growing companies. Angels also often use an IPO as a time to exit the company, although they retain some investment position more frequently than do venture capitalists.

The IPO process is time-consuming and expensive, since fees must be paid to both the underwriter(s) and the attorneys who prepare the voluminous documentation, including a detailed prospectus.

Reverse Merger

As an alternative to issuing stock either through an IPO or a DPO, a company can become publicly traded through a process known as *reverse merger*. This is when a privately held company merges into a publicly traded but dormant company (sometimes called a *shell company*).

A reverse merger is much less expensive than issuing new stock through an IPO or even a DPO. It also takes a lot less time and relieves you of the anxiety of waiting for your IPO to drag along through the registration process while the market is moving down or your industry is being hit by bad news.

Your attorney or accountant or one of their contacts might have access to a "clean shell" that you can buy. A clean shell is a company without a lot of legal liabilities hanging over it. (You don't want to buy a company that ceased to exist because of asbestos-related lawsuits, for example.)

In addition, you may be able to find a shell that has a significant tax-loss carryforward. If the public company's operations continually lost money, the company may have ceased to operate but still have tax losses that can be used in future years to offset taxable income—such as from your operations if you buy the shell.

Once you have gone public through a reverse merger, you still need to raise additional capital; a corporate shell is just a vehicle. You can now issue shares through a secondary public offering, a stock offering after the initial one that made the shell public. You can issue warrants to current shareholders, allowing them to purchase more shares at a specified price for a specified period of time.

Also, once you have acquired a public shell, many more investors might be willing to engage in a private exempt stock offering.

Of course, there are some pitfalls to reverse mergers. Once you resuscitate a dormant public company, shareholders from the past might come out of the woodwork. These shareholders often maintain a constant downward pressure on your stock, seeing any increase in the share price not as evidence that you are going to make good but as an opportunity to get out of a dud investment for at least a few pennies on their investment dollar.

Creditors from the previous operations can also make claims against you and drain capital that would be better spent building the business.

Finally, there is always the possibility that irregularities occurred in trading of the shell company stock, most likely toward the end of the company's operating life, especially if the stock was delisted from an exchange and forced to trade on so-called Pink Sheets or the OTC Bulletin Board, two mechanisms for brokers to buy and sell low-value stocks. These are the least regulated tiers of the stock market, so brokers and/or the company's owners and managers may have manipulated trades. This also will not help your relations with stockholders.

Before engaging in a reverse merger, it's important that you and your attorney, accountant, and/or other business advisor research the entity carefully.

Investment Agreement: Get It in Writing— and Get It Right

The first rule of investment agreements is that you must insist on a written agreement with every investor and professional who performs services for your company. Some people say they need written agreements only for big deals or deals involving strangers.

Nothing could be further from the truth. Handshake deals can breed misunderstandings because you or the other party may not have thought of certain details, you may forget some points involved in the deal, or you and the other party may have different interpretations of a particular element of the deal.

A written agreement is a formal recognition of an arrangement that acts as a reference point for all parties and an enforceable instrument if one party or another does not perform as expected. It clearly describes the complete terms agreed to and states that additional terms can be enforced if necessary.

Standard practice dictates that attorneys be involved in the final drafting of all agreements and transactions. Entrepreneurs too often try to save money by picking up appropriate forms from office supply stores or using agreement forms that come in small-business legal kits. They say they will use a lawyer only for "really important agreements."

The first rule of investment agreements is that you must insist on a written agreement with every investor and professional who performs services for your company.

Saving money by not having lawyers draft agreements is a false economy. By saying that you do not need to know about the clauses in the documents you will execute, you are entrusting your future to your own legal judgment or that of other businesspeople.

Types of Equity Investment Offerings

There are three types of equity investment offerings that can be made by a start-up or growing business:

▶ Private placements, using either a term sheet or a private placement memorandum (PPM)

▶ Direct public offering of common stock (DPO)

▶ Initial public offering of common stock (IPO)

As stated earlier, all investment offerings are regulated by the Securities and Exchange Commission (SEC) and/or state securities regulators. In order to produce the documentation necessary for these types of offerings, you need to hire an attorney competent in securities law and such securities offerings.

A private placement of equity securities may be documented with a term sheet or a more detailed private placement memorandum. A term sheet is simply an agreement between you and an individual investor. It is typically used in transactions involving professional VC investors. The rest of this chapter describes the standard clauses of a term sheet.

Term Sheets

A term sheet is merely a starting point for negotiations. You will have an opportunity to review it with your counsel, decide which terms you would like to have changed, and begin negotiations.

A term sheet is, in effect, a proposal; it summarizes the key investment terms (e.g., how much the investor will be paying for your company's equity securities). The venture capitalist or sophisticated angel investor will draft a term sheet that outlines what you need to provide if you want the money.

A term sheet is merely a starting point for negotiations. You will have an opportunity to review it with your counsel, decide which terms you would like to have changed, and begin negotiations. However, the reality is that most venture capitalists are fairly adamant about the terms of their agreements, and your negotiating leverage depends on how attractive your business opportunity is.

In many respects, a term sheet is like a letter of intent. It lays out the general parameters around which the deal is to be constructed.

A term sheet should be nonbinding, meaning that the party to whom it is presented does not have to accept it. It is not binding until both parties—the entrepreneur and the investor—sign it.

Investors have different ways of making a commitment or beginning the commitment process. Some produce a commitment letter. In his book, *Venture Capital Investing: The Complete Handbook for Investing in Small Private Businesses for Outstanding Profits*, David Gladstone discusses his preference for detailed *commitment letters* instead of term sheets. He suggests this as "an intermediate step between the oral understanding and the legal documents." He believes that a commitment letter allows people to state in business language what they believe the parameters of the deal to be.

Whether you or the venture capitalist use a term sheet or a commitment letter, either document needs to cover five specific items:

1. Terms of the investment
2. Conditions of the loan (if there is one), including collateral
3. A preferred stock arrangement in the case of an equity investment
4. Representations you make about the company
5. Conditions under which the deal will be completed

Here, any document drawn up preliminary to final legal closing documents that lay out the parameters of the relationship will be called a *term sheet*.

Get It in Writing

The assumption is that you seriously discuss an investment in your company only with people you already have a relationship with. You may therefore be tempted to create an agreement based on trust. When discussing the terms and parameters of the deal, someone may say, "That's straightforward, it doesn't need to be written down."

Write it down. Recollection varies with time, events, and emotions.

It is much harder to enforce an agreement that is not in writing. Even if both parties agree to something and even if writing it down will necessitate redrafting the entire document, put it in.

Major Sections of the Term Sheet

The subject of legal agreements is obviously complex and cannot be adequately covered in a few pages. The descriptions given here of major sections of term sheets are informational only. To draw up a term sheet, you should always work with an attorney.

A term sheet consists of five major sections:

1. Defining parties

2. Recitals
3. Business content
4. Financial considerations
5. Boilerplate clauses

Defining Parties

This section states the parties to the agreement. For instance, the agreement is between your company and Uncle Mort or between you and the ABC Venture Partners.

Recitals

Recitals are the "whereas" and "wherefore" clauses that state the purpose of the agreement, as generally understood by both parties. Typically the recitals will indicate that the agreement provides for a cash investment in the company in exchange for certain considerations.

Business Content

This section is about the operations of the business. This includes the role each party will play in this joint undertaking. Any board representation, consulting, or other role the VC will play is spelled out in this section.

Financial Considerations

This section describes what the investor gets in return for the money being invested in the business. Business content and financial considerations are the sections of the agreement that are most often negotiated.

*B*oilerplate" is the standard clauses in every agreement that ensure that the parties understand the mechanics of doing what they are agreeing to do.

Boilerplate Clauses

"Boilerplate" is the standard clauses in every agreement that ensure that the parties understand the mechanics of doing what they are agreeing to do. Within these clauses, there is room to describe the specific circumstances under which the agreement is being put into effect.

Boilerplate clauses, though standard, affect conduct or interaction between the parties. For this reason, they are important and you should understand them. The details of these clauses tie them to the specific situation covered by the agreement.

Though the details are usually straightforward, some of them could be the basis for negotiation if either party wishes. Also, some lawyers differ on which clauses are boilerplate and which should be written more specifically to the particular situation.

The following are a few of the important boilerplate clauses, around which there may be some discussion.

Integration/Entire Agreement

This clause states that the agreement being entered into supersedes any previous agreement, written or oral, between the parties regarding any of the included subjects.

Dispute Resolution, Jurisdiction, and Governing Law

The parties may agree in advance to an approach, a formula, or a process for resolving any dispute that they cannot resolve amicably.

Lawyers argue long and hard over this clause. Especially when companies are incorporated in different states, each attorney wants disputes to be litigated in court in his or her home state under that state's rules and procedures.

The reality when dealing with a VC or sophisticated angel is a variant of the Golden Rule: whoever has the cash gets to pick where any dispute will be settled. More companies are therefore turning to alternative dispute resolution (ADR) for settling disputes, such as mediation and/or arbitration.

In mediation, a neutral third party facilitates discussions between the parties in dispute in an effort to find a workable solution.

In arbitration, each party presents its case to a single arbitrator or a panel of arbitrators that considers each side and then rules in favor of one or the other. Arbitration can be binding or nonbinding.

In cases of mediation or nonbinding arbitration, a party that does not feel a proposed extrajudicial solution is appropriate can still take the case to court. This means the issue of jurisdiction is not necessarily dead.

Certain clauses are in every agreement, but their content varies depending on the nature of the agreement. You need to pay attention to these.

Binding on the Parties, Successors, and Assignees. Under this clause, anyone who inherits or obtains your interest in the property that is the subject of the agreement is bound by the terms of the agreement unless there is a statement exempting or relieving the person or persons of those obligations.

Severability. This clause states that if one clause in the agreement is found in court to be invalid, it is not applicable; however, the rest of the agreement may still be valid and enforceable.

Confidential Information

This clause describes how the parties will handle confidential information.

Each party must keep confidential any information it learns about the other party in the course of the agreement and their work together.

Notices

During the term of the agreement, notices may be sent from one party to the other. In investor agreements, such notices may be about stockholder meetings, successful sales, personnel changes, or possible defaults on covenants in other agreements.

The parties should provide in the agreement the addresses to which such notices should be sent. The address should be one at which someone is always available to receive notices and correspondence that may come via special mail service.

Term. The term is the length of time the agreement—and therefore the arrangement between the parties—remains in force. The reference date is usually in the paragraph where the parties are named (e.g., "This agreement is made between X and Y on ABC date").

* * *

Now you know the basics of a term sheet, which is primarily the business content and financial and associated business terms of the basic agreement. After the entrepreneur and the investor have negotiated and accepted the term sheet, the complete agreement is prepared. The next and final discussion of equity-investor arrangements covers the investment agreements

Chapter 12

Need a Lotta Money to Go Big Time, Part 3

A fter the entrepreneur and the investor have negotiated and accepted the term sheet, which is primarily the business content and financial and associated business terms of the basic agreement, the complete agreement is prepared.

This chapter discusses the terms and conditions of the investor agreement. Not all clauses will be in every agreement and there may be others not covered here.

The Investment Agreement, Specific Clauses: Know Your Rights and Responsibilities

Knowing what these terms entail and what effect they can have on your company can help you design your game plan for dealing with investors who ask for these specific clauses and for your capital-raising strategy in general.

At the time you execute a major investment agreement, there may also be other agreements that must be put together. These often include an agreement regarding the transfer and voting of the securities being divided up, agreements creating a company stock purchase plan for employees, an agreement outlining the stock option program for key employees, and employment agreements for key personnel.

As you move in your capital-raising tours from friends and family to angels and to venture capitalists, investment agreements become more complex.

Private placement memoranda drawn up for friends and family investors are simple for two reasons. First, no single investor at this point will be a major equity holder in the company. Therefore, there is little likelihood that any investor will make substantive demands. Second, they are usually not sophisticated investors and usually not knowledgeable about the nuances of these investments.

This is not to say that you should take advantage of your friends and family. On the contrary, treating them fairly can create important allies down the road. You should create a basic set of arrangements for all friends and family equity stake holders who make their investments during a particular round of financing and treat them all equally.

A *round* is defined by the pricing of the securities being offered. Everyone who is offered the opportunity to buy equity securities at a particular time must be offered the same terms. Sometimes the round will also be defined by a total amount of money needed; if that amount is not raised, the financing round may be canceled. In such an instance, all funds are held in escrow until the total amount of funding is secured.

Most term sheets are not binding. When parties agree on a term sheet, it means they are agreeing to go forward and ultimately close on the agreement. If the parties can't come to an agreement on the term sheet, there will be no closing. The final agreement usually is binding and may include some kind of a penalty clause if for some reason the parties cannot close.

Closing is when funds pass from the investor to the company and a security (stock, convertible stock, or debentures) passes from the company to the investor. Although it is expected the closing will occur, there are occasions when a term sheet is signed and closing never occurs. Closing is always contingent on satisfactory outcome of the investor's due diligence of the company.

Again, it's important to stress that when you deal with professional venture capitalists, they will present you with the term sheet. The professional venture capitalist is almost always investing funds raised from passive investors and has a fiduciary responsibility to those investors to negotiate vigorously for the most favorable terms.

Investment Agreement Structure

The agreement has three main purposes:

1. Summarize the key financial terms.
2. State major legal conditions.
3. Provide information about the company's status.

A typical investment agreement contains more than two dozen terms. We have organized them into six categories, although in an agreement they are not necessarily placed together:

- ▶ Initial capitalization
- ▶ Capital structure (rights)
- ▶ Capital structure (restrictions)
- ▶ Management control
- ▶ Information
- ▶ Legal issues

In each of these categories, there are two to ten or more specific terms. Many of these items will not be necessary for simple agreements between entrepreneurs and angels.

Initial Capitalization

There are four clauses in this category:

- ▶ amount of financing
- ▶ price per share
- ▶ type of security
- ▶ use of funds

Figure 12-1 shows who these issues affect.

Amount of Financing

This clause states simply the amount of money the investor is investing.

Price per Share

This clause determines how many shares of stock will be issued in exchange for the investment being made. The price per share is determined as a part of defining the company's valuation both pre-closing (before the investment is made) and post-closing (after the investment is made).

	Friends and Family	Angel	Venture Capitalist
Amount of Financing	✔	✔	✔
Price per Share	✔	✔	✔
Type of Security	✔	✔	✔
Use of Funds		✔	✔

Figure 12-1. Initial capitalization

Remember: the percentage of a company an investor is buying is determined by the post-closing value. For instance, if the pre-closing value is $4 million and an investor invests $1 million, the investor is not buying 25 percent of the company ($1 million = 25 percent of $4 million) but rather 20 percent ($1 million = 20 percent of $4 million pre-closing valuation plus $1 million invested = $5 million post-closing valuation).

If the investor is a venture capitalist firm, it may act as *lead firm* in a *syndicate* of investors. Many venture capitalists do not want to take the entire risk of backing an entrepreneurial company. In addition, especially with highly technical new companies, a VC firm may want to bring in a firm with specific experience in a certain technological area.

Type of Security

*P*arties to an investor agreement have relationships at several levels: finance, legal, and management. It is too easy to focus on one relationship and its issues and neglect the others.

As we've pointed out, venture capitalists and most angels do not like to invest in a straight common stock deal. Venture capitalists and sophisticated angels usually take preferred stock that is convertible to common stock. The agreement must spell out the exact type of security.

The stock sold in each financing round is designated as a *series*. For instance, the first round of stock is called Series A preferred stock. Preferred stock purchased by VC firms and sophisticated angels usually has all the features of a corporate bond (e.g., a regular dividend). However, preferred stock looks better than debt on the entrepreneurial company's balance sheet when it comes time to raise further capital. Usually the dividend payments are accrued rather than distributed and are paid out at conversion in the form of extra common stock or when the investment is redeemed.

Each successive round of equity financing must involve negotiation of concessions with the owners of the previous round's equity in terms of each series of stock's value and the ranking of each round's investors—that is, the order in which any assets would be distributed in case of bankruptcy proceedings.

Use of Funds

Investors are concerned about how funds will be used. Venture capitalists are particularly concerned that company founders not use the proceeds of any future round of financing to buy out some of their stock, partially cashing out their equity interest in the company, or to pay themselves fat salaries.

Accordingly, in the term sheet, use of funds will be limited usually to working capital (ongoing operations), acquisitions of other companies, or plant and equipment. Sometimes other restrictions are placed on the use of funds.

Venture capitalists are particularly concerned that company founders not use the proceeds of any future round of financing to buy out some of their stock.

Capital Structure (Rights)

This is the category in which the most clauses fall. Here "rights" refers to those granted to the investor (which often result in restrictions on the entrepreneur). These are the clauses in this category:

- ▶ antidilution
- ▶ conversion
- ▶ dividends and interest
- ▶ future stock purchases
- ▶ liquidation preference
- ▶ participation protection
- ▶ redemption (put provision)
- ▶ registration rights
- ▶ tagalong rights
- ▶ unlocking provisions

Figure 12-2 shows who this category affects.

Antidilution

An antidilution clause is common in agreements with angels and venture capitalists; it can also be used in agreements with friends and family and other "seed-stage" investors.

An antidilution clause enables investors to keep a constant share of the company's equity, ensuring that later investors will not receive a larger percentage of the company. Remember: at the time each successive round of financing is organized, the company is revalued. This means that an investor who purchases 500,000 shares in the third round will be buying a different

	Friends and Family	Angel	Venture Capitalist
Anti-dilution	✔	✔	✔
Conversion	✔	✔	✔
Dividends			✔
Future Stock Purchases		✔	✔
Liquidation Preference			✔
Participation Protection			✔
Redemption ("put" provision)		✔	✔

Registration Rights
   Demand registration
   "Piggyback" rights
		✔
		✔
			✔
			✔

"Tag-along" Rights		✔	✔
Unlicking Provisions		✔	✔

Figure 12-2. Capital structure: rights

percentage of the company than an investor who purchased 500,000 shares in the first or second round.

An antidilution clause may give investors preemptive rights to purchase new stock at a later date at the offering price. It may give them the benefit of a reduced effective price per share if the company issues its shares at a lower price in a later round of financing.

Conversion

Conversion rights offer the investor the option to exchange his or her initial preferred stock for common stock at a fixed price during an agreed-upon time frame. Conversion rights may be triggered if there is an IPO or if control of the company changes (i.e., a sale). The conversion may be adjusted for dividends, changes in the capitalization of the company, or stock splits.

Dividends and Interest

Some types of securities provide for dividend and interest payments. Both dividends and interest may be deferred. Most VCs defer both until there is a conversion or sale. Also, an investor may, as a concession to investors in later rounds of financing, waive the interest if he or she converts to common stock.

Future Stock Purchases

Investors often want the right of first refusal on any future sales of stock by the company in order to increase their share in a promising company. Exercising this right also prevents or minimizes dilution.

Investors often want the right of first refusal on any future sales of stock by the company in order to increase their share in a promising company.

Liquidation Preference

This right protects investors in the event that the company suddenly loses value or closes. Holders of the preferred shares are entitled to be "first out" before holders of common stock. In other words, if the company goes into a liquidation or bankruptcy, the preferred-stock investors get anything left over after the lawyers, creditors, and debt holders, and ahead of the entrepreneur, who always holds common stock.

Venture capitalists usually set a time when they will at least calculate a liquidation value for their investment, even if they do not actually liquidate their position. The investor sets a target for receiving its original investment plus some gain, often stated as a multiple of the investment. A merger or acquisition or any change in control of the company is usually "deemed to be a liquidation"—often called a "liquidity event" in agreements—and the liquidation guidelines apply.

Participation Protection

This clause requires the original investors to invest with each successive round of financing proportionately to his or her original pro-rata share of the company. The clause benefits the entrepreneur, because it raises more money when he or she might need it. It also counters dilution of the early investors' equity and forces the entrepreneur to give up equity in order to bring in new investors. Venture capitalists often require that original investors invest in successive rounds of financing. Very few, if any, sophisticated investors agree to such a clause.

Redemption ("Put" Provision)

A so-called "put" provision is commonly used to force the company to buy back a specified portion of an investor's stock at a given time and for a predetermined price.

Registration Rights

There are a number of types of registration rights. The two most common are demand rights and a "piggyback" provision.

In order for a company to conduct any public offering of capital stock, it must register the stock with the SEC and comply with the securities laws of any state in which the offering will be made.

In order for a company to conduct any public offering of capital stock, it must register the stock with the SEC and comply with the securities laws of any state in which the offering will be made. In the case of initial public offerings (IPOs), pre-IPO owners of stock who do not sell at the time of the IPO are often restricted from selling for months or even more than a year after the IPO. Venture capitalists, angels, and other passive investors can cash out of their investments if the company engages in an IPO by registering their stock, which then becomes part of the sale to the public. Very rarely do venture capitalists, angels, and other passive investors hold stock after the IPO.

Under a *demand* registration, investors can force the company to register the investors' shares regardless of whether any other shares are being registered.

"Piggyback" rights guarantee an investor that the company will register his or her stock with the SEC at the same time as it registers its own stock.

"Tagalong" Rights

Under this clause, also called *co-sale* rights, if an entrepreneur decides to sell all or part of his or her shares to a third party, investors are allowed to "tag along" on the sale. This clause may be written in such a way that an entrepreneur may not sell his or her stock unless the buyer agrees to purchase an equal proportion from the investors who have tagalong rights.

Some VCs also insist on "drag-along" rights, which enable them to drag the company's founders along into the sale as well.

Unlocking Provisions

Early investors, especially angels, are most likely to ask for an "unlocking" provision that calls for the company to buy out their position in the event that the company receives a valid offer to buy and rejects it. This clause gives angels some control, even though they may not have board influence over any possible sale of the company.

It also unlocks them later on when venture capitalists assume control, in case the venture capitalists' interests do not totally coincide with the angels'. For instance, if two years after a venture capitalist invests in the company, an offer is made that the venture capitalist doesn't deem good enough, an angel may feel that he or she, after being invested for five or six years, has earned enough and should get out. This clause allows that exit.

Capital Structure (Restrictions)

Venture capitalists and some angels impose restrictions and limitations on the entrepreneur in order to protect their investments, including the following:

▶ founder stock restrictions

▶ founder vesting

▶ right of first refusal

Figure 12-3 shows who this category affects.

	Friends and Family	Angel	Venture Capitalist
Founder Stock Restrictions			✔
Founder Vesting			✔
Right of First Refusal		✔	✔

Figure 12-3. Capital structure: restrictions

Founder Stock Restrictions

This clause is concerned with transfers of the entrepreneur's stock to third parties. It may include prohibitions against special treatment of the founder's stock for estate planning or gifts. It usually contains the investor's right of first refusal and co-sale issues, if they are not explicitly established in a section by that name.

Founder Vesting

An investor may insist that a founder give up some of his or her stock to the investor if the company fails to meet particular milestones or if the founder leaves the company. By taking control of more stock if milestones are not met, the investor is, in effect, revaluing the company because of lost opportunity.

At the time of the investment, a key factor in any venture capitalist's decision to invest is the quality of management and of the founder(s). The investor usually wants to retain the founder(s) for as long as possible and does this by allowing the founder(s) to have access to blocks of stock according to a preset schedule.

Agreements that force the founder(s) to remain with the company for a predetermined period of time in order to be able to retain stock are often referred to as "golden handcuffs." Since investors invest in entrepreneurs as

An investor may insist that a founder give up some of his or her stock to the investor if the company fails to meet particular milestones or if the founder leaves the company.

177

much or more than in their ideas, the company's value is inextricably bound up in keeping the founder(s) in the company.

Right of First Refusal

This clause usually gives the venture capitalist the first chance to buy any stock that another investor wishes to sell. This allows the VC firm to increase its holding in the company without having to go through an entire recapitalization process. This also prevents stock from falling into the hands of others who might challenge the VC firm for control of the company.

Management Control

One of the major issues concerning the investor is management control. Especially for venture capitalists, having some degree of control over management's decision making is absolutely essential in order to protect the investors' interests.

Figure 12-4 shows who finds each of these issues important.

	Friends and Family	Angel	Venture Capitalist
Board of Directors		✔	✔
Veto Rights		✔	✔

Figure 12-4. Management control

Board of Directors

Directors make fundamental decisions that guide the company's activities on behalf of their various constituencies. The issue around the board of directors is how many directors each investor or investor group will be allowed to name. The condition usually sets out the total number of directors on the board and the number of directors that each stock class can elect.

Usually the clause dictates that the bylaws authorize an odd number of directors (often no more than five). On a board of five seats, usually two would be representatives of the major-investor VC firm (which holds preferred stock and has the right to name two directors, thereby holding 40 percent of the board control), two would be named by the common-stock owners (founders) as a group, and one board member would be an independent upon whom the founders and investors mutually agree. In addition, there is usually a provision that a given percentage of the board members (usually less than a majority) can call a special meeting.

Veto Rights

The other means of control a major investor can obtain is veto rights. A clause can specify the kinds of issues over which the investor will have a veto without having to have a vote of the board. This is very typical in deals with VC firms. The kinds of things over which venture capitalists usually want veto rights are changes in the capital stock structure, merger or sale, changes in control of the company, declaration of dividends, major capital expenses, taking on debt, and even the "burn rate" (the rate at which the company uses cash).

Information

Interaction between the entrepreneur and an investor always begins with the entrepreneur providing the potential investor with a business plan and associated back-up materials. The negotiation phase is likely to generate more requests for information.

After the deal closes, the investor wants to make sure he or she is kept abreast of developments that affect the company and the investment. An agreement may contain clauses that guarantee that an investor will receive specific types of information.

Figure 12-5 shows who finds each of these issues important.

	Friends and Family	Angel	Venture Capitalist
Disclosure of other stockholder terms		✔	✔
Reporting (information rights)		✔	✔
Representations and warranties		✔	✔

Figure 12-5. Information

Disclosure of Other Stockholder Terms

Information about investors in prior rounds (amount invested, price per share, and equity stake) is always provided in the documentation for a subsequent financing round.

Reporting (Information Rights)

Sophisticated investors insist that the company report to them on all significant matters. They want information on monthly financial statements, budgets, agreements executed by the company (some of which may need their concurrence) and any changes in the company's business plan. Although friends and family do not always insist on this clause, you should provide these investors with some reporting.

Representations and Warranties

There are usually from five to 25 clauses in this section. They state that you are fully disclosing all matters concerning the company to your investors and potential investors. They state that the investor is investing on the basis of the information you are providing.

While there may be exceptions or qualifications noted to aspects of the information provided, the key is that the investor must have all the information he or she needs. This includes information regarding insurance coverage and corporate assets, as well as information about any litigation pending and compliance with laws and regulations.

Legal Issues

Legal issues cover a broad spectrum and deal with interactions between the entrepreneur and the investor. An investor is normally in for the long haul and wants the best possible working relationship with an entrepreneur. Investors also want a relationship that protects their investment.

Figure 12-6 shows who finds each of these issues important.

Assignment

An assignment clause deals with the conditions under which an investor may transfer securities to other parties. It could, for example, allow a VC firm to make distributions to its limited partners.

Confidentiality

Some investors, especially venture capitalists, may require an entrepreneur to keep negotiations and the potential investment confidential, at least until the deal closes.

	Friends and Family	Angel	Venture Capitalist
Assignment	✔		✔
Confidentiality			✔
Indemnification			✔
Legal Fees and Expenses			✔
Purchase Agreement			✔

Figure 12-6. Legal issues

Indemnification

The indemnification clause is directly tied to the representations and warranties you make. The clause makes you responsible for settling any legal dispute between you and another party that you did not disclose in your representations or about which you were not completely honest in your warranties.

In addition, the indemnification clause requires that the company obtain directors' and officers' (D&O) insurance. The purpose of a D&O policy is to protect the directors and officers of a corporation from liability in the event of a claim or lawsuit against them for wrongdoing in connection with the company's business. This insurance covers board members in their deliberations; with D&O insurance, you indemnify any venture capitalist or angel who sits on your board. This clause may also require the company to act as a responsible party when incurring liabilities, such as those associated with stock registration, and compensate investors for any expenses they incur in this regard.

Legal Fees and Expenses

Under this clause, the investor is able to recover reasonable costs associated with the closing, including fees for legal counsel as well as expenses for documentation, review of closing documents, and other matters.

Definitive Agreements

A closing requires that separate definitive agreements be drawn up before the investment is made. These include the following:

- ▶ a purchase agreement
- ▶ an investor rights agreement
- ▶ a stockholder/shareholder agreement
- ▶ a preferred stock registration

There may be other separate definitive agreements as well. And, as we noted at the start of Chapter 11, "The job's not over until the paperwork is done."

Appendix A

Glossary

THIS GLOSSARY CONTAINS KEY WORDS THAT MAY BE UNFAMILIAR TO the new entrepreneur. Many important words are defined in the text the first time they are used. You may see other words during your reading that you would like to include. Space has been provided under the entries for each letter to add words that are of particular importance to you.

Accelerator: A service company that provides a range of business services for enterprises, such as helping to find capital, personnel, and offices and providing consulting services.

Angel: Someone who invests money in new or growing ventures.

Arm's-length transaction: A business deal in which the people involved have no relationship with each other that could make the terms more beneficial than they would be to unrelated parties.

Asset: An item that has a financial value and can be used in an exchange for something else of value or sold for cash.

Blue-sky laws: State regulations that govern the issue and trading of securities.

Broker: Someone who arranges deals between buyers and sellers for a commission, often a percentage of the value of the transaction.

Capital: Money or something that can be traded or buy something that acts as money.

Capital gain: The increase in value of a stock or real asset (minus its cost).

Collateral: Anything of value that is used to secure a loan and that a lender can take if the borrower does not pay according to the terms of the loan.

Convert debt-to-equity: A common practice of lenders to exchange the debt of a company for a share of ownership, either arranged in advanced as a condition of a loan or decided upon by both parties at any time after the loan is made.

Discounted cash flow: Adjustment of the real worth of a future money stream by calculating in terms of its net present value, to account for the effect of inflation.

Distribution: Payment made by a company in the form of a dividend on a company's stock, capital gains from the sale of stock, or repurchase of the stock by the company.

Early-stage company: Company that is newly formed or in its early growth phases.

Equity: Ownership interest in a company.

Equity capital infusion: Additional capital obtained for shares of ownership in the company.

Equity investor: Someone who provides money for a company in exchange for a percentage of ownership in the company.

Escrow: Money that is set aside for a transaction and then released when the only when certain specified conditions of the transaction are met.

Fiduciary: Relating to a position of trust or to a person who holds a position of trust, often used in *fiduciary responsibility,* by which someone is trusted to manage financial resources ethically.

Finder: Someone who arranges deals between buyers and sellers for a commission, often a percentage of the value of the transaction. Finders are similar to brokers, although many states have licensing requirements for brokers and not for finders. In some states, finders may be prohibited for receiving compensation in stock.

Guarantee: Agreement by which someone takes on the risk of a party to a financial transaction.

Guarantor: Individual, company, or organization that provides a guarantee.

Incubator: Entity (usually consisting of real estate and professional resources) designed to support entrepreneurs and start-up ventures at minimum cost until they reach a given level of viability.

Initial public offering (IPO): The first time that a company makes its stock available to the public through a stock exchange.

Installment: Partial payment of a debt according to a preset schedule of payments as specified in the terms of the agreement that creates that debt.

Interest-only loan: Loan for which the debtor pays the lender an agreed-upon rate of interest for some term without paying any principal.

IPO: See *initial public offering*.

Liability: Financial obligation of an individual or company to pay money for any reason.

Loan guarantee: Provision for a loan whereby a person or an organization such as the Small Business Administration assumes responsibility for paying the lender if the borrower fails to do so.

Lump-sum payout: Payment in full to a designated payee that satisfies the obligation of the payer.

Portfolio company: Term used by an investment company for any company in which it is invested.

Private-equity funding: Investment in a company from private sources in exchange for ownership in that company.

Private-placement memorandum (PPM): A simplified version of the full business prospectus that describes the company in terms of its business areas, marketing strategy, finances, and board of directors and officers.

Proceeds: Total amount of money resulting from a transaction..

Prospectus: Comprehensive business plan that a company usually issues at the time of an *initial public offering* (IPO) listing all the opportunities and risks involved in investing in the company.

Qualify: To make sure that a prospective buyer or investor is seriously interested in a transaction and can afford to buy or invest.

Return-on-investment (ROI): A standard financial term defining the amount or percent that an investor will receive for making an investment.

Risk capital: Money that is invested with no assurance that it will be returned, as in the case of a start-up venture.

Securities: Documents that record an investment, identifying it (as stock, bond, or other) and the owner.

Seed funding: Funds provided to begin a new venture, usually the first funds.

Small Business Administration (SBA): A federal agency established in 1953 to "aid, counsel, assist, and protect ... the interests of small business concerns," which it does through information, advice, and loan guarantees.

Small Business Development Center (SBDC): A facility that is part of a network across the United States established and operated by the Small Business Administration (SBA) to help owners of small businesses with financial and other needs.

Start-up: Newly formed company.

Tax-advantaged investment: An investment that generates a tax credit, a tax deduction, or a tax deferral.

Taxable investment: Commitment of money in order to earn a financial return that will generate a tax liability.

Term sheet: Document that contains the terms and conditions under which an investment is made in a privately held company, including the percent of equity (ownership) the investor will receive.

Trust fund: An amount of money set aside for the benefit of one or more individuals and entrusted to the legal of an individual or an organization (trustee) with the fiduciary responsibility of distributing money according to guidelines set by the individual or organization establishing the fund.

Underwriting: Process by which an investment banker raises capital from investors on behalf of a corporation that is issuing securities (either equity or debt) or a stock brokerage house takes all of the stock a company wants to sell and assumes the risk for selling it to investors.

Valuation: Process of determining the current worth of an asset or company, often for the purpose of determining the price of company shares to sell to prospective investors.

Venture capital (VC) fund: Pool of money provided by wealthy individuals or companies and managed by venture capitalists in investments of greater risk that offer higher returns. Also known simply as *venture capital*.

Venture capitalist: Investor who provides capital to small companies.

Appendix B

U.S. Small Business Administration Microloan Program

Participating Intermediary Lenders

Alabama

Birmingham Business Resource Center
110 12th Street North
Birmingham, AL 35203
Executive Director: Robert Dickinson, Jr.
Microloan Contact: Rodney E. Evans
E-mail: info@bbrc.biz
Phone: (205) 250-6380
Fax: (205) 250-6384
Service Area: Jefferson County
URL: www.bbrc.biz

Southeast Community Capital Corporation
1020 Commerce Park Drive
Oak Ridge, TN 37830
Executive Director: Clint Gwin
Microloan Contact: David Bradshaw
E-mail: gwin@sccapital.org,
bradshaw@sccapital.org
Phone: (865) 220-2025
Fax: (865) 220-2024
Service Area: Bibb, Blount, Calhoun,
Chambers, Chilton, Colbert, Coosa,
Cullman, De Kalb, Elmore, Etowah,
Fayette, Franklin, Hale, Jackson,
Lauderdale, Lawrence, Limestone,
Macon, Madison, Marion, Marshall,
Morgan, Pickens, Randolph, St. Clair,
Shelby, Talladega, Tallapoosa,
Tuscaloosa, Walker, and Winston
URL: www.sccapital.org

Community Equity Investments, Inc.
302 North Barcelona Street
Pensacola, FL 32501
Executive Director: Daniel Horvath
Microloan Contact: Elbert Jones
E-mail: bigdanfla@aol.com,
eljojr@aol.com, ceii2234@aol.com
Phone: (850) 595-6234
Fax: (850) 595-6264
Service Area: Baldwin, Mobile,
Washington, Clarke, Monroe, Escambia,
Conecuh, Covington, Geneva, Coffee,
Dale, Henry, and Houston counties
URL: www.ceii-cdc.org

Arizona

Prestamos CDFI, LLC (formerly Chicanos
Por La Causa, Inc.)
1112 E. Buckeye Road
Phoenix, AZ 85034-4043
Executive Director: Pete Garcia
Microloan Contact: Joe Martinez
E-mail: jmartinez@tiempoinc
Phone: (602) 258-9911
Fax: (602) 252-0484
Service Area: Urban Maricopa and Pima
counties, Graham and Gila counties
(including Point of Pines Reservation and
the Southwestern area of Fort Apache
Reservation), Coconino and Mohave
counties (including the Kaibab,
Havasupai, and Hualapai Reservations
and western portions of the Navajo and
Hopi Reservations), Yavapai, and La Paz
Counties
URL: www.cplc.org

**PPEP Microbusiness and Housing
Development Corporation, Inc.**

820 East 47th Street, Suite B-14
Tucson, AZ 85713
Executive Director: Frank Ballesteros
Microloan Contact: Frank Ballesteros
E-mail: fballesteros@ppepruralinst.org
Phone: (520) 889-4203
Fax: (520) 889-5319
Service Area: Cochise, Santa Cruz, Pinal,
Yuma, rural Pima, and rural Maricopa
Counties including the Fort Mcdowell,
Gila River, Maricopa, Papago, Salt River,
and San Xavier Indian Reservations
URL: www.azsmallbusinessloans.com

Self-Employment Loan Fund, Inc.
1601 North 7th Street, Suite 340
Phoenix, AZ 85006
Executive Director: Caroline Newsom
Microloan Contact: Caroline Newsom
E-mail: self@uswest.net
Phone: (602) 340-8834
Fax: (602) 340-8953
Service Area: Maricopa County
URL: www.selfloanfund.org

**Microbusiness Advancement Center of
Southern Arizona**
30 N. Commerce Park Loop, #160
Tucson, AZ 85745
Executive Director: Mary Gruensfelder-
Cox
Microloan Contact: Debbie Chandler
E-mail: mgcox@mac-sa.org, dchan-
dler@mac-sa.org
Phone: (520) 620-1241
Fax: (520) 622-2235
Service Area: Southern Arizona (Pima,
Cochise, and Santa Cruz Counties)
URL: www.mac-sa.org

Arkansas

Southern Financial Partners

605 Main Street, Suite 203
Arkadelphia, AR 71923
Executive Director: Bryn Bagwell
Microloan Contact: Kelly Woodson
E-mail: bbagwell@ehbt.com, kwood-
son@ehbt.com
Phone: (870) 246-9739
Fax: (870) 246-2182
Service Area: Southern and extreme
northeast areas of Arkansas including
Arkansas, Ashley, Bradley, Calhoun,
Chicot, Clark, Clay, Cleveland,
Columbia, Craighead, Dallas, Desha,
Drew, Garland, Grant, Greene,
Hempstead, Hot Spring, Howard,
Jefferson Lafayette, Lawrence, Lincoln,
Little River, Lonoke, Miller, Mississippi,
Montgomery, Nevada, Ouachita,
Phillips, Pike, Poinsett, Polk, Prairie,
Pulaski, Randolph, Saline, Sevier, and
Union Counties
URL: www.southernfinancialpartners.org

FORGE (Financing Ozarks Rural Growth and Economy)

208 East Main
P.O. Box 1138
Huntsville, AR 72740
Executive Director: Barb Kempke-Becker
Microloan Contact: Charlie Stockton
E-mail: barb@forgeonline.com,
charlie@forgeonline.com
Phone: (479) 738-1585, (800) 394-5057
Fax: (479) 738-6288
Service Area: Crawford, Baxter, Yell,
Perry, Conway, Boone, Madison,
Marion, Carroll, Franklin, Pope, Benton,
Washington, Searcy, and Newton
URL: www.forgeonline.com

California

Arcata Economic Development Corporation

100 Ericson Court, Suite 100
Arcata, CA 95521
Executive Director: Jim Kimbrell
Microloan Contact: Arianne Knoeller or
Kelly Denny
E-mail: arianek@Reninet.com
Phone: (707) 822-4616
Fax: (707) 822-8982
Service Area: Del Norte, Humboldt,
Lake, Mendocino, Siskiyou, and Trinity
Counties
URL: www.aedc1.org

California Coastal Rural Development Corporation

221 Main Street, Suite 300
P.O. Box 479
Salinas, CA 93906
Executive Director: Herb Aarons
Microloan Contact: Ruth Moran
E-mail: herb_aarons@calcoastal.org,
ruth_moran@calcoastal.org
Phone: (831) 424-1099
Fax: (831) 424-1094
Service Area: Santa Clara, Santa Cruz,
Monterey, San Benito, San Luis Obispo,
Santa Barbara, and Ventura Counties
URL: www.calcoastal.org

CDC Small Business Finance Corporation

2448 Historic Decatur Road, Suite 200
San Diego, CA 92106
President: Kurt Chilcott
Microloan Contact: Susan Lamping

Phone: (619) 291-3594
Fax: (619) 291-6954
E-mail: slamping@cdcloans.com
Service Area: San Diego
URL: www.cdcloans.com

Oakland Business Development Corporation
519 17th Street, Suite 100
Oakland, CA 94612
Executive Director: Michael McPherson
Microloan Contact: Nicole Levine
E-mail: nicole@obdc.com
Phone: (510) 763-4297 x 103
Fax: (510) 763-1273
Service Area: Alameda and Contra Costa Counties
URL: www.obdc.com

Pacific Coast Regional Small Business Development Corporation
3255 Wilshire Boulevard
Los Angeles, CA 90010
President: Mark Robertson, Sr.
Microloan Contact: Selena Davis.
Phone: (213) 739-2999 x 222
Fax: (213) 739-0639
E-mail: mark.robertson@pcrcorp.org,
selena.davis@pcrcorp.org
Service Area: South Los Angeles County
URL: www.pcrcorp.org

Sierra Economic Development District
560 Wall Street, Suite F
Auburn, CA 95603
Executive Director: Sandy Sindt
Microloan Contact: Tom Dille
E-mail: sedd@sedd.org, dille@sedd.org
Phone: (530) 823-4703
Fax: (530) 823-4142
Service Area: Modoc, El Dorado, Lassen,

Nevada, Plumas, Sierra, and Placer Counties
URL: www.sedd.org

Southeast Asian Community Center
875 O'Farrell Street
San Francisco, CA 94109
Executive Director: Philip Tuong Duy Nguyen
Microloan Contact: Victor Hsi
E-mail: seaccphilip@juno.com
Phone: (415) 885-2743
Fax: (415) 885-3253
Service Area: Alameda, Contra Costa, Marin, Merced, Sacramento, San Francisco, San Joaquin, San Mateo, Santa Clara, and Stanislaus Counties
URL: www.seacc.us

Valley Economic Development Corporation
5121 Van Nuys Boulevard, 3rd Floor
Van Nuys, CA 91403
Executive Director: Roberto Barragan
Microloan Contact: *Lisa Winkle*
E-mail: roberto@vedc.org, info@vedc.org
Phone: (818) 907-9977
Fax: (818) 907-9720
Service Area: Los Angeles and Orange County
URL: www.vedc.org

Valley Small Business Development Corporation
7035 N. Fruit Avenue
Fresno, CA 93711
Executive Director: Michael E. Foley
Microloan Contact: Stanley Tom
E-mail: requestinfo@vsbdc.com
Phone: (559) 438-9680
Fax: (559) 438-9690

Service Area: Fresno, Kings, Kern, Stanislaus, Madera, Mariposa, Merced, Tuolumne, and Tulare Counties
URL: www.vsbdc.com

Colorado

Colorado Enterprise Fund
1888 Sherman Street, Suite 530
Denver, CO 80203
Executive Director: Cecilia H. Prinster
Microloan Contact: Angela Valdez
E-mail: microloans@coloradoenterprise-fund.org
Phone: (303) 860-0242
Fax: (303) 860-0409
Service Area: City of Denver, and Adams, Arapahoe, Boulder, Broomfield, Denver, Douglas, El Paso, Jefferson, Larimer, Morgan, and Weld Counties
URL: www.coloradoenterprisefund.org

Region 10 League for Economic Assistance and Planning (LEAP)
300 North Cascade Street, Suite 1
P.O. Box 849
Montrose, CO 81401
Executive Director: Paul Gray
Microloan Contact: Jim Kidd
E-mail: paul@region10.net, info@region10.net
Phone: (970) 249-2436
Fax: (970) 249-2488
Service Area: West Central area including Delta, Gunnison, Hinsdale, Montrose, Ouray, and San Miguel Counties
URL: www.region10.net

Connecticut

Community Economic Development Fund
430 New Park Avenue
West Hartford, CT 06110
Executive Director: Donna Wertenbach
Microloan Contact: Sarahi Jordan
E-mail: info@cedf.com, wertenbach@cedf.com, jordan@cedf.com
Phone: (860) 249-3800
Fax: (860) 249-2500
Service Area: Connecticut
URL: www.cedf.com

Connecticut Community Investment Corporation
100 Crown Street
New Haven, CT 06510
Executive Director: Salvatore J. Brancati, Jr.
Microloan Contact: Gary Toole, John Torello
E-mail: loans@ctcic.org
Phone: (203) 776-6172
Fax: (203) 776-6837
Service Area: Connecticut
URL: www.ctcic.org

Delaware

Wilmington Economic Development Corporation
100 W. 10th Street, Suite 706
Wilmington, DE 19801
Executive Director: **Charles H. W. Effinger, Jr.**
Microloan Contact: **Margo J. Reign**
E-mail: info@wedco.org
Phone: (302) 571-9088
Fax: (302) 652-5679
Service Area: New Castle County, in the

cities of Wilmington, Newark, New
Castle, Middletown, Odessa, and
Townsend
URL: www.wedco.org

District of Columbia

H Street Community Development Corporation
501 H Street, NE
Washington, DC 20002
Executive Director: William Barrow
Microloan Contact: Yulonda Queen
E-mail: yulonda.queen@hstreetcdc.org
Phone: (202) 544-8353
Fax: (202) 544-3051
Service Area: "underdeveloped neighbor-
hoods throughout Washington, D.C."
URL: www.hstreetcdc.org

Enterprise Development Group
1038 South Highland Street
Arlington, VA 22204
Executive Director: Tsehaye Teferra
Microloan Contact: Michelle Wilson
E-mail: edgloan@entdevgroup.org
Phone: (703) 685-0510
Fax: (703) 685-4200
Service Area: District of Columbia
URL: www.entdevgroup.org

Florida

Central Florida Community Development Corporation
847 Orange Avenue
Daytona Beach, FL 32114
P.O. Box 15065
Daytona Beach, FL 32115
Executive Director: Gerald O. Chester
Microloan Contact: Louis Halley

E-mail: geraldc@cfcdc.com,
louish@cfcdc.com
Phone: (386) 258-7520
Fax: (368) 238-3428
Service Area: Brevard, Flagler, St. Johns,
and Volusia Counties
URL: www.cfcdc.com

Clearwater Neighborhood Housing Services, Inc.
608 North Garden Avenue
Clearwater, FL 33755
Executive Director: Isay M. Gulley
Microloan Contact: John J. Moloney
E-mail: igulley@hotmail.com,
jmoloney82@hotmail.com
Phone: (727) 442-4155
Fax: (727) 446-4911
Service Area: City of Clearwater and
Pinellas County
URL: NA

Community Enterprise Investments, Inc.
302 North Barcelona Street
Pensacola, FL 32501
Executive Director: Daniel R. Horvath
Microloan Contact: Percy Goodman
E-mail: dhorvath@ceii-cdc.org, pgood-
man@ceii-cdc.org
Phone: (850) 595-6234
Fax: (850) 595-6264
Service Area: Florida Panhandle includ-
ing Bay, Calhoun, Escambia, Gadsden,
Gulf, Jackson, Holmes, Liberty, Leon,
Franklin, Wakulla, Walton, Washington,
Okaloosa, and Santa Rosa Counties
URL: www.ceii-cdc.org

Minority/Women Business Enterprise Alliance, Inc.
625 E. Colonial Drive

Orlando, FL 32803
Executive Director: Geovanny Sepulveda
Microloan Contact: Geovanny Sepulveda
E-mail: geovanny4@hotmail.com,
alliance@allianceflorida.com
Phone: (407) 428-5860
Fax: (407) 428-5869
Service Area: Orange, Osceola, Lake,
Seminole, Polk, Hillsborough, Sumter,
Brevard, Volusia, and Marion Counties
URL: www.allianceflorida.com

Partners for Self-Employment, Inc., d.b.a. Micro-Business, USA

3000 Biscayne Boulevard, Suite 102
Miami, FL 33137
Executive Director: Miltoria Fordham
Microloan Contact: Miltoria Fordham
E-mail: toria@microbusinessusa.org
Phone: (877) 722-4505, (305) 438-1407
x 204
Fax: (305) 438-1411
Service Area: Miami-Dade, Broward,
Palm Beach, and Pinellas Counties
URL: www.microbusinessusa.org

The Business Loan Fund of the Palm Beaches, Inc.

1016 North Dixie Highway, 2nd Floor
West Palm Beach, FL 33401
Executive Director: John B. Brown
Microloan Contact: John B. Brown
E-mail: blfpb@evcom.net
Phone: (561) 838-9027
Fax: (561) 838-9029
Service Area: Palm Beach County,
Hendry, Indian River, Martin, Palm
Beach County Development Regions,
and St. Lucie
URL: NA

Georgia

Small Business Assistance Corporation

111 E. Liberty Street, Suite 100
P.O. Box 10750
Savannah, GA 31412-0950
Executive Director: Tony O'Reilly
Microloan Contact: Tony O'Reilly
E-mail: toreilly@sbacsav.com,
sbac@sbacsav.com
Phone: (912) 232-4700
Fax: (912) 232-0385
Service Area: Appling, Atkinson, Brooks,
Bacon, Berrien, Ben Hill, Bryan, Bulloch,
Bleckley, Brantley, Coffee, Charlton,
Camden, Clinch, Candler, Cook,
Chatham, Dodge, Emanuel, Echols,
Effingham, Evans, Glynn, Irwin,
Johnson, Jeff Davis, Laurens, Liberty,
Long, Lowndes, Lanier, McIntosh,
Montgomery, Pierce, Tift, Turner, Telfair,
Truetlen, Toombs, Tattnall, Ware,
Wilcox, Wayne, and Wheeler Counties
URL: www.sbacsav.com

Southeast Community Capital

1020 Commerce Park Drive
Oak Ridge, TN 37830
Executive Director: Clint Gwin
Microloan Contact: David Bradshaw
E-mail: gwin@sccapital.org,
bradshaw@sccapital.org
Phone: (865) 220-2025
Fax: (865) 220-2024
Service Area: Barrow, Bartow, Carroll,
Cherokee, Dade, Elbert, Fannin, Floyd,
Franklin, Gordon, Gwinnett, Hall, Hart,
Heard, Paulding, Pickens, Polk,
Stephens, Union, Walker, and Whitfield
URL: www.sccapital.org

Hawaii

Pacific Gateway Center
720 North King Street
Honolulu, HI 96817
Executive Director: Tin Myaing Thein
Microloan Contact: NA
E-mail: myaing@pacificgateway.org,
info@pacificgateway.org
Phone: (808) 845-3918
Fax: (808) 842-1962
Service Area: Hawaii
URL: www.pacificgateway.org

Idaho

Panhandle Area Council
11100 Airport Drive
Hayden, ID 83835-9743
Executive Director: James Deffenbaugh
Microloan Contact: Kay Kitchel
E-mail: jimd@pacni.org,
kkitchel@pacni.org
Phone: (208) 772-0584
Fax: (208) 772-6196
Service Area: Northern panhandle,
including Benewah, Bonner, Boundary,
Kotenai, and Shoshone Counties
URL: www.pacni.org

Illinois

Accion Chicago, Inc.
1618 W 18th Street, Suite 200
Chicago, IL 60608
President: Jonathan Brereton
Microloan Contact: Heather Rogers
E-mail: jbrereton@accionchicago.org,
hrogers@accionchicago.org,
info@accionchicago.org
Phone: (312) 275-3000

Fax: (312) 275-3010
Service Area: Cook County (including
parts of Chicago), Lake, McHenry,
DeKalb, Kane, Dupage, Kendall,
Grundy, Kankakee, Will, and Lasalle
Counties
URL: www.accionchicago.org

**Justine Petersen Housing and
Reinvestment Corporation**
5031 Northrup Avenue
St. Louis, MO 63110
Executive Director: Robert Boyle
Microloan Contact: Sheri Flanigan-
Vazquez
E-mail: rboyle@justinepetersen.org,
sflanigan@justinepetersen.org
Phone: (314) 664-5051 x 117
Fax: (314) 644-5364
Service Area: Clinton, Jersey, Madison,
and St. Clair Counties
URL: www.justinepetersen.org

Indiana

SEED Corp.
501 N. Morton Street, Suite 106
Bloomington, IN 47404
Executive Director: Terri Brown
Microloan Contact: Charlotte Zietlow /
Beth Kuebler
E-mail: info@seed-corp.org
Phone: (812) 323-7827
Fax: (812) 335-7352
Service Area: Morgan, Owen, Greene,
Lawrence, Monroe, Brown, Jackson,
Bartholomew, Decatur, and Jennings
Counties
URL: www.seed-corp.org

Iowa

Siouxland Economic Development Corporation

428 Insurance Center
507 7th Street, Room 428
P.O. Box 1077
Sioux City, IA 51102
Executive Director: Ken Beekley
Microloan Contact: Glenda Castleberry
E-mail: ken@simpco.org, glenda@simpco.org
Phone: (712) 279-6286
Fax: (712) 279-6920
Service Area: Cherokee, Ida, Monona, Plymouth, Sioux, and Woodbury Counties
URL: www.siouxlandedc.com

Kansas

South Central Kansas Economic Development District Inc.

209 East William Street, Suite 300
Wichita, KS 67202-4012
Executive Director: William Bolin
Microloan Contact: Christie Henry
E-mail: bbolin@sckedd.org,
christie@sckedd.org
Phone: (316) 262-7035
Fax: (316) 262-7062
Service Area: Butler, Chautauqua, Cowley, Elk, Greenwood, Harper, Harvey, Kingman, Marion, McPherson, Reno, Rice, Sedgwick, and Sumner Counties
URL: www.sckedd.org

Growth Opportunity Connection (Go Connection)

4747 Troost Avenue, Suite 211
Kansas City, MO 64110
Executive Director: Alan Corbet
Microloan Contact: Rebecca Gubbels
E-mail: info@goconnection.org
Phone: (816) 235-6146
Fax: (816) 235-6586
Service Area: Wyandotte, Johnson, Douglas, and Leavenworth Counties
URL: www.goconnection.org

Kentucky

Community Ventures Corporation

1450 North Broadway
Lexington, KY 40505
Executive Director: Kevin R. Smith
Microloan Contact: David Collins / Tyrone Tyra
E-mail: info@cvcky.org
Phone: (859) 231-0054, (800) 299-0267
Fax: (859) 231-0261
Service Area: Anderson, Boone, Bourbon, Boyle, Campbell, Clark, Estill, Fayette, Franklin, Gallatin, Garrard, Grant, Harrison, Jessamine, Kenton, Lincoln, Madison, Mercer, Nicholas, Pendleton, Powell, Scott, and Woodford Counties
URL: www.cvcky.org

Kentucky Highlands Investment Corporation

362 Old Whitley Road
P.O. Box 1738
London, KY 40743-1738
Executive Director: Jerry Rickett
Microloan Contact: Cindy Bowles
E-mail: cbowles@khic.org
Phone: (606) 864-5175
Fax: (606) 864-5194

Service Area: Bell, Clay, Clinton, Cumberland, Estill, Harlan, Jackson, Knox, Laurel, Lee, Leslie, Letcher, Lincoln, Madison, McCreary, Owsley, Perry, Pulaski, Rockcastle, Russell, Wayne, and Whitley Counties
URL: www.khic.org

Louisville Central Development Corporation/Business Plus
1407 West Jefferson Street, Suite 200
Louisville, KY 40203
Executive Director: Sam Watkins Jr.
Microloan Contact: Kirk Bright
E-mail: NA
Phone: (502) 583-8821
Fax: (502) 589-1173
Service Area: Jefferson County—Primary focus: Enterprise Empowerment Zone
URL: NA

Purchase Area Development District
1002 Medical Drive
P.O. Box 588
Mayfield, KY 42066
Executive Director: Henry Hodges
Microloan Contact: Norma Reed Prouitt
E-mail: henry.hodges@mail.state.ky.us, webmaster@purchaseadd.org
Phone: (270) 247-7171
Fax: (270) 251-6110
Service Area: Ballard, Calloway, Carlisle, Fulton, Graves, Hickman, McCracken, and Marshall Counties
URL: www.purchaseadd.org

Louisiana
Newcorp Business Assistance Center
1600 Canal Street, Suite 601
New Orleans, LA 70112

Executive Director: Vaughn R. Fauria
Microloan Contact: Romona D. Summers
Phone: (504) 539-9340
Fax: (504) 539-9343
E-mail: newcorpinfo@newcorpbac.net
Service Area: Louisiana
URL: www.newcorpbac.net

Maine
Androscoggin Valley Council of Governments
125 Manley Road
Auburn, ME 04210
Executive Director: Robert J. Thompson
Microloan Contact: Greg Whitney
E-mail: gwhitney@avcog.org, avcog@avcog.org
Phone: (207) 783-9186
Fax: (207) 783-5211
Service Area: Androscoggin, Franklin, and Oxford Counties
URL: www.avcog.org

Coastal Enterprises Inc.
36 Water Street
P.O. Box 268
Wiscasset, ME 04578
Executive Director: Ronald Phillips
Microloan Contact: Michael Finnegan
E-mail: jgs@ceimaine.org, cei@ceimaine.org
Phone: (207) 882-7552
Fax: (207) 882-7308
Service Area: Statewide excluding Aroostock, Piscataquis, Washington, Oxford, Penobscot, and Hancock Counties
URL: www.ceimaine.org

Community Concepts Inc.
17-19 Market Square
P.O. Box 278
South Paris, ME 04281
Executive Director: Charleen Chase
Microloan Contact: Walter Riseman
E-mail: wriseman@community-con-
cepts.org, info@community-concepts.org
Phone: (207) 743-7716
Fax: (207) 743-6513
Service Area: Oxford County
URL: www.community-concepts.org

Northern Maine Development Commission
11 West Presque Isle Road
P.O. Box 779
Caribou, ME 04736
Executive Director: Robert Clark
Microloan Contact: Duane Walton
E-mail: rclark@nmdc.org,
dwalton@nmdc.org
Phone: (207) 498-8736, (800) 427-8736
(in state)
Fax: (207) 493-3108
Service Area: Aroostook
URL: www.nmdc.org

Eastern Maine Development Corporation
40 Harlow Street
Bangor, ME 04401
Executive Director: Jonathan Daniels
Microloan Contact: NA
E-mail: jdaniels@emdc.org,
lending@emdc.org, info@emdc.org
Phone: (207) 942-6389
Fax: (207) 942-3548
Service Area: Hancock, Penobscot,
Piscataquis, and Washington Counties
URL: www.emdc.org

Maryland

H Street Community Development Corporation
501 H Street, NE
Washington, DC 20002
Executive Director: William Barrow
Microloan Contact: Yulonda Queen
E-mail: yulonda.queen@hstreetcdc.org
Phone: (202) 544-8353
Fax: (202) 544-3051
Service Area: Montgomery and Prince
George's Counties
URL: www.hstreetcdc.org

Enterprise Development Group
1038 South Highland Street
Arlington, VA 22204
Executive Director: Tsehaye Teferra
Microloan Contact: Michelle Wilson
E-mail: edgloan@entdevgroup.org
Phone: (703) 685-0510
Fax: (703) 685-4200
Service Area: Prince George's and
Montgomery Counties
URL: www.entdevgroup.org

Massachusetts

Transportation Lending Services
1341 G Street, NW, 10th Floor
Washington, DC 20005
Executive Director: Dale J. Marsico
Microloan Contact: Patrick Kellogg
E-mail: kellogg@ctaa.org
Phone: (202) 415-9682
Fax: (202) 737-9197
Service Area: North Central
Massachusetts—county subdivisions of
Athol, Winchendon, Gardner,
Templeton, Phillipston, Orange, Erving,

Wendell, Montague, Gill, and Greenfield Counties
URL: www.ctaa.org/transitfunding/

Dorchester Bay Economic Development Corporation
594 Columbia Road, Suite 302
Dorchester, MA 02125
Executive Director: Cristo R. Banda
Microloan Contact: Cristo R. Banda
E-mail: cbanda@dbedc.com
Phone: (617) 825-4200
Fax: (617) 825-3522
Service Area: Suffolk and Norfolk Counties
URL: www.dbedc.com

Economic Development Industrial Corporation of Lynn
3 City Hall Square, Room 307
Lynn, MA 01901
Executive Director: Peter M. DeVeau
Microloan Contact: Peter M. DeVeau
E-mail: pdeveau@shore.net
Phone: (781) 581-9399
Fax: (781) 581-9731
Service Area: City of Lynn
URL: www.lynndevelopment.com/edic_home.htm

Jewish Vocational Service Inc.
29 Winter Street
Boston, MA 02108-4799
Executive Director: Barbara Rosenbaum
Microloan Contact: Erik Korsh
E-mail: ekorsh@jvs-boston.org
Phone: (617) 451-8147
Fax: (617) 451-9973
Service Area: Greater Boston with special emphasis on businesses in the Boston Enterprise Zone / Boston Empowerment

Zone, and businesses in Mattapan, Dorchester, Roxbury, Hyde Park, and Jamaica Plain
URL: www.jvs-boston.org

Jobs for Fall River Inc./Fall River Office of Economic Development
1 Government Center
Fall River, MA 02722-7700
Executive Director: Kenneth Fiola
Microloan Contact: Stephen Parr
E-mail: info@froed.org
Phone: (508) 324-2620
Fax: (508) 677-2840
Service Area: City of Fall River
URL: www.froed.org

South Eastern Economic Development (SEED) Corportation
80 Dean Street
Taunton, MA 02780
Executive Director: Maria Gooch-Smith
Microloan Contact: Laurie Walsh
E-mail: info@seedcorp.com
Phone: (508) 822-1020
Fax: (508) 880-7869
Service Area: SE Massachusetts—Norfolk, Bristol, Plymouth, Barnstable, Dukes, and Nantucket Counties
URL: www.seedcorp.com

Western Massachusetts Enterprise Fund, Inc.
308 Main Street
P.O Box 1077
Greenfield, MA 01302
Executive Director: Christopher Sikes
Microloan Contact: Moon Morgan
E-mail: loaninfo@wmef.org
Phone: (413) 774-4033
Fax: (413) 774-3673

Service Area: Berkshire, Franklin Counties, the towns of Chester and Chicopes within Hampden County, Springfield, the towns of Athol, Petersham, Phillipston, and Royalston within Worcester County and Hampshire County
URL: www.wmef.org

Michigan

The Center for Empowerment and Economic Development (CEED)
2002 Hogback Road, Suite 12
Ann Arbor, MI 48105
Executive Director: Michelle Richards
Microloan Contact: Michelle Richards
E-mail: info@miceed.org
Phone: (734) 677-1400
Fax: (734) 677-1465
Service Area: Washtenaw, Oakland, Wayne, Macomb, Lenawee, Jackson, Hillsdale, Monroe, and Livingston Counties
URL: www.miceed.org

Community Capital Development Corporation (MI)
805 Welch Boulevard
Flint, MI 48504
Executive Director: Harold Hill
Microloan Contact: Jatasha Washington
E-mail: ccdc@tir.com
Phone: (810) 239-5847
Fax: (810) 239-5575
Service Area: Genesee County
URL: NA

Kent Area MicroBusiness Loan Services
233 East Fulton Street, Suite 101
Grand Rapids, MI 49503

Executive Director: Edward L. Garner
Microloan Contact: Edward L. Garner
E-mail: NA
Phone: (616) 771-6880
Fax: (616) 771-8021
Service Area: Kent County
URL: NA

Northern Initiatives (Northern Economic Initiative Corporation)
University Center
Northern Michigan University
Marquette, MI 49855
P.O. Box 7009
Marquette, MI 49855
Executive Director: Dennis West
Microloan Contact: Todd Horton
E-mail: dwest@niupnorth.org, thorton@niupnorth.org
Phone: (906) 228-5571, (800) 254-2156
Fax: (906) 228-5572
Service Area: Upper Peninsula of Michigan
URL: www.niupnorth.org

Rural Michigan Intermediary Relending Program, Inc.
121 East Front Street, Suite 201
Traverse City, MI 49686
Executive Director: Michael Haddad
Microloan Contact: Stephen Spencer
E-mail: mhaddad@timbc.com
Phone: (231) 941-5858
Fax: (231) 941-4616
Service Area: Emmet, Charlevoix, Antrim, Leelanau, Benzie, Grand, Traverse, Kalkaska, Manistee, Wexford, Missaukee, Cheboygan, Presque Isle, Otsego, Montmorency, Alpena, Crawford, Oscoda, Alcona,

Roscommon, Ogemaw, Iosco, Osceola, Mason, and Lake Counties
URL: NA

Saginaw Economic Development Corporation
301 E. Genesee, 3rd Floor
Saginaw, MI 48607
Executive Director: Leslie Weaver
Microloan Contact: Leslie Weaver
E-mail: SEDCLW@aol.com
Phone: (989) 759-1395
Fax: (989) 754-1715, (989) **759-1734**
Service Area: Saginaw County
URL: NA

Minnesota

Minneapolis Consortium of Community Developers
3137 Chicago Avenue
Minneapolis, MN 55407
Executive Director: Jim Roth
Microloan Contact: Dave Chapman
E-mail: jroth@mccdmn.org, dchapman@mccdmn.org, info@mccdmn.org
Phone: (612) 789-7337
Fax: (612) 822-1489
Service Area: Portions of the City of Minneapolis
URL: www.mccdmn.org

Southern Minnesota Initiative Foundation
525 Florence Avenue
P.O. Box 695
Owatonna, MN 55060-0695
Executive Director: Carol Cerney
Microloan Contact: Diane Lewis
E-mail: dianel@smifoundation.org
Phone: (507) 455-3215
Fax: (507) 455-2098

Service Area: Sibley, Nicollett, LeSueur, Rice, Wabasha, Brown, Watonwan, Blue Earth, Waseca, Dodge, Olmsted, Winona, Martin, Faribault, Freeborn, Mower, Fillmore, and Houston
URL: www.smifoundation.org

Southwest Initiative Foundation (formerly Southwest Minnesota Foundation)
15 3rd Avenue NW
P.O. Box 428
Hutchinson, MN 55350
Executive Director: Sherry Ristau
Microloan Contact: Bernadette Berger
E-mail: sherryr@swifoundation.org, bernyb@swifoundation.com, info@swifoundation.org
Phone: (320) 587-4848, (800) 594-9480
Fax: (320) 587-3838
Service Area: 18 counties of Southwest Minnesota—Big Stone, Chippewa, Cottonwood, Jackson, Kandiyphi, Lac qui Parle, Lincoln, Lyon, McLeod, Meeker, Murray, Nobles, Pipestone, Renville, Rock, Swift, and Yellow Medicine
URL: www.swifoundation.com

Northeast Entrepreneur Fund, Inc.
8355 Unity Drive, Suite 100
Virginia, MN 55792
Executive Director: Mary Mathews
Microloan Contact: Bob Voss
E-mail: info@entrepreneurfund.org
Phone: (218) 749-4191 or (800) 422-0374
Fax: (218) 749-5213
Service Area: Aitkin, Carlton, Cook, Itasca, Koochiching, Lake, Cass, Pine, and St. Louis Counties
URL: www.entrepreneurfund.org

Northwest Minnesota Foundation

4225 Technology Drive, NW
Bemidji, MN 56601
Executive Director: John Ostrem
Microloan Contact: Tim Wang
E-mail: johno@nwmf.org,
timw@nwmf.org, nwmf@nwmf.org
Phone: (218) 759-2057, (800) 659-7859
(in state)
Fax: (218) 759-2328
Service Area: Beltrami, Clearwater,
Hubbard, Kittsson, Lake of the Woods,
Mahnomen, Marshall, Norman,
Pennington, Polk, Red Lake, and
Rousseau Counties
URL: www.nwmf.org

WomenVenture

2324 University Avenue, W, Suite 200
St. Paul, MN 55114
Executive Director: Tené Wells
Microloan Contact: Heidi Pliam
E-mail: hpliam@womenventure.org
Phone: (651) 646-3808
Fax: (651) 641-7223
Service Area: Cities of Minneapolis and
St. Paul and, Anoka, Carver, Chisago,
Dakota, Hennepin, Isanti, Ramsey, Scott,
Washington, Steele, and Wright Counties
URL: www.womenventure.org

Mississippi

Friends of Children of Mississippi, Inc.

939 North President Street
Jackson, MS 39202
Executive Director: Marvin Hogan
Microloan Contact: Stephanie Williams
E-mail: eagleeye@misnet.com
Phone: (601) 353-3264

Fax: (601) 714-4278
Service Area: Mississippi
URL: NA

Missouri

Growth Opportunity Connection (Go Connection)

4747 Troost Avenue, Suite 211
Kansas City, MO 64110
Executive Director: Alan Corbet
Microloan Contact: Rebecca Gubbels
E-mail: info@goconnection.org
Phone: (816) 235-6146
Fax: (816) 235-6586
Service Area: Platte, Jackson, Clay, and
Cass Counties
URL: www.goconnection.org

Justine Petersen Housing and Reinvestment Corporation

5031 Northrup Avenue
St. Louis, MO 63110
Executive Director: Robert Boyle
Microloan Contact: Sheri Flanigan-
Vazquez
E-mail: rboyle@justinepetersen.org,
sflanigan@justinepetersen.org
Phone: (314) 664-5051 x 117
Fax: (314) 664-5364
Service Area: Counties of Franklin,
Jefferson, Lincoln, St. Charles, St. Louis,
Warren, and the City of St. Louis
URL: www.justinepetersen.org

Resources for Missouri, Inc. (formerly Rural Missouri, Inc.)

1014 Northeast Drive
Jefferson City, MO 65109
Executive Director: Ken Lueckenotte
Microloan Contact: Zola Finch

E-mail: ken@rmiinc.org, zola@rmiinc.org
Phone: (573) 635-0136, (800) 234-4971
Fax: (573) 635-5636
Service Area: Statewide excluding Platte, Jackson, Clay, and Cass Counties
URL: www.rmiinc.org

Montana

Montana Community Development Corporation

110 East Broadway, 2nd Floor
Missoula, MT 59802
Executive Director: Rosalie Sheehy Cates
Microloan Contact: Brad Fredericks
E-mail: rcates@mtcdc.org, bfredericks@mtcdc.org, info@mtcdc.org
Phone: (406) 728-9234
Fax: (406) 542-6671
Service Area: Lake, Mineral, Missoula, Ravalli, and Sanders Counties
URL: www.mtcdc.org

Nebraska

Rural Enterprise Assistance Project (REAP)–Center for Rural Affairs

145 Main Street
P.O. Box 136
Lyons, NE 68038
Executive Director: Chuck Hassebrook
Microloan Contact: Peggy Mahaney
E-mail: chuckh@cfra.org, peggym@cfra.org, info@cfra.org
Phone: (402) 687-2100
Fax: (402) 687-2200
Service Area: Adams, Antelope, Arthur, Banner, Blaine, Boone, Box Butte, Boyd, Brown, Buffalo, Burt, Butler, Cass, Cedar, Chase, Cherry, Cheyenne, Clay, Colfax, Cuming, Custer, Dakota, Dawes, Dawson, Deuel, Dixon, Dodge, Douglas, Dundy, Fillmore, Franklin, Frontier, Furnas, Gage, Garden, Garfield, Greeley, Hall, Hamilton, Harlan, Hayes, Hitchcock, Holt, Hooker, Howard, Jefferson, Johnson, Kearney, Keith, Keya Paha, Kimball, Knox, Lancaster, Lincoln, Logan, Loup, Madison, McPherson, Merrick, Morrill, Nance, Nemaha, Nuckolls, Otoe, Pawnee, Perkins, Phelps, Pierce, Platte, Polk, Red Willow, Richardson, Rock, Saline, Sarpy, Saunders, Scottsbluff, Seward, Sheridan, Sherman, Sioux, Stanton, Thayer, Thomas, Thurston, Valley, Washington, Wayne, Webster, Wheeler, and York Counties
URL: www.cfra.org

West Central Nebraska Development District, Inc.

201 East 2nd Street, Suite C
P.O. Box 599
Ogallala, NE 69153
Executive Director: Martin O'Haus
Microloan Contact: Paul Rausch
E-mail: mowcndd@lakemac.net
Phone: (308) 284-6077
Fax: (308) 284-6070
Service Area: Arthur, Chase, Dawson, Dundy, Frontier, Furnas, Gosper, Grant, Hayes, Hitchcock, Hooker, Keith, Lincoln, Logan, Perkins, Red Willow, Thomas, and McPherson Counties
URL: NA

Community Development Resources (NE)

285 S. 68th Street Place, Suite 520
Lincoln, NE 68510

Executive Director: Rick Wallace
Microloan Contact: Brad From
E-mail: rwallace@cdr-nebraska.org
Phone: (402) 436-2386
Fax: (402) 436-2439
Service Area: Lancaster and Lincoln
Counties
URL: www.cdr-nebraska.org

Nevada

Nevada Microenterprise Initiative
113 West Plumb Lane
Reno, NV 89509
Phone: (775) 324-1812
Fax: (775) 324-1813
Executive Director: NA
Microloan Contact: **Tamra Arellano**
E-mail: tarellano@4microbiz.org,
info@4microbiz.org
1600 E. Desert Inn Road, Suite 203
Las Vegas, NV 89109
Phone: (702) 734-3555
Fax: (702) 734-3530
Executive Director: NA
Microloan Contact: Anna Siefert
E-mail: asiefert@4microbiz.org,
info@4microbiz.org
Service Area: Nevada
URL: www.4microbiz.org

New Hampshire

Northern Community Investment Corporation
347 Portland Street
P.O. Box 904
St. Johnsbury, VT 05819
Executive Director: NA
Microloan Contact: Suzanne L. Roberts

E-mail: suzanne@ncic.org, ncic@ncic.org
Phone: (802) 748-5101
Fax: (802) 748-1884
Service Area: Grafton, Carroll, and Coos
Counties
URL: www.ncic.org

New Jersey

Regional Business Assistance Corporation
247 East Front Street
Trenton, NJ 08611
Executive Director: William Pazmino
Microloan Contact: NA
E-mail: info@rbacloan.com
Phone: (609) 396-2595, (866) 396-2595
Fax: (609) 396-2598
Service Area: Bergen, Burlington,
Hunterdon, Mercer, Middlesex,
Monmouth, Morris, Somerset, Sussex,
and Warren Counties
URL: www.rbacloan.com

Greater Newark Business Development Consortium, Inc.
744 Broad Street, 26th Floor
Newark, NJ 07102-3802
Executive Director: Mark L. Quinn
Microloan Contact: Desiree Sealey
E-mail: dsealey@gnbdc.org,
staff@gnbdc.org
Phone: (973) 242-4134
Fax: NA
Service Area: New Jersey
URL: www.gnbdc.org

UCEDC
Liberty Hall Corporate Center
1085 Morris Avenue, Suite 531
Union, NJ 07083
Executive Director: Maureen Tinen

Microloan Contact: Ellen McHenry
E-mail: emchenry@ucedc.com,
info@ucedc.com
Phone: (908) 527-1166
Fax: (908) 527-1207
Service Area: New Jersey
URL: www.ucedc.com

Cooperative Business Assistance Corporation

328 Market Street
Camden, NJ 08102
Executive Director: R. Michael Diemer
Microloan Contact: Harry W. Stone, CPA
E-mail: info@cbaclenders.com
Phone: (856) 966-8181
Fax: (856) 966-0036
Service Area: Atlantic, Camden, Cape May, Cumberland, Gloucester, and Salem Counties
URL: www.cbaclenders.com

New Mexico

Women's Economic Self-Sufficiency Team

414 Silver SW
Albuquerque, NM 87102-3239
Executive Director: Agnes Noonan
Microloan Contact: Debbie Baca
E-mail: albuquerquehq@wesst.org
Phone: (505) 241-4753, (800) GO.WESST (469-3778)
Fax: (505) 241-4766
Service Area: New Mexico
URL: www.wesst.org

New York

Adirondack Economic Development Corporation

60 Main Street, Suite 200
P.O. Box 747
Saranac Lake, NY 12983-0747
Executive Director: Ernest Hohmeyer
Microloan Contact: Beverly Deso
E-mail: beverly@aedconline.com,
info@AEDConline.com
Phone: (518) 891-5523, (888)-243-AEDC (2332)
Fax: (518) 891-9820
Service Area: Clinton, Essex, Franklin, Fulton, Hamilton, Herkimer, Jefferson, Lewis, Oneida, Oswego, St. Lawrence, Saratoga, Warren, and Washington Counties
URL: www.aedconline.com

Alternatives Federal Credit Union

125 N. Fulton Street
Ithaca, NY 14850
Executive Director: William Myers
Microloan Contact: Michael Culotta
E-mail: michael@alternatives.org,
afcu@alternatives.org
Phone: (607) 273-4611, (877) 273-AFCU (2328)
Fax: (607) 277-6391
Service Area: Schuyler, Tompkins, Tioga, Cortland, Chemung, and Broome Counties
URL: www.alternatives.org

Buffalo Economic Renaissance Corporation (BERC)

Office of Strategic Planning
920 City Hall
Buffalo, NY 14202
Executive Director: Timothy E. Wanamaker
Microloan Contact: Marie F. Currie

E-mail: mcurrie@berc.org
Phone: (716) 842-6923
Fax: (716) 842-6942
Service Area: City of Buffalo
URL: www.berc.org

Buffalo and Erie County Industrial Land Development Corporation

275 Oak Street
Buffalo, NY 14203
Executive Director: Charles E. Webb
Microloan Contact: David Kerchoff
E-mail: dkerchof@ecidany.com, info@ecidany.com
Phone: (716) 856-6525
Fax: (716) 856-6754
Service Area: Erie County
URL: www.ecidany.com

Columbia Hudson Partnership (Hudson Development Corporation)

444 Warren Street
Hudson, NY 12534-2415
Executive Director: James P. Galvin
Microloan Contact: NA
E-mail: partner@chpartnership.com
Phone: (518) 828-4718
Fax: (518) 828-0901
Service Area: Columbia and Green Counties
URL: www.chpartnership.com

Community Development Corporation of Long Island

2100 Middle Country Road, Suite 300
Centereach, NY 11720-3576
Executive Director: Wilbur Klatsky
Microloan Contact: Trevor E. Davis
E-mail: tdavis@cdcli.org
Phone: (631) 471-1215
Fax: (631) 471-1210

Service Area: Suffolk and Nassau Counties
URL: www.cdcli.org

Manhattan Borough Development Corporation

55 John Street, Suite 1701
New York, NY 10038
Executive Director: Ollie Chapman
Microloan Contact: David Gale
E-mail: NA
Phone: (212) 791-3660
Fax: (212) 571-0873
Service Area: Borough of Manhattan
URL: NA

Albany-Colonie Regional Chamber of Commerce

107 Washington Avenue
Albany, NY 12210-2200
Executive Director: Lyn Taylor
Microloan Contact: Walter Burke
E-mail: walterb@ac-chamber.org, info@ac-chamber.org
Phone: (518) 431-1400, (518) 453-5223 (Walter Burke)
Fax: (518) 431-1339
Service Area: Albany, Rensselaer, Saratoga, Schenectady, Schoharie, Greene, Fulton, and Montgomery Counties
URL: ac-chamber.org

New York Association for New Americans, Inc.

17 Battery Place
New York, NY 10004-1102
Executive Director: Yanki Tshering
Microloan Contact: Leonid Ostrovsky
E-mail: ytshering@nyana.org, lostrovsky@nyana.org

207

Phone: (212) 898-4112, (212) 425-2900
Fax: (212) 425-7260
Service Area: Borough of Queens,
Manhattan, the Bronx, Brooklyn, and
Staten Island
URL: nyana.org

Renaissance Economic Development Corporation
1 Pike Street
New York, NY 10002
Executive Director: Benjamin Warnke
Microloan Contact: Susan Yee
E-mail: benjamin@renaissance-ny.org,
info@renaissance-ny.org
Phone: (212) 964-6002
Fax: (212) 964- 6003
Service Area: Boroughs of Brooklyn,
Manhattan, and Queens
URL: renaissance-ny.org

Rural Opportunities Enterprise Center, Inc.
400 East Avenue
Rochester, NY 14607
Executive Director: Stuart J. Mitchell
Microloan Contact: Lee Beaulac
E-mail: lbeaulac@ruralinc.org
Phone: (585) 340-3387, (585) 340-3705
Fax: (585) 340-3326
Service Area: Onandaga, Ulster, Monroe,
Schuyler, Chemung, Allegheny,
Cattaraugus, Cayuga, Chatauqua,
Dutchess, Erie, Genessee, Greene,
Livingston, Niagara, Ontario, Orange,
Orleans, Putnam, Seneca, Steuben,
Sullivan, Wayne, Wyoming, and Yates
Counties
URL: www.ruralinc.org

North Carolina

Neuse River Development Authority, Inc.
233 Middle Street, Suite 206
P.O. Box 111
New Bern, NC 28563
Executive Director: Donald T. Stewart
Microloan Contact: Larry Riter
E-mail: lriter@nrda.org, info@nrda.org
Phone: (252) 638-6724
Fax: (252) 638-1819
Service Area: Carteret, Craven, Duplin,
Greene, Jones, Johnston, Lenoir, Onslow,
Pamlico, and Wayne Counties
URL: www.nrda.org

Self-Help Ventures Fund
301 West Main Street
P.O. Box 3619
Durham, NC 27702-3619
Executive Director: Martin Eakes
Microloan Contact: Annie Scorza
E-mail: bob@self-help.org
Phone: (919) 956-4400, (800) 476-7428
Fax: (919) 956-4600
Service Area: Statewide excluding
Watauga, Avery, Mitchell, and Yancey
Counties
URL: www.self-help.org

W.A.M.Y. Community Action, Inc.
152 Southgate Drive, Suite 2
P.O. Box 2688
Boone, NC 28607
Executive Director: Angela Miller
Microloan Contact: Dave Lindsey
E-mail: wamyloan@boone.net
Phone: (828) 264-2421, (828) 765-9123
(Dave Lindsey)
Fax: (828) 264-0952
Service Area: Watauga, Avery, Mitchell,

and Yancey Counties
URL: www.wamyca.org

North Dakota

Dakota Certified Development Corporation

51 Broadway, Suite 500
Fargo, ND 58102
Executive Director: Toby Sticka
Microloan Contact: Justin Pearson
E-mail: toby@dakotacdc.com,
justin@dakotacdc.com, info@dako-
tacdc.com
Phone: (701) 293-8892
Fax: (701) 293-7819
Service Area: Grand Forks, Devils Lake,
Minot, Williston, and Dickinson
Counties
URL: www.dakotacdc.com

Lake Agassiz Regional Development Corporation

417 Main Avenue
Fargo, ND 58103
Executive Director: Irvin D. Rustad
Microloan Contact: Darin Bullinger
E-mail: info@lakeagassiz.com
Phone: (701) 235-1197
Fax: (701) 235-6706
Service Area: Griggs, Bismarck, Mandan,
Jamestown, and Valley City
URL: www.lakeagassiz.com/lardc/lardc-
main.html

Ohio

Community Capital Development Corporation (OH)

900 Michigan Avenue
Columbus, OH 43215-1165

Executive Director: Brad Shimp
Microloan Contact: Stephanie Mendivil
E-mail: brad.shimp@ccdcorp.org, ste-
fanie.mendivil@ccdcorp.org
Phone: (614) 645-0387
Fax: (614) 645-8588
Service Area: Franklin, Delaware,
Fairfield, Licking, Union, Pickaway,
Fayette, and Madison Counties
URL: www.ccdcorp.org

Enterprise Development Corporation

9030 Hocking Hills Drive
The Plains, OH 45780-1209
Executive Director: Gary Seeley
Microloan Contact: NA
E-mail: gseeley@edcseo.org, edcseo@edc-
seo.org
Phone: (740) 797-9646, (800) 822-6096
Fax: (740) 797-9659
Service Area: Adams, Ashland, Athens,
Belmont, Brown, Carroll, Columbiana,
Coshocton, Gallia, Guernsey, Harrison,
Highland, Holmes, Jackson, Jefferson,
Knox, Lawrence, Meigs, Monroe,
Morgan, Muskingum, Hocking, Noble,
Perry, Pike, Ross, Scioto, Tuscarawas,
Vinton, and Washington Counties
URL: www.edcseo.org

Hamilton County Development Company, Inc.

1776 Mentor Avenue
Cincinnati, OH 45212
Executive Director: David K. Main
Microloan Contact: Andrew Young
E-mail: maind@hcdc.com,
lawalden@hcdc.com
Phone: (513) 631-8292, (888) 504-
HCDC (4232)

Fax: (513) 631-4887
Service Area: City of Cincinnati, Adams, Brown, Butler, Clermont, Clinton, Hamilton, Warren, and Highland Counties
URL: www.hcdc.com

Kent Regional Business Alliance (OH)
Room 300-A
College of Business Administration
Kent State University
Kent, OH 44242-0001
Executive Director: Linda Yost
Microloan Contact: NA
E-mail: loans@krba.biz, krba@krba.biz
Phone: (330) 672-1275
Fax: (330) 672-9338
Service Area: Ashtabula, Geauga, Trumbull, Portage, Columbiana, Carroll, Holmes, Coshocton, Tuscarawas, Stark, and Harrison Counties
URL: www.krba.biz

Women's Network (Women's Organization for Mentoring, Entrepreneurship, and Networking)
526 South Main Street, Suite 235
Akron, OH 44311-1058
Executive Director: Janice Robinson
Microloan Contact: NA
E-mail: women@ald.net
Phone: (330) 379-9280, (330) 379-2772
Fax: (330) 379-3454, (330) 379-9283
Service Area: Cuyahoga, Lake, Lorain, Mahoning, Medina, Stark, Summit, and Wayne Counties
URL: NA

WECO Fund, Inc.
WECO Building
1745 Rockwell Avenue

Cleveland, OH 44104
Executive Director: Christine Henry
Microloan Contact: Bob Schordock
E-mail: bob@wecofund.com
Phone: (216) 458-0250
Fax: (216) 458-0257
Service Area: Cuyahoga County
URL: www.wecofund.com

Oklahoma

Greenwood Community Development
131 North Greenwood Avenue, 2nd Floor
Tulsa, OK 74120
Executive Director: Reuben Gant
Microloan Contact: Lamar Guillory
E-mail: rgant@tulsacoxmail.com
Phone: (918) 585-2084
Fax: (918) 585-9268
Service Area: Northwest Tulsa County
URL: NA

Little Dixie Community Action
209 N. 4th Street
Hugo, OK 74743
Executive Director: Randall Erwin
Microloan Contact: Tommy Butler
E-mail: rerwin@littledixie.org, tbutler@littledixie.org
Phone: (580) 326-3351
Fax: (580) 326-2305
Service Area: Choctaw, McCurtain, and Pushmataha Counties
URL: www.littledixie.org

Rural Enterprises of Oklahoma, Inc.
2912 Enterprise Boulevard
P.O. Box 1335

Durant, OK 74702
Executive Director: Tom Seth Smith
Microloan Contact: Debbie Partin
E-mail: tomsmith@ruralenterprises.com,
debbiep@ruralenterprises.com
Phone: (580) 924-5094, (800) 658-2823
Fax: (580) 920-2745
Service Area: Statewide excluding Adair,
Canadian, Cherokee, Cleveland, Craig,
Creek, Delaware, Haskell, Hayes,
Hughes, Kay, Latimer, Leflore, Lincoln,
Logan, McIntosh, Muskogee, Noble,
Nowata, Okfuskee, Oklahoma,
Okmulgee, Osage, Ottawa, Pawnee,
Payne, Pittsburg, Pottawatomie, Rogers,
Seminole, Sequoyah, Wagoner,
Washington, and Wayne Counties includ-
ing the city of Tulsa
URL: www.ruralenterprises.com

Tulsa Economic Development Corporation
907 South Detroit Avenue, Suite 1001
Tulsa, OK 74120
Executive Director: Rose M. Washington
Microloan Contact: Peggy L. Prudom
E-mail: rose@tulsaedc.com, peggy@tul-
saedc.com
Phone: (918) 585-8332
Fax: (918) 585-2473
Service Area: Adair, Canadian, Cherokee,
Cleveland, Craig, Creek, Delaware,
Haskell, Hughes, Kay, Latimer, Leflore,
Lincoln, Logan, McIntosh, Muskogee,
Noble, Nowata, Okfuskee, Oklahoma,
Okmulgee, Osage, Ottawa, Pawnee,
Payne, Pittsburg, Pottawatomie, Rogers,
Seminole, Sequoyah, Wagoner, and
Washington Counties including the city
of Tulsa

URL: www.www.tulsaedc.com

Oregon

Cascades West Financial Services, Inc.
1400 Queen Avenue SE, Suite 205-C
Albany, OR 97222
Executive Director: Jim Kaitschuck
Microloan Contact: Brenda Baze
E-mail: jkaitsch@ocwcog.org,
bbaze@ocwcog.org
Phone: (541) 967-8551
Fax: (541) 967-4651
Service Area: Benton, Lane, Lincoln,
Linn, Marion, Polk, and Yamhill
Counties
URL: www.cascadeswest.com

**SOWAC Microenterprise Development
Center** (formerly Southern Oregon
Women's Access to Credit, Inc.)
33 North Central #418
Medford, OR 97501
Executive Director: NA
Microloan Contact: Dennis Davis
E-mail: dpdavis@sowac.org
Phone: (541) 779-3992, (866) 608-6094
Fax: (541) 779-5195
Service Area: Jackson, Josephine,
Klamath, and Lake Counties
URL: www.sowac.org

**Oregon Association of Minority
Entrepreneurs Credit Corporation**
4134 N. Vancouver Avenue
Portland, OR 97217
Executive Director: Samuel Brooks
Microloan Contact: Sanford Maddox
E-mail: sanford@oame.org
Phone: (503) 249-7744
Fax: (503) 249-2027

Service Area: Multnomah, Washington, Clackamas, Columbia, Tillamook, Clatsop, and Hood Counties
URL: www.oame.org

Umpqua Community Development Corporation
738 SE Kane Street
Roseburg, OR 97470
Executive Director: Betty Tamm
Microloan Contact: Matt Morrow
E-mail: btamm@umpquacdc.org, mmorrow@umpquacdc.org
Phone: (541) 673-4909
Fax: (541) 673-5023
Service Area: Coos, Curry, and Douglas Counties
URL: www.umpquacdc.org

Pennsylvania

Aliquippa Alliance for Unity and Development
524 Franklin Avenue
Aliquippa, PA 15001
Executive Director: **Jonathan Pettis**
Microloan Contact: Patricia Kribbs
E-mail: jpettis@aaud.org, pkribbs@aaud.org
Phone: (724) 378-7422
Fax: (724) 378-9976
Service Area: Beaver, Butler, and Lawrence Counties
URL: www.aaud.org

Community First Fund
44 N Queen Street
P. O. Box 524
Lancaster, PA 17608-0524
Executive Director: Daniel Betancourt
Microloan Contact: Jim Hufford

E-mail: dbetancourt@commfirstfund.org, jhufford@commfirstfund.org
Phone: (717) 393-2351
Fax: (717) 393-1757
Service Area: Lancaster, York, Berks, Dauphin, Lebanon, Cumberland, Perry, and Adams Counties
URL: www.commfirstfund.org

Community Loan Fund of Southwestern Pennsylvania, Inc.
1920 Gulf Towers
707 Grant Street
Pittsburgh, PA 15219
Executive Director: Mark Peterson
Microloan Contact: Laura Swiss
E-mail: mpeterson@clfund.com, lswiss@clfund.com, info@clfund.com
Phone: (412) 201-2450
Fax: (412) 201-2451
Service Area: Allegheny, Armstrong, Beaver, Butler, and Indiana Counties
URL: www.clfund.com

Northeastern Pennsylvania Alliance
1151 Oak Street
Pittston, PA 18640-3795
Executive Director: Tom Pellegrini
Microloan Contact: John Wozniak
E-mail: tpellegrini@nepa-alliance.org, jwozniak@nepa-alliance.org, info@nepa-alliance.org
Phone: (570) 655-5581
Fax: (570) 654-5137
Service Area: Carbon, Lackawanna, Luzerne, Monroe, Pike, Schuylkill, and Wayne Counties
URL: www.nepa-alliance.org

MetroAction, Inc.
222 Mulberry Street

P.O. Box 431
Scranton, PA 18501-0431
Executive Director: Kristine Augustine
Microloan Contact: Christina Hitchcock
E-mail:
kaugustine@scrantonchamber.com,
chitchcock@scrantonchamber.com,
Phone: (570) 342-7711
Fax: (570) 347-6262
Service Area: Luzerne, Lackawanna, and
Monroe Counties
URL: www.metroaction.org

North Central Pennsylvania Regional Planning and Development Commission

651 Montmorenci Avenue
Ridgway, PA 15853
Executive Director: Howard Glessner
Microloan Contact: Patricia Brennan
E-mail: pbrennen@ncentral.com,
ncprpdc@ncentral.com
Phone: (814) 773-3162
Fax: (814) 772-7045
Service Area: Cameron, Clearfield, Elk,
Jefferson, McKean, and Potter Counties
URL: web2.ncentral.com/ncprpdc

Northwest Pennsylvania Regional Planning and Development Commission

395 Seneca Street
P.O. Box 1127
Oil City, PA 16301
Executive Director: Denise G.
McCloskey
Microloan Contact: Lynn E. Rough
E-mail: denisem@nwcommission.org,
lynnr@nwcommission.org,
nwinfo@nwcommission.org
Phone: (814) 677-4800
Fax: (814) 677-7663

Service Area: Clarion, Crawford, Erie,
Forest, Lawrence, Mercer, Warren, and
Venango Counties
URL: www.nwcommission.org

Philadelphia Commercial Development Corporation

1441 Sansom Street, Suite 300
Philadelphia, PA 19102
Executive Director: Curtis Jones, Jr.
Microloan Contact: NA
E-mail: econ@pcdc1.com
Phone: (215) 790-2200
Fax: (215) 790-2222
Service Area: Philadelphia
URL: www.philadelphiacommercial.com

SEDA-Council of Governments

201 Furnace Road
Lewisburg, PA 17837
Executive Director: Dennis E. Robinson
Microloan Contact: John K. Reichard
*E-mail: derobins@seda-cog.org,
reichard@seda-cog.org, admin@seda-cog.org*
Phone: (570) 524-4491
Fax: (570) 524-9190
Service Area: Centre, Clinton, Columbia,
Juniata, Lycoming, Mifflin, Montour,
Northumberland, Perry, Snyder, and
Union Counties
URL: www.seda-cog.org

Southern Alleghenies Planning and Development Commission

541 58th Street
Altoona, PA 16602
Executive Director: Edward M. Silvetti
Microloan Contact: Stephen Metzger
E-mail: metzger@sapdc.org,
sapdc@sapdc.org

Phone: (814) 949-6545
Fax: (814) 949-6505
Service Area: Bedford, Blair, Cambria,
Fulton, Huntingdon, and Somerset
Counties
URL: www.sapdc.org

Washington County Council on Economic Development
40 S. Main Street, Lower Level
Washington, PA 15301
Executive Director: Malcolm Morgan
Microloan Contact: Alan A. Hill
E-mail: wcced@pulsenet.com
Phone: (724) 225-8223
Fax: (724) 225-8202
Service Area: Southwestern area of
Pennsylvania—Greene, Fayette,
Washington, and Westmoreland
Counties—and Monongalia County in
West Virginia
URL: www.washingtoncountypa.org

Puerto Rico

Economic Development Corporation of San Juan (Corporación para el Fomento
Económico de la Ciudad Capital,
COFECC)
1103 Avenida Muñoz Rivera
P.O. Box 191791
Río Piedras, PR 00926
P.O. Box 191791
San Juan PR
00919-1791
Executive Director: Giovanna Piovanetti
Microloan Contact: Giovanna Piovanetti
E-mail: gpiovanetti@cofecc.net,
cofecc@cofecc.net
Phone: (787) 756-5080, (787) 753-4585

Fax: (787) 753-8960
Service Area: Puerto Rico
URL: www.cofecc.net

Rhode Island

Rhode Island Coalition for Minority Investment
216 Weybosset Street, 2nd Floor
Providence, RI 02903
Executive Director: Denise A. Barge
Microloan Contact: Karriem Kanston
E-mail: dbarge@midcri.com,
kkanston@midcri.com, ricmi.info@mid-cri.com
Phone: (401) 351-2999
Fax: (401) 351-0990
Service Area: Rhode Island
URL: www.midcri.com/ricmi.htm

South Carolina

Business Carolina, Inc.
1441 Main Street, Suite 900
Columbia, SC 29201
Executive Director: Mike Sandusky
Microloan Contact: Ed Kesser
E-mail: msandusky@businesscarolina.net,
ekesser@businesscarolina.net
Phone: (803) 461-3801, (800) 756-4353
Fax: (803) 461-3826
Service Area: Abbeville, Aiken,
Allendale, Anderson, Bamberg, Barnwell,
Beaufort, Berkeley, Calhoun, Charleston,
Cherokee, Chester, Chesterfield,
Colleton, Darlington, Dillon, Dorchester,
Edgefield, Fairfield, Florence,
Georgetown, Greenville, Greenwood,
Hampton, Horry, Jasper, Lancaster,
Laurens, Lexington, Marion, Marlboro,
McCormick, Newberry, Oconee,

Orangeburg, Pickens, Richland, Saluda, Spartanburg, Union, and York Counties
URL: www.businesscarolina.net

Charleston Citywide Local Development Corporation

75 Calhoun Street, 3rd Floor
Charleston, SC 29401
Executive Director: Sharon Brennan
Microloan Contact: Patrick King
E-mail: brennans@ci.charleston.sc.us, kingp@ci.charleston.sc.us
Phone: (843) 724-3796
Fax: (843) 724-7354
Service Area: City of Charleston
URL: www.ci.charleston.sc.us

Santee-Lynches Regional Development Corporation

36 West Liberty Street
P.O. Box 1837
Sumter, SC 29150
Executive Director: James Darby Jr.
Microloan Contact: Walter Dunlap
E-mail: slrdc@slcog.org
Phone: (803) 775-7381
Fax: (803) 773-9903
Service Area: Clarendon, Kershaw, Lee, and Sumter Counties
URL: www.slcog.state.sc.us/depart.html

South Dakota

Lakota Fund

Trade Center
P.O. Box 340
Kyle, SD 57752
Executive Director: Dowell Caselli-Smith
Microloan Contact: Tony Taylor
E-mail: dsmith@lakotafund.org, ttaylor@lakotafund.org
Phone: (605) 455-2500
Fax: (605) 455-2585
Service Area: Bennett County, Pine Ridge Indian Reservation, and areas of Shannon and Jackson Counties that are surrounded by Indian Lands, and exclusive of Northern Jackson County
URL: www.lakotafund.org

Tennessee

Economic Ventures, Inc.

1545 Western Avenue, Suite 110
Knoxville, TN 37921
Executive Director: Allison Sousa
Microloan Contact: Vicki Riggs
E-mail: NA
Phone: (865) 524-0360
Fax: (865) 524-3437
Service Area: Anderson, Blount, Campbell, Clairborne, Cocke, Grainger, Hamblen, Jefferson, Knox, Loudon, Monroe, Morgan Roane, Scott, Sevier, Union, Greene, Hancock, Hawkins, Sullivan, Washington, Johnson, Carter, and Unicoi Counties
URL: NA

LeMoyne-Owen College Community Development Corporation

802 Walker Avenue, Suite 5
Memphis, TN 38126
Executive Director: Jeffrey T. Higgs
Microloan Contact: Austin Emeagwai
E-mail: contact@loccdc.org
Phone: (901) 508-2823
Fax: (901) 942-6448
Service Area: Memphis and Shelby County
URL: www.loccdc.org

Southeast Community Capital Corporation
1020 Commerce Park Drive
Oak Ridge, TN 37830
Executive Director: Clint Gwin
Microloan Contact: David Bradshaw
E-mail: gwin@sccapital.org,
bradshaw@sccapital.org
Phone: (865) 220-2025
Fax: (865) 220-2024
Service Area: Tennessee
URL: www.sccapital.org

Woodbine Community Organization
222 Oriel Avenue
Nashville, TN 37210
Executive Director: Cathie Dodd
Microloan Contact: NA
E-mail: nashrm@aol.com
Phone: (615) 833-9580
Fax: (615) 833-9727
Service Area: Cheatham, Davidson, Dickson, Houston, Humphrey, Montgomery, Robertson, Rutherford, Stewart, Sumner, Williamson, and Wilson Counties
URL: www.woodbinecommunity.org

Texas

ACCION Texas, Inc.
2014 S. Hackberry Street
San Antonio, TX 78210
Executive Director: Janie Barrera
Microloan Contact: Mario Riojas
E-mail: info@acciontexas.org
Phone: (210) 226-3664, (888) 215-2373
Fax: (210) 533-2940
Service Area: Arkansas, Atascosa, Austin, Bandera, Bastrop, Bee, Bexar, Blanco, Brewster, Brooks, Brownsville, Burnet,
Cameron, Caldwell, Calhoun, Comal, Concho, Corpus Christi, Crockett, Culberson, Dallas, DeWitt, Dimmit, Duval, Edwards, El Paso, Fayette, Fort Worth, Frio, Gillespie, Goliad, Gonzales, Green, Guadalupe, Harris, Hays, Houston, Hidalgo, Hudspeth, Irion, Jackson, Jeff Davis, Jim Hogg, Jim Wells, Karnes, Kendall, Kenedy, Kerr, Kimble, Kinney, Kleberg, Lampasas, Laredo, LaSalle, Lavaca, Lee, Live Oak, Llano, Loving, Mason, Maverick, Medina, McAllen, McCulloch, McMullen, Menard, Midland/Odessa, Nueces, Pecos, Presidio, Real, Reeves, Real, Reeves, Refugio, San Antonio, San Patricio, San Saba, Schleicher, Starr, Sutton, Tarrant, Tom Green, Travis, Uvalde, Val Verde, Victoria , Webb, Willacy, Zapata, and Zavala Counties
URL: www.acciontexas.org

Business Resource Center Incubator
401 Franklin Avenue
Waco, TX 76701
Executive Director: NA
Microloan Contact: NA
E-mail: info@brc-waco.com
Phone: (254) 754-8898
Fax: (254) 756-0776
Service Area: Bell, Bosque, Coryell, Falls, Hill, and McLennan Counties
URL: www.brc-waco.com

BiG AUSTIN—Businesses Investment Growth
1050 East 11th Street, Suite 350
Austin, Texas 78702
Executive Director: Jeannette Peten
Microloan Contact: Ligia Trevino
E-mail: ligia@bigaustin.org,

info@bigaustin.org
Phone: (512) 928-8010
Fax: (512) 926-2997
Service Area: Travis, Williamson, Hays, Bastrop, Blanco, Burnet, Burleson, Milam, Gillespie, Lampasas, Lee, Llano, Mason, Mcculloch, and San Saba Counties
URL: www.bigaustin.org

Neighborhood Housing Services of Dimmitt County, Inc.

301 Pena Street
Carrizo Springs, TX 78834
Executive Director: Manuel Estrada, Jr.
Microloan Contact: Manuel Estrada, Jr.
E-mail: nhsdc_mestrada@sbcglobal.net
Phone: (830) 876-5295
Fax: (830) 876-4136
Service Area: Dimmit, La Salle, Zavala Edwards, Kinney, Real, Uvalde, Val Verde, and Maverick Counties
URL: NA

Rural Development and Finance Corporation

230 Pereida Street
San Antonio, TX 78210
Executive Director: Gloria Guerrero
Microloan Contact: Jimmy Z. Palacio
E-mail: Gloria.Guerrero@rdfc.org
Phone: (210) 212-4552
Fax: (210) 212-9159
Service Area: Cameron, El Paso, Starr, Hidalgo, Willacy, Maverick, Dimmit, Webb, Zapata, and Zavala Counties
URL: www.rdfc.org

South Texas Business Fund (formerly San Antonio Local Development Company)
City of San Antonio's Development and

Business Services Center
1901 South Alamo Street, Suite 283
San Antonio, TX 78204
Executive Director: Ramiro Cavazos
Microloan Contact: Mike Mendoza
E-Mail: mmendoza@sotexbizfund.com
Phone: (210) 207-3932
Fax: (210) 207-3939
Service Area: Atascosa, Bandera, Bexar, Comal, Frio, Gillespie, Guadalupe, Karnes, Kendall, Kerr, Medina, San Antonio, and Wilson Counties
URL: www.sotexbizfund.com

Southern Dallas Development Corporation

351 W. Jefferson Boulevard, Suite 600, LB 106
Dallas, TX 75208
Executive Director: Charles McElrath
Microloan Contact: Victor Elmore
E-mail: info@sddc.org
Phone: (214) 948-7800
Fax: (214) 948-8104
Service Area: Portions of the City of Dallas
URL: www.sddc.org

The Corporation for Economic Development of Harris County, Inc.

11703 ½ Easttex Freeway
Houston, TX 77039
Executive Director: Jacqueline Griffin
Microloan Contact: Valerie Boudreaux-Allen
E- mail: jgriffin@cedhc.com, info@cedhc.com
Phone: (281) 590-5600
Fax: (281) 590-5605
Service Area: Brazoria, Chambers, Fort

Bend, Galveston, Harris, Liberty, Montgomery, and Waller Counties
URL: www.cedhc.com

Vermont

Economic Development Council of Northern Vermont, Inc.
2 N. Main Street, Suite 301
St. Albans, VT 05478
Executive Director: Connie Stanley-Little
Microloan Contact: Tammy L. Underwood
E-mail: tlu@sover.net, edcnv@sover.net
Phone: (802) 524-4546
Fax: (802) 527-1081
Service Area: Chittenden, Franklin, Grand Isle, Lamoille, and Washington Counties
URL: www.edcnv.org

Northern Community Investment Corporation
347 Portland Street
P.O. Box 904
St. Johnsbury, VT 05819
Executive Director: NA
Microloan Contact: Suzanne L. Roberts
E-mail: suzanne@ncic.org, ncic@ncic.org
Phone: (802) 748-5101
Fax: (802) 748-1884
Service Area: Caledonia, Essex, and Orleans Counties
URL: www.ncic.org

Opportunities Credit Union (formerly Vermont Development Credit Union)
18 Pearl Street
Burlington, VT 05401
Executive Director: Caryl J. Stewart
Microloan Contact: Lejla Sehovic

E-mail: lsehovic@oppsvt.org, info@oppsvt.org
Phone: (802) 865-3404, (800) 865-8328
Fax: (802) 862-8971
Service Area: Addison, Bennington, Orange, Rutland, Windham, and Windsor Counties
URL: www.oppsvt.org

Virginia

Lynchburg Business Development Centre, Inc.
147 Mill Ridge Road
Lynchburg, VA 24502
Executive Director: Catherine McFaden
Microloan Contact: Byron Steward
E-mail: loanfundmgr@lbdc.com
Phone: (434) 582-6100
Fax: (434) 582-6106
Service Area: Amherst, Appomattox, Bedford, and Campbell Counties, cities of Lynchburg and Bedford, the Town of Amherst, and Altavista
URL: www.lbdc.com

Center for Community Development, Inc.
440 High Street, Suite 204
Portsmouth, VA 23704
Executive Director: Bruce Asberry
Microloan Contact: Monique Harrell
E-mail: profit1@ccdi-va.net
Phone: (757) 399-0925
Fax: (757) 399-2642
Service Area: Chesapeake, Essen, Gloucester, Hampton, King and Queens, King William, Mathews, Middlesex, Newport News, Norfolk, Portsmouth, Suffolk, and Virginia Beach
URL: www.ccdi-va.net

Crater Development Company

1964 Wakefield Street
P.O. Box 1808
Petersburg, VA 23805
Executive Director: Dennis K. Morris
Microloan Contact: Harpal S. Malik
E-mail: dmorris@cpd.state.va.us, hmalik@cpd.state.va.us,
craterpd@cpd.state.va.us
Phone: (804) 861-1666
Fax: (804) 732-8972
Service Area: Counties of Brunswick,
Dinwiddie, Greensville, Isle of Wight,
Prince George, Southampton, Surry, and
Sussex, and the Cities of Colonial
Heights, Emporia, and Franklin
URL: www.craterpdc.state.va.us/CDC/
cdc_main.htm

Enterprise Development Group

1038 South Highland Street
Arlington, VA 22204
Executive Director: Tsehaye Teferra
Microloan Contact: Michelle Wilson
E-mail: edgloan@entdevgroup.org
Phone: (703) 685-0510
Service Area: Prince William, Arlington,
and Fairfax Counties and the cities of
Alexandria and Falls Church
URL: www.entdevgroup.org

People Incorporated of Southwest Virginia

1173 West Main Street
Abingdon, VA 24210
Executive Director: Robert G. Goldsmith
Microloan Contact: Philip Black
E-mail: rgoldsmith@peopleinc.net,
pblack@peopleinc.net,
info@peopleinc.net

Phone: (276) 623-9000, (276) 466-6527
Fax: (276) 628-2931
Service Area: Counties of Bland,
Buchanan, Carroll, Dickenson, Floyd,
Grayson, Lee, Russell, Scott, Smyth,
Tazewell, Washington, and Wise, and
cities of Bristol, Galax, and Norton
URL: www.peopleincorp.org

Piedmont Housing Alliance

111 Monticello Avenue, Suite 104
Charlottesville, VA 22902
Executive Director: Stuart C. Armstrong
Microloan Contact: NA
E-mail: pha@avenue.org
Phone: (434) 817-2436
Fax: (434) 817-0664
Service Area: Counties of Albemarle,
Fluvanna, Greene, Louisa, Nelson,
Orange, and Madison, and the City of
Charlottesville
URL: avenue.org/pha

Richmond Economic Development Corporation

411 E. Franklin Street, Suite 203
Richmond, VA 23219
Executive Director: Stephen J. Schley
Microloan Contact: Brenda L. Lewis
E-mail: sjschley@redcfinance.org,
blewis@redcfinance.org
Phone: (804) 780-3012, (804) 780-3023
Fax: (804) 788-4310
Service Area: City of Richmond
URL: www.redcfinance.org

Business SEED (Total Action Against Poverty)

210 South Jefferson Street

P.O. Box 2868
Roanoke, VA 24011
Executive Director: Chris Scott
Microloan Contact: Diane Johns
E-mail: chris.scott@businessseed.com,
diane.johns@businessseed.com
Phone: (540) 344-7006
Fax: (540) 344-6998
Service Area: Alleghany, Bath, Botetourt,
Craig, and Roanoke Counties including
the cities of Clifton Forge, Covington,
Roanoke, and Salem
URL: www.businessseed.com

Capital Source (formerly Virginia
Community Development Loan Fund)
1624 Hull Street
Richmond, VA 23234
Executive Director: Tim Hayes
Microloan Contact: Taisha Robinson
E-mail: thayes@mycapsource.org, trobin-
son@mycapsource.org
Phone: (804) 233-2014
Fax: (804) 233-2158
Service Area: Counties of Henrico,
Chesterfield, Goochland, Hanover,
Powatan, and the cities of Petersburg
and Hopewell
URL: www.mycapsource.org

Washington

Community Capital Development
1437 South Jackson, Suite 201
Seattle, WA 98144
P.O. Box 22283
Seattle, WA 98122
Executive Director: Jim Thomas
Microloan Contact: NA
E-mail: artm@seattleccd.com, info@seat-
tleccd.com
Phone: (206) 324-4330 x 104
Fax: NA
Service Area: Adams, Chelan, Douglas,
Grant, Kittitas, Klickitat, Okanogan,
Yakima, King, Pierce, Skagit, San Juan,
Snohomish, Island, Kitsap, and
Whatcom
URL: www.seattleccd.com

Oregon Association of Minority Entrepreneurs Credit Corporation
4134 N. Vancouver Avenue
Portland, OR 97217
Executive Director: Samuel Brooks
Microloan Contact: Sanford Maddox
E-mail: sanford@oame.org
Phone: (503) 249-7744
Fax: (503) 249-2027
Service Area: Clark County
URL: www.oame.org

Tri-Cities Enterprise Center Corporate Office
2000 Logston Boulevard
Richland, WA 99354-5300
Executive Director: Stanley Stave
Microloan Contact: Katie Fast
E-mail: kfast@enterprisecenter.net,
info@enterprisecenter.net
Phone: (509) 375-3268 x 112
Fax: (509) 375-4838
Service Area: Benton, Franklin,
Columbia, Garfield, Asotin, Whitman,
and Spokane Counties
URL: www.enterprisecenter.net

Washington CASH (Community Alliance for Self-Help)
1912 East Madison Street
Seattle, WA 98122

Executive Director: Melany Brown
Microloan Contact: Andrew Nichols
E-mail: melany@washingtoncash.org,
andrew@washingtoncash.org,
info@washingtoncash.org
Phone: (206) 352-1945
Fax: (206) 352-1899
Service Area: Clark, Cowlitz, Island,
King, Kitsap, Lewis, San Juan, Skagit,
Snohomish, Thurston, and Whatcom
Counties
URL: www.washingtoncash.org

**Rural Community Development
Resources, Inc.** (formerly Washington
Association of Minority Entrepreneurs)
24 South 3rd Avenue
Yakima, WA 98902
President and CEO: Luz Bazan Gutierrez
E-mail: delnorte@nwinfo.net
Phone: (509) 453-5133
Fax: (509) 453-5165
Service Area: Mattawa and Othello in
Grant County; Moses Lake and Royal
City in Adams County; Walla Walla
County; and Pasco in Franklin County
URL: NA

West Virginia

**Lightstone Foundation and Community
Development Corporation**
HC 63, Box 73
Lightstone Lane
Sugar Grove, WV 26815
Executive Director: Michelle Marshall
Microloan Contact: Norma Jean Propst
E-mail: loans@lightstone.org, info@light-
stone.org
Phone: (304) 249-5200

Fax: (304) 249-5310
Service Area: West Virginia
URL: www.lightstone.org
Mountain CAP of West Virginia, Inc.
105 Jerry Burton Drive
Sutton, WV 26601
Executive Director: Mary Chipps
Microloan Contact: Tara Rexroad
E-mail: trexroad@mountaincap.com,
mountaincap@mountaincap.com
Phone: (304) 765-7738, (800) 850-7738
Fax: (304) 765-7308
Service Area: Barbour, Braxton, Clay,
Fayette, Gilmer, Lewis, Nicholas,
Randolph, Roane, Upshur Raleigh,
Harrison, and Webster Counties
URL: www.mountaincap.com

**Washington County Council on Economic
Development**
40 S. Main Street, Lower Level
Washington, PA 15301
Executive Director: Malcolm Morgan
Microloan Contact: Alan A. Hill
E-mail: wcced@pulsenet.com
Phone: (724) 225-8223
Fax: (724) 225-8202
Service Area: Monongalia County
URL: www.washingtoncountypa.org

Wisconsin

Advocap, Inc.
19 West First Street
P.O. Box 1108
Fond du Lac, WI 54936-1108
Executive Director: Michael Bonertz
Microloan Contact: Kathy Doyle
E-mail: mikeb@advocap.org,
kathyd@advocap.org

Phone: (920) 922-7760, (800) 631-7760
Fax: (920) 922-7214
Service Area: Fond du Lac, Green Lake,
and Winnebago Counties
URL: www.advocap.org

Impact Seven, Inc.
147 Lake Almena Drive
Almena, WI 54805
Executive Director: William Bay
Microloan Contact: Inger Sanderud
E-mail: impact@impactseven.org
Phone: (715) 357-3334
Fax: (715) 357-6233
Service Area: Statewide with the excep-
tions of Fond du Lac, Green Lake,
Kenosha, Milwaukee, Osaukee, Racine,
Walworth, Waukesha, Washington, and
Winnebago Counties and inner-city
Milwaukee
URL: www.impactseven.org

**Lincoln Neighborhood Redevelopment
Corporation**
2266 S. 13th Street
Milwaukee, WI 53215
Executive Director: Michael Gapinski
Microloan Contact: Matthew Maigatter
Phone: (414) 671-5619
Fax: (414) 385-3270
E-mail: lnrc@cbgmail.com
Area Served: Greater Milwaukee SMSA
URL: NA

Northeast Entrepreneur Fund, Inc.
1401 Tower Avenue, Suite 302
Superior WI 54880
Executive Director: Mary Mathews
Microloan Contact: Robert Voss
E-mail: info@entrepreneurfund.org
Phone: (800) 422-0374

Fax: (715) 392-6131
Service Area: Douglas County
URL: www.entrepreneurfund.org

**Wisconsin Women's Business Initiative
Corporation**
2745 North Dr. Martin Luther King Jr.
Drive
Milwaukee, WI 53212
Executive Director: Wendy Werkmeister
Microloan Contact: Carol N. Maria
E-mail: info@wwbic.com
Phone: (414) 263-5450
Fax: (414) 263-5456
Service Area: Brown, Dane, Dodge,
Jefferson, Kenosha, Milwaukee,
Ozaukee, Racine, Rock, Walworth, and
Washington Counties
URL: www.wwbic.com

Wyoming

Wyoming Women's Business Center
University of Wyoming Campus
Education Annex/Business & Technology
Center
Rooms 155 and 158
13th and Lewis Streets
P.O. Box 3661
Laramie, WY 82071
P.O. Box 764
Laramie, WY 82073
Executive Director: Rosemary Bratton
Microloan Contact: Andrea L. Presse
Phone: (307) 766-3084, (888) 524-1947
(in Wyoming)
Fax: (307) 766-3085
E-mail: wwbc@uwyo.edu
Service Area: Wyoming
URL: www.wyomingwomen.org

Appendix C

Entrepreneur Profile

T HE *ENTREPRENEUR PROFILE HAS NINE QUESTIONS, EACH OF WHICH* demand some level of analysis. The answers you give to these nine questions may differ at each stage at which you are seeking capital. (Feel free to photocopy this page and use it regularly.)

1. **Who are you as an entrepreneur?**

2. **What is the geographic area in which you want to start (operate) your venture?**

3. **What type of business are you in?**

4. What and where is your market?

5. What round of financing are you seeking? (i.e., seed, mezzanine, third-round VC, etc.)

6. How much money do you need in this round of financing?

7. What do you need the money for at this time?

8. How quickly do you need the money?

9. Are you looking to raise capital through debt or equity sale?

Appendix D

Angel Investment Memorandum

StartUp, Inc.: Summary of Terms for Proposed Convertible Preferred-Stock Investment

Issuer: StartUp, Inc. ("Company").

Investor: VC, L.P. ("Investor").

Amount of Investment: $_____ (the "Investment Amount").

Ownership: _____ % (based on $_____ fully diluted, post-money valuation with _____ common equivalents).

Type of Security: Series A Convertible Preferred Stock ("Preferred").

Use of Proceeds: The funds will be used to fund working capital and continued growth of the Company.

Conditions to Closing:

(1) Investor shall complete its due diligence investigation of all aspects of the Company. During the due diligence investigation, the Company agrees to provide Investor and its accountants, attorneys, and other agents and representatives complete access to the Company's facilities, employees, books, records, customers, prospective business pipeline, and suppliers.

(2) The Company shall have provided to the Investor (a) annual financial statements for the fiscal year ended December 31, 20___, and (b) financial statements for the most recent year-to-date period. [subject to availability]

225

(3) All documents required by the Investor, including without limitation a Securities Purchase Agreement, a Shareholder Agreement, an Investor Rights Agreement, and all required agreements with management and employees.

(4) Absence of litigation or adverse proceedings against the Company.

(5) No material adverse changes shall have occurred with respect to the Company.

Investor shall be under no obligation to continue with its due diligence investigation or to extend the financing contemplated herein if, at any time, the results of its due diligence investigation are not satisfactory to the Investor for any reasons at its sole discretion. In such event, the Investor shall immediately notify the Company, in which case the "Exclusivity" paragraph shall no longer be binding on the Company. In addition, the Company acknowledges that the pre-money valuation contemplated herein is preliminary and subject to the verification of a number of factors to be confirmed in due diligence.

With the Company's complete cooperation, Investor agrees to complete its due diligence investigation on the Company on or prior to _____, 20____.

Anticipated Closing: Assuming satisfactory completion of the due diligence investigation and timely acceptance of this term sheet, the Investor expects to negotiate and complete definitive documentation with the Company by or before _____, 20____ (the date of completion of definitive documentation is the "Closing Date").

Rights, Preferences, Privileges, and Restrictions of Preferred

(1) **Conversion:** Each share of Preferred will be convertible at any time, at the option of the holder, into one share of Common Stock of the Company. The conversion rate will be subject to appropriate adjustment in the event of stock splits, stock dividends, recapitalizations, etc. and as set forth in paragraph (6) below. The Preferred will be automatically converted into Common Stock, at the then applicable conversion rate, in the event of an underwritten public offering of shares in which the net proceeds to the Company are not less than $_____ and the per share issue price is at least [4X] the conversion price per share.

(2) **Mandatory Redemption:** Redeemable at the holders' option at the stated value (plus accrued or accumulated and unpaid dividends thereon) upon the death or voluntary departure of [Founder] or the [fifth] anniversary of the issuance of the Preferred or the [] [insert other performance milestones].

(3) **Liquidation Preference:** In the event of any liquidation or winding up of the

Company, the holders of Preferred will be entitled to receive in preference to the Common Stock an amount equal to the stated value (plus accrued or accumulated and unpaid dividends to the date of redemption, to the extent of retained earnings) and to receive a pro rata (in kind) distribution of the amount payable to the holders of Common Stock on an as if converted basis.

A consolidation or merger of the Company (in which the shareholders of the Company before the merger or consolidation do not, after such transaction, own greater than 50.1% of the voting control of the successor corporation) or sale of all or substantially all of its assets will be deemed to be a liquidation for purposes of the liquidation preference for those holders of Preferred that do not convert prior to the closing of such transaction.

(4) **Dividend Provisions:** The Preferred shall be entitled to semiannual cumulative dividends, which shall accrue at the per share annual rate of [8%] of stated value. Such dividends shall be payable, at the Company's option, either in cash or in kind, upon any conversion of the Preferred or any distribution that is calculated on an as if converted basis. The Preferred will also share pari passu on an as if converted basis in any dividends declared on the Common Stock.

(5) **Voting Rights:** Except as with respect to the election of directors and certain protective provisions for extraordinary events or significant changes in the nature of the Company's business, all matters requiring shareholder approval will be submitted to the holders of Preferred and Common, voting together as a single class. The holders of Preferred will have the right to that number of votes equal to the number of shares of Common issuable upon conversion of the Preferred.

(6) **Antidilution Protection:** The conversion price will be subject to weighted average adjustments for certain issuances below the conversion price then in effect to persons other than officers, employees or consultants.

Information Rights: The Company will timely furnish the Investor with annual, quarterly, and monthly (actual to budget) financial statements.

Registration Rights:

(1) **Demand Rights:** The holders of the Preferred (or Common Stock issued upon conversion of the Preferred) will have the right, on two occasions, to require the Company to file a Registration Statement covering Common Stock issuable upon conversion of the Preferred (subject to certain standard conditions). These rights shall be exercisable at any time after the earlier of six months after the Company's initial public offering and three years from the Closing Date.

(2) **Registration on Form S-3:** In addition to the rights under paragraph (1), holders of the Preferred (or Common Stock issued upon conversion of the Preferred) will have the right to require the Company to file an unlimited number of Registration Statements on Form S-3 (subject to certain standard conditions), if such Form is available.

(3) **Piggyback Registration:** The Investors will be entitled to unlimited "piggyback" registration rights on all registrations of the Company, subject to underwriters' cutbacks.

(4) **Registration Expenses:** All customary registration expenses will be borne by the Company.

Shareholders Agreement:

The Company will secure a Shareholders Agreement among the Investor, the Company, and all principal shareholders, providing the Investor with the following:

(1) **Preemptive Right:** Investor will have a right of first refusal with respect to any proposed sale of Common Stock or securities convertible into Common Stock by the Company to the extent necessary for the Investor to maintain its percentage interest in the Common Stock on an as converted basis, which right will terminate upon a public offering.

(2) **Right of First Refusal:** The Company, and then Investor, will have a right of first refusal with respect to any proposed resale of Common Stock by any stockholder, which right will terminate upon a public offering.

(3) **Co-Sale Provision:** The current holders of Common Stock will grant Investor a right to participate on a pro rata basis in any sales of the Company's Common Stock made by them.

(4) **Take-Along Provision:** The current holders of Common Stock will agree to enter into any sale transaction with respect to their Common Stock or the Company that is approved by the holders of a majority of the issued and outstanding capital stock of the Company.

Board Representation:

The Board will consist of [7] members. Unless a default under the Purchase Agreement occurs, and is continuing, the Preferred will elect [2] directors, the Common will elect [3] directors, and together they will elect the [sixth and seventh] directors. The charter or bylaws will contain appropriate protective provisions under the laws of the Company's jurisdiction of incorporation.

Preferred Protective

Provisions: The Company shall not amend its charter or bylaws or take any other corporate action without the approval by the holders of at least a [majority/super-majority] of the then outstanding Preferred, if such amendment or corporate action would:

- in any manner (a) authorize, create, amend or issue any class or series of capital stock ranking, either as to payment of dividends, distribution of assets or redemption, prior to or on parity with the Preferred or (b) authorize, create, amend or issue any shares of any class or series or any bonds, debentures, notes or other obligations convertible into or exchangeable for, or having optional rights to purchase, any shares having any such priority or on parity with the Preferred;

- in any manner alter or change the designation or the powers, preferences or rights or the qualifications, limitations or restrictions of the Preferred;

- reclassify shares of Common Stock, or any other shares of any class or series of capital stock hereinafter created junior to the Preferred into shares of any class or series of capital stock ranking, either as to payment of dividends, distribution of assets or redemption, prior to or on parity with the Preferred;

- increase the authorized number of shares of Preferred, issue additional shares of Preferred or authorize any other class or series of capital stock of the Company or its subsidiaries;

- result in any substantial change in the nature of the business engaged in by the Company;

- create, authorize, reserve or involve the issuance of more than an aggregate of _____ shares of Common Stock in connection with options to purchase shares of Common Stock heretofore or hereafter issued to officers, employees or directors of the Company pursuant to any plan, agreement or other arrangements, including without limitation, options granted pursuant to the [insert names of any plan(s)];

- result in the redemption, repurchase or other acquisition by the Company of capital stock or other securities of the Company or its subsidiaries, except for (a) contractually obligated, nondiscretionary repurchases or other acquisitions of capital stock of the Company from employees of the Company upon such employees' termination of employment from the Company pursuant to the terms and conditions of agreements which provide the Company the right to repurchase such capital stock upon such termination of employment and (b) the redemption or repurchase of the Preferred pursuant to the terms thereof;

- result in (a) any liquidation, dissolution, winding-up or similar transaction of the Company or its subsidiaries or (b) a sale of all or substantially all of the assets of the Company or its subsidiaries or a merger, consolidation, sale of capital stock or other transaction in which the holders of capital stock of the Company and its subsidiaries, in the aggregate, immediately prior to such transaction will not hold, immediately after such transaction, more than 50 percent of the aggregate voting power of outstanding capital stock of the surviving corporation;

- result in the incurrence of additional indebtedness of the Company or its subsidiaries, including, without limitation, any loan agreement, promissory note (or other evidence of indebtedness), mortgage, security agreement or lease, or any commitment for any of the foregoing, whether in a single transaction or a series of related transactions, in an amount exceeding [$50,000];

- result in a sale, lease or assignment of any assets of, or interests in assets held by, the Company or its subsidiaries outside the ordinary course of business, or a series of related sales, leases or assignments, having an aggregate value exceeding [$50,000];

- result in a capital expenditure of the Company in excess of [$50,000];

- result in the removal or election of any corporate officer, or the termination or hiring of any employee earning annualized compensation in excess of [$100,000];

- result in the formation of a contract or any other transaction with any holder of Common Stock or any affiliate of any holder of Common Stock;

- result in the hiring or engagement, as an employee, consultant or service provider, of any member of, or entity controlled by, any holder of Common Stock's family or any other person or entity affiliated with any holder of Common Stock;

- result in additional securities of the Company's subsidiaries being issued or would in any way alter the current ownership structure of the Company's subsidiaries;

- in any way amend, alter, restate or otherwise change its charter or bylaws, or those of the Company's subsidiaries, as they are currently in effect;

- reduce the amount payable to the holders of Preferred upon (a) the voluntary or involuntary liquidation, dissolution or winding up of the Company or (b) any acquisition of all or substantially all of the assets of the Company, or an acquisition of the Company by another corporation or entity by consolidation, merger or other reorganization or combination in which the holders of the Company's outstanding voting stock immediately prior to such transaction do not own, immediately after such transaction, securities representing more than 50 percent (50%) of the voting power of the corporation or other entity surviving such transaction; or

- result in the grant of registration rights to any other class or series of capital stock of the Company or its subsidiaries more favorable than or on parity with those granted to the holders of the Preferred.

Employment Contract: The Company shall enter into an employment contract with [Founders] on mutually agreeable terms including appropriate nondisclosure and noncompetition covenants.

Noncompetition Agreements: Unless such agreements already exist in a form satisfactory to the Investor, the Company shall enter into one-year noncompetition agreements with all officers and key employees identified by Investor.

Key Man Insurance: The Company shall obtain and maintain term life insurance on [Founder] for $_____, with proceeds payable to the Company, for the purpose of redeeming the Preferred if the Investor elects to redeem. [tied to redemption trigger for death of Founder]

Exclusivity: Except with respect to the Company's discussions with _____, for a period of [30 days] from the date of acceptance of this term sheet, the Company and each principal shareholder of the Company shall (i) deal exclusively with the Investor in connection with the issuance or sale of any equity or debt securities or assets of the Company or any merger or consolidation involving the Company; (ii) shall not solicit, or engage others to solicit, offers for the purchase or acquisition of any equity or debt securities or assets of the Company or for any merger or consolidation involving the Company; (iii) shall not negotiate with or enter into any agreements or understandings with respect to such transaction; and (iv) shall inform the Investor of any such solicitation or offer. Each of the parties agrees to cooperate and negotiate in good faith during the exclusive period.

Expenses: If the Closing occurs or if the Investor does not proceed with the transaction due to material misrepresentation to Investor by the Company regarding its business, then the Company will bear the Investor's out-of-pocket, legal, consulting, and other expenses incurred with respect to the transaction, up to a maximum of [$30,000].

Other Conditions: The Company shall take any and all necessary actions with respect to amending its charter to [consolidate all existing classes of capital stock into a single class of voting Common Stock and] permit the issuance of the Preferred with its attendant rights, preferences, privileges and restrictions.

Expiration: This proposal shall expire _____, 20____.

Except for the terms of this Summary under the heading "Exclusivity," and "Expenses" which upon execution will be binding on the parties, this letter is not a binding agreement or an offer. This letter does not contain all material terms upon which the parties intend to agree and is only intended to provide a basis on which to begin to work on a final agreement. A binding commitment will only be made pursuant to the execution of a definitive purchase agreement mutually acceptable to the Company and the Investor and only after all of the Conditions and Conditions Precedent noted above have been satisfied.

We look forward to working with you to complete our due diligence and continuing the relationship that we have developed to date.

VC, L.P.

By: _____

Title: _____

StartUp, Inc.

By: _____

Title: _____

Appendix E

Law Firm Criteria and Evaluation

Use the chart on the next page as a tool for evaluating law firms you might work with in developing your finance plan for your business.

Item	Firm 1	Firm 2	Firm 3
Compatibility Integrity Ability to work together			
Competence/Track Record IPOs DPOs PPMs Term sheets			
Commitment Level of contact Resources Interest			
Contacts Angels Venture Capitalists Underwriters			
Costs IPO DPO PPM Term Sheet			
Overall impression of value added			
Other Comments			

Scale: 1 = low to 10 = high

Index

Additional Titles in Entrepreneur's Made Easy Series